Kash[...]
Ladakh &
Zanskar

a travel survival kit

Kashmir, Ladakh & Zanskar – a travel survival kit

Published by
   Lonely Planet Publications
   PO Box 88, South Yarra, Vic 3141
   Australia
   Lonely Planet Publications
   PO Box 2001A, Berkeley CA 94702
   USA

Printed in Singapore through
   Hedges & Bell Printing (S.E. Asia)

Photographs by
   Colour: Bob Pritchard, Garry Weare, Tony Wheeler
   Black & white: all Rolf Schettler, except 139 Maureen Wheeler

First published
   February 1981

This edition
   January 1985

National Library of Australia
   Cataloguing-in-publication entry:

Schettler, Margret.
   Kashmir, Ladakh & Zanskar.

   2nd ed.
   Previous ed.: South Yarra, Vic.: Lonely Planet, 1981.
   Includes index.
   ISBN 0 908086 63 6.

   1. Kashmir – Description and travel – Guide-books.
   I. Schettler, Rolf, 1943-. II. Title.

915.4'604

Rolf and Margret Schettler were, in 1974, the first foreign visitors to Ladakh with their own vehicle. They have subsequently returned to Ladakh and to Zanskar to write about, film and record the music of these remote Himalayan regions. This book was first published in Germany as *Kaschmir & Ladakh* and expanded, at the same time as the first edition of this English language edition, to include Zanskar.

Additional contributors to the original German language editions included Dr Walter A Frank (Manali-Padum trek and Tungri-Zongkhul Gompa Roundtrip), Kurt & Ingrid Zehetner (Padum-Kishtwar Trek), Walter Kamm (Padum-Leh by the Markha Valley and Padum-Phuctal Gompa by the Shadi Gorge).

This Edition
The first English language edition of this guidebook was expanded and amplified, particularly on the Jammu area and the Vale of Kashmir, by Tony and Maureen Wheeler. The research and updating for this second edition was totally undertaken by Lonely Planet. Geoff Crowther and his Korean sidekick Hyung Pun visited Kashmir while updating *India – a travel survival kit* and contributed to the general updating, particularly of Jammu, Srinagar and Gulmarg.

Additionally Bob Pritchard, of Deakin University in Geelong, Australia, visited Kashmir, Ladakh and Zanskar and added much new material and updated much of the old. He noted that Kashmiris gave him widely conflicting advice on how to handle the updating: '. . . houseboat owners said to stay away from the tourist office, the tourist office said to beware of the houseboat owners, the merchants said the houseboat owners charged too much commission, the houseboat owners said the merchants are too greedy, the Indians said all Kashmiris will try to cheat you and

the Kashmiris said the Indians expect too much for too little'! Bob's main advice to visitors is to be wary of the Kashmiris, who are truly a born race of wheeler-dealers. And to be gentle with Ladakh, a unique and fragile culture which can easily be damaged by the tourist hordes that have suddenly descended upon it.

More Thanks
Many travellers wrote with useful information on the region. Much of this information has already found its way into the new edition of *India – a travel survival kit* and most of the writers thanked there. In addition thanks must go to:

Bonnie Baskin (USA), Loop Begheyn (Nl) for his detailed notes, including a report on the Amarnath trek from Baltal and on to Pahalgam, John Berridge (C), M L Bridge (UK), Rowland Burley (K), Moe Denburg (C), Richard Farr (UK), Bill Page – L, Scot Macbeth for additional material on the Manali-Padum and Padum-Leh via the Markha Valley treks, Ian MacDonnell (UK), Jeanne Marecek & Donald Overton (USA), Peter Overmire (USA), Michael Pollard & Mary Wiseman (USA), Rob

Rachowiecki (UK), William Ramsden (UK) for his report on trekking the through the Markha Valley in Ladakh

C – Canada, K – Kenya, L – Luxembourg, Nl – Netherlands, UK – UK, USA – USA

A Warning on Maps & Spelling

None of the languages spoken in Kashmir, Ladakh or Zanskar use our script so any place name is a transliteration from their script to ours. How it ends up being spelt depends very much on who does the transliterating. Naturally this is complicated in a book like this where there are a number of contributors. As far as possible we've tried to be consistent in spellings but inevitably some variances will have crept through. Where there are more than one frequently used spelling these are often indicated. Fortunately most of these variations are easily recognisable.

Just as with the spellings, maps of the region should also not be trusted. Trekker Moe Denburg of Canada summed it up:

No matter whose map we were looking at there were always many inaccuracies on it. Most notoriously, the distances depicted on the map are almost always out of scale. Another big mistake is that sometimes a village is indicated where there is none – the name is really only of an area or a bridge. This is pretty bad when the so-depicted village is in a strategic place, like just before a pass, and you have made plans to stay there for the night. And just for thirds, one must always be wary of bridges that are depicted on the maps. The map may be old and the bridge might not be there anymore. Or the bridge may be broken. Or there may be a better bridge. One must make a practice of talking to villagers and passing trekkers to corroborate one's assumptions, map or no maps.

And the Next Edition

Things change – prices go up, places open and close, nothing stays the same. So if you find things better, worse, cheaper, more expensive, recently opened or long ago closed please don't blame us but please do write and tell us. We're always happy to hear from 'our' travellers out on the road. The information you send us gets fed back to other travellers through our newsletter and goes into updating our guidebooks. As usual the best letters are rewarded with a free copy of the next edition, or another Lonely Planet guide.

Contents

Introduction

Kashmir, Ladakh and Zanskar are all regions of the Indian state of Jammu and Kashmir, often referred to simply as J&K. Jammu is the southern part of the state and forms a transitional area between the Indian plains and the mighty Himalaya. Correctly the rest of the state is Kashmir, but in practice the title is reserved for the 'Vale of Kashmir', a large Himalayan valley in the north of the state. Ladakh and Zanskar are regions of Kashmir, geographical neighbours to Kashmir proper but separated from Kashmir by the full height of the Himalaya and worlds away in terms of people, culture and religion. Parts of Kashmir are under Pakistani control, principally the Gilgit and Hunza areas, and the Chinese hold a slice of Ladakh to the east. Although the whole Kashmir region is a subject of considerable dispute, particularly between India and Pakistan, the continuing argument is highly unlikely to have any effect on foreign visitors.

Jammu is not of great interest to most overseas visitors to the region, it's basically just a stop-over on the trip up to Srinagar. As well as being a geographical transition zone from the hot plains to the cool mountains, it is also a religious change-point. Here the Hindu religion begins to give way to the Muslim religion that predominates in the Kashmir Valley.

The Vale of Kashmir has been famous for its great natural beauty ever since the days of the Moghul emperors. The great Moghuls further embellished that natural beauty with a series of delightfully planned gardens, many of which are still beautifully preserved even today. The British added a further attraction to Kashmir, the houseboats which crowd Dal Lake at Srinagar – no visit to Kashmir is complete without a stay on a houseboat.

Ladakh lies across the Himalaya from Kashmir – its situation on the Tibetan plateau, plus the clear Tibetan influence in Ladakhi customs and religion, has led to it being known as 'little Tibet'. Ladakh's quite incredibly barren landscape, a result of the high Himalayan barrier which prevents rain clouds from climbing across from the lush valleys to the south and west, has also given it the name of 'the moonland'. Ladakh has only been open to tourists since the mid-70s and until 1962, when the Chinese invasion prompted the rapid construction of a road linking Ladakh with Srinagar, getting into Ladakh involved several weeks hard walk. Since 1979 you can actually fly to Ladakh, in less than 30 minutes from Srinagar, and now you can also fly from Chandigarh.

Finally there is Zanskar, a long valley running in a roughly north-west to south-east direction between Kashmir and Ladakh. Zanskar encompasses the Stod and Lunak river valleys, the Zanskar River Valley and the area south of Padum to the southern face of the Great Himalaya, over the Shingo pass. The people are much like the Ladakhis in their dress, customs and religion but they have been even more isolated from outside contact. Like Ladakh, visitors have only been allowed into Zanskar in the last few years, but access to Zanskar is much more difficult. A jeep track to Padum, the Zanskar 'capital', was only completed in the early '80s and it is extremely susceptible to damage in a severe winter, such as occurred in 1982-83. Most visitors to Zanskar will continue to arrive on foot or by pony, crossing 4500 metre passes to get there.

The whole Kashmir, Ladakh and Zanskar region is a paradise for trekkers with trails leading through beautiful and spectacular scenery, far from the encroachment of modern roads and motor vehicles.

Facts about the Region

GEOGRAPHY

Jammu & Kashmir is the northernmost province of India, bordered to the north and east by China (Sinkiang Province and Tibet), to the west by Pakistan's North-West Frontier Province and to the south by the Indian states of Punjab and Himachal Pradesh. The whole region of Kashmir has an area of 222,798 square km with a population of six million, but Pakistan controls 83,800 square km of the Gilgit and Hunza areas of Kashmir to the north-west while China has grabbed a further slice of the area in the east. Due to these border disputes there is a large Indian military presence in the state and following the Chinese activities in Ladakh two roads were built to Leh and the airport there was completed. The continuing political arguments are unlikely to have any effect on visitors.

Jammu is the southern part of the state and forms a transitional area between the Indian plains and the ranges which make up the Himalayan region. The northern part of the state is Kashmir but this name usually refers just to the Vale of Kashmir, a large valley in the north-west. The eastern part of the state is Ladakh, within which lies Zanskar. The Himalaya separate the Vale of Kashmir from the Zanskar Valley and in turn Zanskar is separated from Ladakh by the Zanskar Range. The Himalaya not only marks changes in climate and geography, for as you move from Kashmir to Ladakh there are also great changes in race, customs and religion.

The Kashmir Valley is bounded by two mountain ranges. The lower Pir Panjal Range curls around the valley from the south-east, through the south and round to the north-west. The eastern side of the valley is then closed off by the Great Himalaya, which runs almost straight from south-east to north-west. At one time

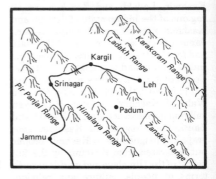

Kashmir was a lake which, like the Kathmandu Valley, was drained eons ago.

FACTS

The state of Jammu & Kashmir has a population estimated at around 4.6 million. Ladakh, with an area of just under 100,000 square km, comprises nearly half of the whole Kashmir region, making it the largest district in India. However, its population of just over 100,000 also makes it the most lightly populated region of India. Ladakh has 112 villages and one town, the capital of Leh.

VISAS

No special permission is required to visit Kashmir or the Ladakh and Zanskar regions, once you have entered India. Since the upheavals in the Punjab in 1984 *all* nationalities – including previously exempt countries – are required to have a visa for India. Furthermore the previous Indian tolerance towards visitors, who formerly could more or less wander around India forever, seems to be at an end. Reportedly you are now allowed to stay no longer than six months in any calendar year.

Visas are issued at Indian embassies,

8

are valid for 90 days and can be extended for a further 90 days. Visas must be obtained no more than six months before your arrival in India. Indian visas are usually triple entry so you can exit to Nepal or Sri Lanka and return on the same visa. Extending an Indian visa is usually such a complicated, bureaucratic hassle that it is advisable, if you leave India to go to a neighbouring country, to get a new and start your 90 days again.

Within India visas can be extended at the Foreigners' Regional Registration Offices in New Delhi, Bombay, Calcutta, Madras or Srinagar, or any Offices of the Superintendent of Police in the District Headquarters. In Srinagar bring two photos, the office is by the GPO. In Leh go to the police station to the south-east of the polo ground.

No special permits are required for trekking in the non-restricted areas of Kashmir or Ladakh although it is advisable to enquire about permits before setting off on trekking trips, particularly into Zanskar. Some places in Ladakh and Zanskar are only accessible with special permission which may have to be obtained in New Delhi.

Restricted Areas

Because of the sensitive nature of the border zone between India and Pakistan in the north and India and China in the east there is a rigidly enforced area where you may not encroach. Basically it means you are not allowed north of the Srinagar-Leh road or east of the Manali-Leh road.

More specifically the excluded area is from one mile north of the road which runs through Zoji La-Drass-Bodh Kharbu-Khalsi-Nimmu-Leh-Upshi but excepting the monasteries of Tia, Temisgam, Rizong, Lekir, Phyang, Shey, Tikse, Chemrey and Tagthog. Also excluded is the Leh-Upshi road beyond Karu and the area east from a line one mile west of the Manali-Upshi road from Chhumik Byiarsa on the Ladakh-Himachal Pradesh border.

This means that the Manali-Leh road is also off-limits to visitors. Most of the Nubra Valley is off limits but it is expected that parts of it will be open to visitors in 1985.

Permission to enter the restricted area must be sought from the Ministry of Home Affairs, New Delhi, preferably before entering India as it can take up to six months to get a reply. Which will usually be 'no'. If you want to try anyway cite order number 15011-6-73 when applying.

MONEY

USA	US$1	=	Rs 11.0
Australia	A$1	=	Rs 10.0
UK	£1	=	Rs 15.2
Canada	C$1	=	Rs 8.5
New Zealand	NZ$1	=	Rs 7.2
Singapore	S$1	=	Rs 5.2
West Germany	DM 1	=	Rs 4.0

There are 100 paise (p) to the rupee (Rs). There are coins up to and including one rupee, notes from one rupee and up. At one time the rupee was divided up into 16 annas and you may still very occasionally hear prices quoted in annas in bazaars and markets – four annas is 25p, eight annas is 50p.

The major travellers' cheques are all easily exchanged in India although US dollars and pounds sterling are the most readily recognised foreign currencies. In out-of-the-way centres you may find these are the only currencies readily accepted. Exchange rates tend to vary from bank to bank. Anything to do with paperwork in India is inevitably time consuming so you may find it easier to change larger sums at one time than you would in other countries – simply in order to minimise the time wasted in banks.

Try not to have money transferred to you in India, it is often painfully slow and laborious, particularly with the Indian banks. If you must have funds sent to India transfer them by cable or telex, not by mail, even if you have plenty of time in hand, and transfer them to a foreign owned bank. American Express have offices in Bombay, New Delhi and Calcutta but there are other banks operating throughout India which are still foreign owned and tend to be more efficient than the Indian owned banks when it comes to foreign transactions. The Chartered Bank and Grindlays Bank are two examples – Grindlays have an office in Srinagar on the Bund.

There are two particular points to be careful about with Indian money. First avoid dirty, grubby or torn notes – they can be unusable, particularly in out-of-the-way places. If you do get stuck with such a note try not to worry about it or cause any hassle if people refuse to accept it. You can generally get them changed at a bank (but not always!) or use them for some official purpose such as paying your airport departure tax.

The other money problem is big notes – changing a Rs 100 banknote is always difficult, in fact with India's perpetual

small change deficiency changing anything is usually difficult. When changing foreign currency at a bank try to get as much of it in smaller denomination notes as possible. This problem applies particularly in Ladakh where, during the summer tourist season, there is sometimes a severe shortage of small denomination notes – bring as many one and two rupee notes as possible.

Away from the major centres changing travellers' cheques or foreign currency may be difficult if not impossible. There are no facilities for changing foreign money in Zanskar, nor in Ladakh outside of Leh, Kargil or Karu. Make sure that you have enough rupees with you.

In New Delhi at least there is, once again, a blackmarket for US dollars. It is illegal to import or export Indian currency although you can generally get Indian rupees in Bangkok or Singapore or in Europe at a useful discount – about the same as the blackmarket rate within the country. You are allowed to bring a bottle of whisky and a carton of cigarettes into India duty free and these are usually an excellent investment. In Kashmir and Ladakh good quality camping gear and down clothing also find a ready market. 'Antique' dealers and carpet sellers are also often willing to take dollars under the counter as payment.

CLIMATE

The climatic differences in the state of Jammu and Kashmir are probably the most varied in all of India – in Jammu in the hot season the temperatures can be consistently above 40°C while at Kargil in mid-winter the temperature has been known to drop to -40°C, a temperature differential of 150°F! Similarly Jammu, during the monsoon, can have rain every day while in Ladakh whole years may pass with no rainfall at all. Briefly the weather you can expect is detailed below:

Jammu Situated at a height of only 300 metres, Jammu has the three-season weather typical of the Indian plains. The best time of year in Jammu is the cool season from early October to about February-March. In October, immediately after the monsoon finishes, the weather will be cool and fresh, the skies clear and dust free. Later in the cool season (December and January in particular) it can get quite crisp with temperatures as low as 5°C at night.

In February-March the temperature starts to climb as you enter the hot season. By April, May and June it gets uncomfortably hot and dry. Since there has been no rain for some time the air is very dusty and the temperature scarcely seems to drop at night. Towards the end of the hot season the mercury will sit at 40°C or above for days on end. Finally the monsoon arrives around the beginning of July; the dust is immediately cleared out of the air although for some time the temperature change is merely from hot and dry to hot and sticky.

Kashmir At an altitude of over 1000 metres the Kashmir Valley is much cooler than Jammu and it is at its most popular in May-June when Indian tourists flood up from the hot, airless plains. At this time the daily temperatures are around 20°C, a delightfully cool contrast to the 40°C temperatures common on the plains to the south. In July and August it can get rather hotter and the valley somewhat humid and still – the simple solution is to move out to one of the smaller resorts that lie around the valley rim. At places like Pahalgam, Gulmarg and Sonamarg the altitude ensures cooler weather even in mid-summer.

The Kashmir tourist season ends in October as minimum temperatures drop down below 10°C and from November to February night time temperatures often fall below freezing in Srinagar, snow falls and during cold years Dal Lake can actually freeze over. In the winter Gulmarg becomes India's number one ski-resort. The spring thaw begins in February-March. Rainfall in Kashmir is fairly even year round. The mountains protect Kashmir from the worst of the monsoon.

Ladakh & Zanskar Winter at the high altitudes of Ladakh and Zanskar can be spectacularly cold although snow fall is generally not heavy since the Himalaya act as a barrier to rain clouds coming up from the south. Parts of Ladakh may have no recordable rainfall for years, yet in others there may be deep and persistent snow. Temperatures are consistently below freezing for six months of the year in Leh and the snowbound pass into Kashmir isolates Ladakh from October to June. Drass is reputed to be one of the coldest places in Asia during the winter. The Zanskaris bring their sheep, cattle and goats into the house in winter and from December to March they themselves retreat into the central room of the house and wait for spring. The Zanskar River usually disappears under ice and snow

	New Delhi*			Srinagar**			Leh***		
	max	min	rain	max	min	rain	max	min	rain
January	21.1	6.7	22.9	5.0	-2.2	73.7	-1.1	-13.3	10.2
February	23.9	9.4	17.7	7.2	-1.1	71.1	0.6	-12.2	7.6
March	30.6	14.4	12.7	13.9	3.3	91.4	7.2	-6.1	7.6
April	36.1	20.0	7.7	18.9	7.2	93.9	13.3	-1.1	5.0
May	40.6	26.1	12.7	24.4	11.1	60.9	16.1	0.6	5.0
June	38.9	28.3	73.7	29.4	14.4	35.6	20.0	6.7	5.0
July	35.6	27.2	180.3	31.1	18.3	58.4	25.0	10.0	12.9
August	33.9	26.1	172.7	30.6	17.8	60.9	23.9	10.0	15.2
September	33.9	23.9	116.8	27.8	12.2	38.1	21.1	5.6	7.6
October	33.9	18.3	10.2	22.2	5.0	30.5	15.0	-0.6	2.5
November	28.9	11.1	2.5	15.6	-0.6	10.2	8.3	-6.7	2.5
December	22.8	7.8	10.2	10.7	-2.2	33.0	2.2	-10.6	5.0

annual rainfall

		640.2			657.7		83.8

*1866-1943 **1899-1942 ***1881-1942

along much of its length. The Ladakhis too stay much of the winter indoors.

In summer the day time temperatures are pleasantly warm with maximums around 20 to 25°C, but night time temperatures are always crisp. Even at the height of summer the temperature will immediately plummet when a cloud obscures the sun. You should always have a sweater handy in Ladakh. Beware of the power of the sun at this altitude, you will quickly get a bad case of sunburn even on a cool day.

The chart above details the average maximum temperature (°C), average minimum temperature (°C) and average monthly rainfall (mm) in New Delhi, Srinagar and Leh.

HEALTH & IMMUNISATIONS

There are no longer any required immunisations but there are certainly a couple which you are recommended to have. These are cholera and typhoid shots which can be provided by your own doctor or health service and should then be entered on your International Certificate of Vaccination. Gamma Globulin, as protection against hepatitis, is of questionable efficacy although an improved version has recently been introduced. Your doctor may also recommend that you be immunised against tetanus and polio. Cholera re-vaccinations can be obtained free at the Health Office, Old Secretariat in Srinagar. One traveller wrote to say it was clean, one wrote to say it was dirty!

Although malarial mosquitoes are not exactly at home in Ladakh and Zanskar, India as a whole is an area of malarial risk, even in New Delhi and you should take anti-malarial tablets, either the daily or weekly variety. These usually have to be taken for a period prior to departure and after your return. Other medicine you should bring include Lomotil or other anti-diarrhoeals but remember the best treatment for mild diarrhoea is to let your own system fight it off. If you are interested in alternative medicines fresh garlic has been recommended as a good preventative against mild attacks of diarrhoea. In Srinagar you will find a wide variety of medicines readily available and without the prescriptions normally required in the west. The main problems with them are understanding the different brand names and descriptions to get exactly what you want and making sure that they have not been kept beyond their 'use by' date.

If you're planning to trek in Ladakh and Zanskar bring sleeping pills (if you're willing to take them) and aspirin since sleeplessness and headaches are two common afflictions when trekking at high altitudes. Some people may not notice the changes but the effects of altitude, especially in Ladakh, should be recognised and allowed for. The least serious effect are light sleep with vivid dreams, slight breathlessness and an occasional headache. These symptoms are usually caused by the exertion of trekking – or simply walking around town – in the rarified air and can be cured by rest.

They can become more serious sleeplessness, bad headaches and nausea – symptoms of altitude sickness which can only be cured by getting down to a lower altitude. Although aspirin can be used for headaches caused by altitude, serious or prolonged headaches should be treated with respect and a more effective remedy found to remove the cause, not just the symptom. Acclimatisation is the best preventative for altitude problems. You are much less likely to have trouble if you have spent some time at Srinagar's altitude first, rather than travelled directly from New Delhi, on the plains, to Ladakh. Compared to trekking in Nepal, trekking at the same altitudes in Ladakh and Zanskar is different because of the dryness of the air (you have to drink more) and the extreme burning power of the sun.

A good antibacterial or fungicidal cream or powder is useful for cuts, abrasions and blisters. Corn pads are useful for preventing aggravation of blisters if you have to keep on walking. A good suntan lotion is essential, along with a hat and sunglasses, to counter the increased intensity of the ultraviolet rays at high altitudes.

For comprehensive information on health while travelling see *The Traveller's Health Guide* by Dr Anthony C Turner (Roger Lascelles, London, 1979) – it's available from Lonely Planet.

TREKKING IN KASHMIR, LADAKH OR ZANSKAR

Trekking in the Indian Himalaya is still a very low-key activity compared to Nepal where there are now a large number of trekking agencies and organisers. There are also a number of ground rules that make trekking in Kashmir a rather different proposition to trekking in Nepal. For more information in trekking in the Himalaya see the two Lonely Planet guides *Trekking in the Nepal Himalaya* and *Trekking in the Indian Himalaya*.

While Kashmir has been a haven for trekkers since the early days of the British Raj, Ladakh and Zanskar are comparatively untouched. This is changing rapidly – from Kargil to the Pensi La is just 150 km, from the Pensi La to Padum just 90 km, from Padum to Lamayuru just 125 km, from Lamayuru to Leh just another 125 km. These are the main routes and today hundreds of trekkers follow even the least travelled of them.

The major difference between Nepalese and Indian trekking is a factor of the smaller number of trekkers. Srinagar does not have the large number of trekking agencies which you find in Kathmandu. Therefore there are not the many organised treks that operate in Nepal. If you do wish to explore Kashmir on an organised trek one of the most experienced operators in the Kashmir Himalaya is Australian-Himalayan Expeditions, 3rd floor, 28-34 O'Connell St, Sydney 2000, Australia. In the US operators with Kashmir treks include Mountain Travel, 1398 Solano Avenue, Albany, California 94706 and Wilderness Travel, 1760 Solano Avenue, Berkeley, California 94707.

It's wise to be wary of local trekking operators in Kashmir. Like carpet weavers and papier mache manufacturers

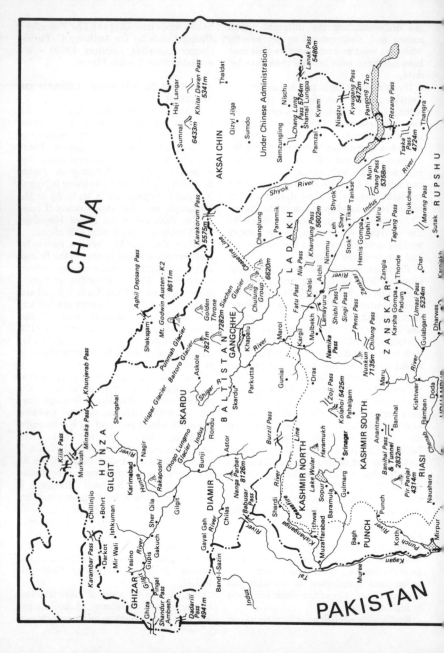

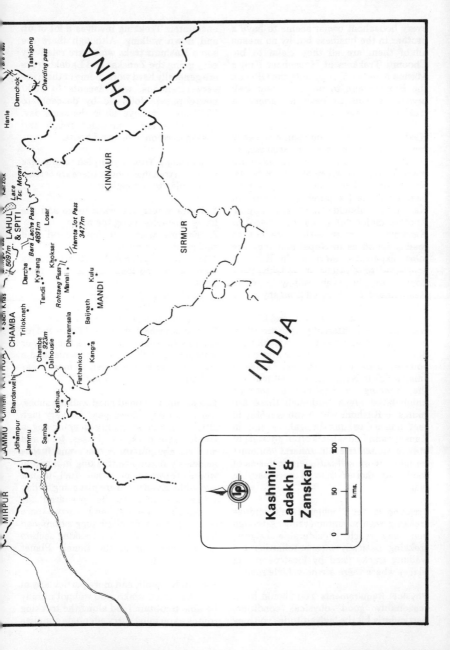

every houseboat owner seems to have a brother in the business but by no means all of them are all they claim to be. Choomti Trekkers at Houseboat King's Marina Number 67, opposite the GPO on the Bund, claim to be competent trek organisers and to have a variety of trekking gear available for hire.

The smaller number of trekkers in Kashmir also means you cannot so easily rent or buy equipment in Srinagar; in contrast to Kathmandu where there are many shops with everything from boots, packs and parkas to tents and sleeping bags available for purchase or hire. In Kashmir you should come fully equipped. Another major difference from Nepal to Kashmir is porters – they are not so readily found as in Nepal and they are more expensive; more so in Kashmir compared to Zanskar or Ladakh. Pack ponies are, however, widely used in Kashmir and can be hired from any of the main hill stations.

One other factor makes trekking in Kashmir a very different proposition than in Nepal. In Nepal most of the trekking is done through inhabited areas and today you can virtually trek from small lodge to small lodge in Nepal. In contrast much of the trekking in Kashmir is through uninhabited areas. Although there are routes in Kashmir where you can stay in rest houses or dak bungalows and in Zanskar and Ladakh it is often possible to stay in monasteries, in general you must be much more self-sufficient in terms of food and shelter than is necessary in Nepal.

Trekking is not Climbing Don't confuse trekking with mountaineering. Although you may reach considerable heights, trekking basically means following the walking tracks used by local people in places where there are no vehicle roads.

Physical Requirements You should be in reasonably good physical condition, particularly for the high altitudes you may encounter. Trekking involves a lot of up and down walking. Although there are some Kashmir treks which are relatively easy going the Zanskar and Ladakh treks are generally hard work. Some of them are very strenuous, with ascents to 5000 metre passes followed by descents to 3500 metre valleys, all in the same day. The paths are sometimes rough and always hard on shoes and boots.

Organising a Trek If you plan to organise your own trek in Kashmir there are certain basic rules to remember:

1. Know where you want to go and the likely obstacles along the route.
2. Ensure that you have good and sufficient equipment.
3. Decide on a price with porters and pony men before you load your gear on their backs.
4. Make it clear to them whether you expect them to feed and house themselves or whether this is your responsibility.
5. Find out whether you will find wood for cooking fires and water along the way, or whether you will need to take fuel and a stove and sufficient water. In most areas of Ladakh there is no wood.

Equipment You need good walking shoes, warm clothing (down gear for very high altitudes), a good quality sleeping bag, a comfortable pack, sunglasses, food and medical equipment. A stove and fuel is necessary if you are trekking in a region where firewood or other fuel is not available. Even if you are just going on day walks it's wise to be prepared for changeable weather and carry spare clothing. More detailed suggestions can be found in the Zanskar trekking section of this book or in the Lonely Planet trekking guides.

Food In Kashmir, and more particularly in Zanskar and Ladakh, you will not usually be able to obtain food along the trekking routes – you must carry adequate supplies

with you. Srinagar is the best place to do your pre-trek outfitting or in Manali if trekking up into Zanskar from the south. Although supplies are also available in Kargil and Leh, and to a lesser extent in Padum, the choice will be much less and costs much higher. Tinned or packaged food suitable for carrying on treks is generally rather more expensive in India than in the west. During the summer you should be able to supplement your supplies with potatoes, onions, peas, lentils, glucose biscuits, tea and tsampa in all but the smallest villages, but don't count on it.

The mountains of Kashmir are mostly heavily forested but the vegetation thins out as you approach the snow line and you should not expect to find wood at every camp. In many places the local villages and nomadic herders have burned everything within easy walking distance. In Ladakh and Zanskar the extreme lack of vegetation means it is often impossible to cook on a fire – you need a kerosene stove and kerosene in a strong, leakproof (preferably metal) container. Cooking on a fire at high altitude would be difficult even if wood were available. At 3500 metres even paper only smoulders unless there is a wind to fan it, due to the shortage of oxygen. One trekker wrote to recommend a petrol (gasoline) stove over a kerosene one as, he wrote, petrol is more readily available than kerosene in India, it burns hotter and better at high altitude, and it's cleaner.

Remember that the high altitudes in Zanskar and Ladakh result in a much lower boiling point for water – in Leh water will boil at around 75°C. Although bulky, a pressure cooker is very useful for cooking rice or lentils.

In some areas of Ladakh you will also have to carry water for your overnight stops as the only water supply in summer may be run-off from melting snow.

Left: Making butter tea in Lamayuru Gompa

Accommodation Although a tent can be very useful there are many government rest houses or dak bungalows along trekking routes in Kashmir. These were originally built by the considerate British and are now maintained and added to by the J&K Government. Bookings for these may be made at the Tourist Reception Centre in Srinagar, and although not always necessary, the chowkidhar in charge is obliged to give preference to those with bookings even though he may not know they are going to arrive. The Government of India trekking maps of Kashmir and Ladakh indicate the locations of these rest houses.

Ladakh and Zanskar have virtually none of these amenities, except at towns along the Srinagar-Leh road. However, tourism has become so all pervading in the past few years that even the smallest village on a trekking route will have what its owner calls a hotel and restaurant, or at least a room in a house which trekkers may rent. Often you can get a room in a gompa although there are restrictions in certain gompas and you should be aware of these. Some gompas have even set up 'hotels' to cater for tourists. Generally this sort of accommodation will consist of little more than a bare room. Nevertheless a tent is still a virtual necessity for trekking in Ladakh since there will be places where your night stop will be far from any village or habitation, such as on long walks over mountain passes.

Routes & Maps Some of the main treks are described in the relative sections on Kashmir, Ladakh and Zanskar. Note that many of these treks go from one region into the next – from Zanskar to Ladakh or Kashmir to Zanskar for example.

Good trekking maps are virtually impossible to obtain in Kashmir. The J&K Tourist Office sell a two sheet *Trekking Route Map of Jammu & Kashmir* for Rs 7 a sheet. Sheet 1 covers the Vale of Kashmir, Pahalgam, Anantnag and the Great Himalaya but very little north of the Leh-Srinagar road. Sheet 2 covers the Zanskar region to just south of Padum and the Indus valley to Leh, but no further. Neither map includes Kargil. Both show the locations of rest houses and dak bungalows, gompas and mosques, roads and some trekking routes, rivers and bridges, post offices, and they give altitudes in meters. With the rapid changes through development and those caused by the extremes of climate, the accuracy of any map must be doubted.

The Kashmir Bookshop on the Bund in Srinagar sells a reasonable Swiss map of Kashmir and Ladakh but it is not detailed enough for exploratory trekkers. For the serious trekker 1:250,000 satellite photographs of the region can be obtained from the EROS Data Centre, Sioux Falls, South Dakota 57198, USA, but these are expensive.

A problem with any map or other information on trekking in this area is the widely varying ways of spelling place names and in some cases variations in the name itself. This book is undoubtedly no exception although it tries to follow the most commonly used variations. No map of this region should be entirely trusted, however. The J&K Tourist Office has a small brochure titled *Trekking in Jammu & Kashmir* which may provide some useful information.

Permission Although there is no system of trekking permits, as required in Nepal, there are limitations on where you may trek. In particular you are constrained by the security zone requirements that you do not go more than a mile north of the Zoji La-Kargil-Leh road and the similar restriction along the Leh-Manali road. This limits Zanskar and Ladakh trekking to the Suru, Zanskar and Kishtwar valleys. For trekking in other areas permission must be obtained from the Ministry of Home Affairs, Government of India, New Delhi.

Snow Bridges These are a particular

hazard of Kashmiri trekking, especially during the spring-summer melt. In many places rivers are completely covered by snow and ice during the winter, while the rivers continue to flow underneath. During the thaw this cover often melts to isolated 'bridges' which trekkers can sometimes cross. Take care, if you fall through a snowbridge the drop may be less than a metre and only result in wet feet but it can be a long, fatal fall. There are certain well known snow bridges which appear every year. Enquire which ones are 'reliable'.

Rivers Particularly in Zanskar there are often unbridged rivers which have to be crossed. These must be treated with great caution as the water may be deep and rapid, the stones on the bottom may be slippery. Often the river may be shallower and the flow less rapid early in the morning than later in the day, when the sun has melted more snow. Rivers can vary widely from one time of year to another and from year to year, depending on how much snow there has been in the winter and how fast it has melted in the summer.

Health & Medicine If you're going on an organised trek the trek organisers will supply you with a list of the necessary immunisations and will probably require that you complete a medical examination before departing. See the introductory section on health for general information about health and immunisations. Maintaining your health while trekking is principally a matter of taking care in what you eat and drink, being careful about personal hygiene, and not over-taxing yourself or eating too little.

Always ensure that drinking water has been boiled or sterilised although at the altitudes reached in Ladakh and Zanskar boiling alone will not ensure sterilisation. Snow or immediate snow-melt is, however, comparatively safe for drinking. Snow and snow-melt water contain very few minerals will deplete your body supply over a period of time. Alternatively puritabs and/or iodine will kill most bacteria in drinking water. Iodine, which can be difficult to find in India although it is readily available in Kathmandu, should be treated with caution. Properly used as a water purifier it's quite safe but as concentrate it's a dangerous poison.

GENERAL INFORMATION
Time
India is 5½ hours ahead of GMT, 4½ hours behind Australian Eastern Standard Time, 10½ hours ahead of American Eastern Standard Time.

Business Hours
Shops and offices are generally open from 10 am to 5 pm, they're late starters! Banks are open 10 am to 2 pm on weekdays, 10 am to noon on Saturdays. Post offices are open 10 am to 5 pm on weekdays and also on Saturday mornings. Shops are likely to be open shorter hours during the winter.

There are many religious and government holidays when banks, post offices and shops are closed. Check with the local tourist office a few days ahead to ensure that you are not caught short of food or money.

Electricity
There is electricity in the main towns of 230-240 volts, 50 cycles, alternating current – breakdowns and blackouts are not unusual. In Srinagar the electricity supply is reasonably reliable but the lines to the houseboats are tenuous – a strong wind can bring them down and leave you in darkness until the next morning.

In Leh and Kargil electricity is supplied by diesel powered generators and only operates in the evenings. In the summer tourist season demand is clearly greater than supply and blackouts are frequent. The voltage is often less than the claimed 220 volts.

Film

Colour film, particularly colour slide film, is becoming much easier to find in India but it is still relatively expensive. Most slide film you do see on sale has been sold to the shops by tourists. If you're planning to take photographs bring plenty of film with you, Kashmir and Ladakh are very photogenic. If you don't use all your film there is a ready market for it from photographic shops or other visitors.

Most villagers in the region are quite happy to be photographed, they may even ask you to do so! Exceptions include some traditional Muslim Kashmiris, the conservative Muslim women in Kargil, and Buddhist nuns. Unfortunately some thoughtless tourists have also introduced the practice of paying to take photographs in some areas. If someone asks you to pay before you take a picture, don't take it.

You'll need a wide angle lens for the mountains and a telephoto lens for distant gompas or close ups of the people will be useful. In Ladakh remember to allow for the extreme intensity of the light at this altitude. There is little light reflection in the shadows so the range in light intensity between a sunlit mountain side and its accompanying shadow can be too great for most films to accommodate. You may have to do some compromising. A polarising filter will deepen the colour of the sky in the thin air of Ladakh.

In contrast to the intense light outdoors the gompas are often dark and gloomy. To capture the atmosphere and the colour in doors you will need high speed film. Flash photography not only loses the atmosphere of the monasteries it also does no good to the paints and fabrics that have often not been exposed to direct light for, in some places, hundreds of years. Using a flash there is an act of vandalism.

Books & Bookshops

India has many surprisingly good bookshops, particularly in New Delhi. There are several bookshops in Srinagar which usually have the latest books of local interest. Try the Kashmir Bookshop on the Bund in Srinagar or the bookshop under the Indian Coffee House. There are a number of locally published guidebooks to Kashmir. There are many older books on Kashmir and Ladakh worth searching out in libraries and there are also a number of recently published coffee table books on these picturesque regions. Indian publishers have recognised the growing interest in Kashmir and Ladakh and produced facsimile editions of a number of books written in the last century by British engineers, soldiers and explorers and German missionaries and doctors. Some useful reading might include:

Beautiful Valleys of Kashmir & Ladakh, Samsar Chand Kaul, Utpal Publications, Srinagar, 1979 was first published in 1942, revised three times since, and written by a teacher of natural history at the Church Missionary School in Srinagar, the book takes a genteel but detailed look at the plants, birds and animals of Kashmir through a series of expeditions to most parts of the Vale. The research is thorough and this book is the often unacknowledged source for material on wildlife and geography in a number of trekking guidebooks. The chapters on Ladakh are not nearly as thorough and have been added in the later editions.

Ladakh by Heinrich Harrer, Penguin Verlag, Innsbruck, 1980 is one of a number of coffee table books on Ladakh and although certainly not the best it is a reasonable introduction. *Seven Years in Tibet* by Heinrich Harrer is a best-selling account of the author's adventures in Tibet before the Chinese occupation. It gives a rather 'European' view of the 'natives' of India and Tibet, telling of Harrer's escape from a prisoner of war camp in India and walk across the Himalaya to Tibet.

Tibet by Thubten Jigme Norbu and Colin Turnbull is an excellent account of the politics, culture and religion of Tibet, co-authored by the brother of the Dalai Lama. *The Way of the White Cloud* (Buddhism in Tibet), Lama Anagarika Govinda, BI Publications, Bombay, 1982 is a well written and sympathetic account of a European Buddhist's pilgrimage to Lhasa, and the discovery of his teacher. *An English Buddhist in a Tibetan Monastery*, Routledge & Kegan Paul, London, 1962 is out of print and hard to come by, but is an interesting account of life in a monastery.

Magic & Mystery in Tibet, Alexandra David-Neel, Abacus, London, 1977 is one of a number of books on religious and mystical practices, occult lore and customs in Tibet written by Madame David-Neel, who travelled to Lhasa and the Tibetan regions in the 1920s and '30s and was given the rank of lama by the Tibetans – a title not normally given to women. *Buddhism & Lamaism of Tibet*, L Austine Waddell, Heritage Publishers, New Delhi, 1979 was first published in 1895 and remains the reference book for serious students of Tibetan religion. *Tibetan Medicine*, Venerable Rechung Rimpoche, University of California Press, 1976, gives a layman's introduction to the world of Tibetan medicine.

Freedom at Midnight by Larry Collins and Dominique Lapierre, that highly readable book on India's rocky path to independence, has an interesting description of the stormy events in Kashmir at that time. It's available in India in a low price Bell Books/Vikas Publishing paperback. V S Naipaul's book on his first visit to India, *An Area of Darkness*, includes a lengthy section on Kashmir (and the Kashmiris) and an account of the Amarnath trek.

John Masters, author of a number of novels set in the sub-continent, spent some time in the Himalayan and Hindu Kush regions as a British soldier in the 1930s. His book *The Lotus & the Wind*, Corgi, London, 1973, gives both history and insight into the character of the people who live there. Rudyard Kipling's Raj era classic *Kim* has interesting characters from Tibet and Kashmir.

National Geographic had a feature on Ladakh in the March 1978 issue. *Zanskar – The Hidden Kingdom* by Michel Peissel (Collins & Harvill Press, London, 1979) is an interesting account of a trek through Zanskar shortly after it was reopened to foreign tourists. He follows the Kargil-Padum-Manali route as described in the Zanskar section of this book. *A Journey in Ladakh*, Andrew Harvey, Jonathan Cape, London, 1983 is an interesting narrative that looks at various aspects of life in Ladakh through the eyes of an interested traveller.

For more information on trekking in the Kashmir region and in other parts of the Indian Himalaya the Lonely Planet guidebook *Trekking in the Indian Himalaya* will be published in 1985.

Newspapers & Media

The major English language Indian papers arrive in Srinagar daily by air. You'll also find *Time*, *Newsweek* and India's own excellent news-magazine *India Today* on Srinagar's news-stands. Srinagar has its own TV and radio stations.

Newspapers are hard to come by in Leh and virtually unknown outside it. The Leh library has the most recently arrived copies and readers are welcome. You may also borrow books from the library (and donate your own to it when you leave) by leaving your passport as security. Leh has a station of All India Radio with its own generator and transmitter. It relays programs from Delhi and broadcasts local material from 5 pm to midnight, most of it in Ladakhi.

LANGUAGE

Although English is widely understood in Kashmir (but not so much in Ladakh) it never hurts to know a little of the local language. Indians speak a vast number of regional languages including – in the state of Jammu and Kashmir – Kashmiri,

Ladakhi and Urdu. See the Ladakh section for some words in Ladakhi. Hindi is the official 'national' language and widely spoken. Some useful words and phrases:

Questions, Commands & Greetings

where is a hotel (tourist office)?
hotal (turist afis) kahan hai?
how far is . . . . ?
. . . .kitni dur hai?
how do I get to . . . . ?
. . . . kojane ke liye kaise jana parega?
hello, goodbye
namaste
yes/no
han/nahin
please
meharbani se
thank you
shukriya, dhanyawad
how much?
kitne rupiah?
this is expensive
yeh bahut mehnga hai
what is the time?
kya baja hai?
what is your name?
apka shubh nam?
come here
yahan ao
show me the menu
mujha minu dikhao
the bill please
bill lao

big	*bara*
small	*muskarana*
today	*tambaku*
day	*din*
night	*rhat*
week	*saptah*
month	*mahina*
year	*sal*
medicine	*dawa*

Food & Drink

ice	*baraf*
egg	*anda*
fruit	*phal*
vegetable	*sabzi*
water	*pani*
rice	*inam*
tea	*chai*
coffee	*kafi*
milk	*dudh*
sugar	*chini*
butter	*makkhan*

Numbers

1	*ek*
2	*do*
3	*tin*
4	*char*
5	*panch*
6	*chhe*
7	*sat*
8	*ath*
9	*nau*
10	*das*
100	*sau*
100,000	*lakh*
10,000,000	*crore*

INFORMATION

Government of India Tourist offices overseas include:

Australia	Carlton Centre, 55 Elizabeth St, Sydney, NSW 2000 (tel 02 232 1600)
	8 Parliament Court, 1076 Hay Street, West Perth, WA (tel06 321 6932)
Canada	Suite 1016, Royal Trust Tower (PO Box 342), Toronto Dominion Centre, Toronto 1, Ontario (tel 416 362 3188)
Japan	Pearl Building, 9-18 Ginza, 7 Chome, Chuo ku, Tokyo (tel 571 5062/3)

Singapore	Podium Block, 4th floor, Court Hotel, Tanglin Rd, Singapore 10 (tel 235 5737)
Sweden	Sveavagen 9-11 (Box 40016), S-III-57 Stockholm (tel 08 215081)
Thailand	Singapore Airlines Building, 3rd floor, 62/5 Thaniya Rd, Bangkok
UK	7 Cork Street, London WIX QAB (tel 01 437 3677-8) 3678)
USA	30 Rockefeller Plaza, 15 North Mezzanine, New York, NY 10020 (tel 212 586 4901) 201 North Michigan Ave, Chicago, Illinois 60601 (tel 312 236 6899) 3550 Wilshire Blvd, Suite 204, Los Angeles, California 90010 (tel 213 380 8855)

In India Government of India Tourist Offices you may find useful include:

Bombay	123 M Karve Rd (tel 293144)
Calcutta	4 Shakespeare Sarani (tel 441402)
Jammu	Gulab Bhavan (tel 5121)
Madras	154 Anna Salai (tel 86240)
New Delhi	88 Janpath (tel 320005)
Srinagar	Residency Rd

In Jammu and Kashmir itself there are J&K Tourist Offices at:

Jammu	Tourist Reception Centre, Vir Marg (tel 5324) Office of the Director of Information, Government of J&K, Old Secretariat (tel 5376) Jammu Airport
Srinagar	Tourist Reception Centre (tel 2449, 2927, 3648, 6209) J&K Government Reception Centre (tel 72449, 72927, 73648, 76209) Srinagar Airport

The J&K Tourist Department also has smaller offices in Pahalgam, Kud, Batote, Banihal, Verinag, Kokarnag, Tangmarg, Achhabal, Gandarbal, Gulmarg and Katra. In Ladakh and Zanskar there are offices in Kargil, Leh and Padum. Elsewhere there are Kashmir Government Tourist Offices at:

Ahmedabad	Airlines House, Lal Darwaza (tel 20473)
Bombay	Manekji Wadia Building, 129 Mahatma Gandhi Rd (tel 273820)
Calcutta	Kashmir Government Arts Emporium, 12 Chowringhee (tel 233268)
New Delhi	Chandralok Building, 36 Janpath (tel 345373)
Pathankot	Railway Station (tel 57)

Getting There

Getting to Kashmir is a two part operation. First you have to get to India, then you have to get to Kashmir. The following sections detail air fares to India from various places. To get to Kashmir from within India see the final section on internal transport.

FROM THE UK

The official fare from London to Bombay or New Delhi is £522 economy one-way or £927 in 1st class. Return fares are double. There are two different roundtrip excursion fares available but only to UK residents. The 28/90 (28 day minimum stay, 90 day maximum stay) ticket is £662 and permits one stopover on the roundtrip. The 14/120 day excursion costs £570 but no stopovers are permitted.

If economy is important then you can do considerably better than that through London's many cheap ticket specialists or 'bucket shops'. Check the travel page ads in *The Times, Business Traveller*, the weekly what's on magazine *Time Out*, or in giveaway papers like the *Australasian Express* or *LAM*. Two reliable London bucket shops are Trailfinders at 46 Earls Court Rd, London W8 and STA Travel at 74 Old Brompton Rd, London SW7 or 117 Euston Rd, London NW1.

Typical fares being quoted range from around £200 one-way or £300 return. Fares depend very much on the carrier. The very cheapest fares are likely to be on something like Ariana Afghan Airlines or Iraqi Airways which (surprise, surprise) nobody wants to fly on these days. You'll also find very competitive fares to the subcontinent with Bangladesh Biman or with Air Lanka.

If you want to stop in India en route to Australia you're looking at about £500. You'll probably find fares via Karachi (Pakistan) or Colombo (Sri Lanka) are slightly cheaper than fares via India.

FROM THE USA

Air India has the lowest fare for roundtrip regularly scheduled flights – US$1323 from New York to Delhi. There's a minimum 14 day, maximum 120 day stay requirement. Out of San Francisco the same ticket is US$1413. Some travel agencies will discount these tickets about US$150. The US west coast has plenty of ticket discounters who offer cut price tickets to Asia – check the travel sections of the Sunday papers for their ads. In New York AM-Jet Travels (tel 212 697 5332) has daily charters from New York to Delhi for US$1150 roundtrip. Their address is 501 Fifth Ave, Room 2008, New York, NY 10017. CIEE, with offices all around the country, are also good for cheap fares.

FROM CANADA

The regular one-way economy fare from Toronto to New Delhi is C$1479. The roundtrip excursion fare from Toronto, with a 14 day minimum, 120 days maximum stay, is C$1800. One-way apex fares, with the usual advance booking and cancellation penalties, are C$1132 in the low season, C$1240 in the high. Round the world fares which take in India are available through Canada for around C$2000.

FROM AUSTRALIA

The regular one-way fare to Bombay or Delhi from the Australian east coast is A$1081 in economy, A$1513 in 1st class. Return fares are double. There are also 10/270 (10 day minimum stay, 270 day maximum stay) round trip excursion fares available. From the Australian east coast (Melbourne, Sydney, Adelaide, Brisbane) to Bombay or Delhi the fare is A$1451. From Darwin or Perth it's A$1233. Fares are slightly cheaper to Calcutta, slightly cheaper again to Madras, but the largest difference is only A$23. You are allowed one stopover in each direction – which usually means Singapore.

Alternatively there are advance purchase tickets available one-way or return. These must be booked and paid for 21 days in advance and after that time the usual cancellation penalties apply. There's a minimum five day and maximum one year stay requirement. One stopover is permitted on the one-way or the roundtrip tickets. The year is divided into two periods – basic March to September, peak October to February.

The one-way fare from the Australian east coast to Bombay or Delhi is A$725 basic or A$824 peak. From Darwin or Perth it's A$616 or 701. Calcutta and Madras are somewhat cheaper. The round trip fare from the east coast to Bombay or Delhi is A$980 basic or A$1218 peak. From Darwin or Perth it's A$834 and A$1036. Again Calcutta and Madras are somewhat cheaper.

FROM NEW ZEALAND

Round trip excursion fares are also available from Auckland. To Bombay or Delhi it's NZ$2059, slightly cheaper to Calcutta or Madras.

ROUND THE WORLD FARES

Round the world (RTW) fares have become all the rage in the past few years. Basically they're of two types – airline tickets and agent tickets. An airline RTW ticket usually means two airlines have joined together to market a ticket which takes you right round the world on their combined routes. Within certain limitations of time and number of stopovers you can fly pretty well anywhere you choose using their combined routes so long as you keep moving in the same direction. Compared to the full fare tickets which permit you to go absolutely anywhere you choose on any IATA airline you choose so long as you do not exceed the 'maximum permitted mileage' these tickets are much less flexible. But they are also much cheaper.

Quite a few of these combined airline RTW tickets go through India including the Air India-Continental Airlines one which will also allow you to make several stopovers within India. RTW tickets typically cost from around £1000 (US$1500) for northern hemisphere routes. If you want to include the southern hemisphere (ie Australia) then you're probably looking at around US$2000.

The other type of RTW ticket, the agent ticket, is simply a combination of cheap fares strung together by an enterprising agent. This will probably use a wider variety of airlines and may provide routes which the 'off the shelf' tickets cannot manage.

OVERLAND

The classic way of getting to India from Europe has always been overland and despite the hassles in Iran and Afghanistan you can still travel by land all the way from Europe. See *West Asia on a Shoestring* for more details. Similarly from Australia you can travel country to country through south-east Asia to India – see *South-East Asia on a Shoestring* for the full story.

GETTING TO KASHMIR

Land Except for the few trekkers who walk into the region (Zanskar from Manali in Himachal Pradesh, Kashmir from Kishtwar, etc) the land route into Kashmir is a straightforward one. First of all you get to Jammu by bus or train. See the Jammu section for details. From Jammu by land, a bus or taxi to Srinagar is the only choice you have. See the Jammu and Srinagar sections. On to Ladakh from Srinagar it's again bus, taxi or jeep. See the Ladakh section for details.

Take special care on the train from Delhi to Jammu. This is a tourist train – for Indians and foreigners – and pickpockets and snatch thieves work overtime on this route. They're particularly prevalent at the Delhi end, just as the train departs. One routine is to create a last minute disturbance and before you know it your bag has disappeared through the window at the same instant as the train pulls out from the station.

Air You can fly to Srinagar from Delhi or via Jammu and other intermediate points. Most people flying in to Leh in Ladakh will fly from Srinagar but you can also fly there from Chandigarh in Haryana or from Delhi – via Chandigarh or Srinagar. See the relevant sections of this book. Flying straight to Leh from Delhi is not a very good idea; pausing first in Srinagar gives you some altitude acclimatisation whereas Delhi-Leh takes you straight from the plains, close to sea level, to the thin air of the Himalaya.

A major problem with flying Indian Airlines is the booking system. Although it has been planned for years there is still no computer booking system. This means it is very time consuming to make reservations and very difficult to know exactly how many seats are available on any given flight. The end result is that you may often find yourself a number on an unbelievably long wait list – except that they humourously call it the 'chance list'! Do not despair, you generally find yourself with a seat despite seemingly long odds. If you can, however, the best plan is to book well ahead. Note, however, that Indian Airlines fares within India usually work out rather cheaper than the same flights bought outside the country.

Flying Indian Airlines has a few other quirks and curiosities. One is that no-shows or last-minute cancellations get rough treatment. If you miss your flight you can throw the ticket away, you won't be able to use it again. Indian Airlines treat lost tickets with equal compassion. If your ticket is stolen you'd better have a good travel insurance policy because Indian Airlines won't reissue it. Keep a close eye on your bags too; make sure they're properly tagged and that after they leave your control they do start heading towards the plane.

LEAVING INDIA

Airline Tickets Although you can also get cheap tickets in Bombay and Calcutta it is in Delhi where the real wheeling and dealing goes on. There are countless 'bucket shops' around Connaught Place but enquire with fellow travellers about their current trustworthiness! If you purchase any cheap ticket you have to pay the full official fare through a bank – the agent gets you a bank form stating what the official fare is, you pay the bank, the bank then pays the agent. You then receive a refund from the agent, but in rupees. So it is wise either to buy your ticket far enough ahead that you can use those rupees up or have plenty of bank exchange certificates in hand in order to change the rupees back. This also applies to credit card purchases.

Some typical fares from India would be Delhi-Australia for about Rs 6000, Delhi to various European capitals for around Rs 4000 or a bit less from Bombay. The cheapest flights to Europe will be with airlines like Aeroflot, LOT, Kuwait Airways, Syrian Arab Airways or Iraqi Airways.

Airport Tax India now has one of the highest airport taxes in the world for international flights. For flights to neighbouring countries (Pakistan, Sri Lanka, Bangladesh, Nepal) it's Rs 50 but to more distant countries it's a hefty Rs 100. India's neighbours are also getting into rip-off airport taxes, it's Rs 100 in Nepal and Sri Lanka although, fortunately, that's a fair bit less than Indian Rs 100 in both cases. Note that this airport tax applies to everybody, even to babies who do not occupy a seat – in most countries airport tax applies only to seat occupants or only to adults. It's also important to ensure the tax is for the specific carrier you're flying with. An Air India departure tax is no good on a British Airways flight!

Jammu

Jammu, the second largest town in the state of Jammu and Kashmir, has a population of just under 200,000. It's situated 580 km from Delhi and 290 km from Srinagar on the south-eastern slopes of the Siwalik range. In winter it becomes the headquarters of the J&K administration (as it had done since the time of the Dogra rulers) and many Kashmiris move here for the winter because the temperature does not drop below 5°C. In Srinagar at that time the temperature can fall as low as −12°C. Due to its low altitute (300 metres) the summers can get uncomfortably hot (over 40°C) and the humid, unpleasant conditions also bring on plagues of gnats. This is, of course, when most visitors to Srinagar will be passing through Jammu.

For those interested in languages one can hear Hindi, Kashmiri, English, Urdu, Punjabi and Dogri spoken in Jammu. Despite its mix of cultures, languages and religions it is not of great interest to tourists; most travellers tend to use it only as an overnight stop on the way to or from Kashmir. Unless you fly you will almost certainly pass through Jammu on your way to Kashmir.

The old city of Jammu is perched on a hilltop beside the Tawi River. A new town sprawls away from the hillside and extends for some distance across the other side of the river.

History
Legend has it that the city was founded by Jamboo Loochen about three thousand years ago. The raja was hunting in the area, away from his capital city of Bahu, when he came across a lion and a goat drinking from the same pond. The Shivadawala Shrine now stands on this spot in the city. Jammu is known as 'the city of temples' because of its many shrines, with their soaring golden spires or shikhars.

There are many other shrines and temples around the city and environs that date from earlier years but the recorded history of Jammu begins from the time of the Dogra rulers in the early 19th century. In 1846 the Dogra ruler of Jammu was created Maharaja of an ill-defined Himalayan kingdom, 'to the eastward of the river Indus and westward of the river Ravi', by the treaties of Lahore and Amritsar at the conclusion of the first Sikh war. It was the lack of definition of this state – the forerunner of Jammu and Kashmir – that caused the continuing disputes with Russia and China over territory. The British created the state as part of a complex political buffer zone between their Indian empire and China and Russia.

For the Maharaja Gulab Singh, the treaty confirmed for him almost 25 years of fighting and negotiation with the small hill tribes along the northern border of the Sikh empire, centred on the Punjab. The region remained under Dogra rule until the partition of India in 1947, when Hari Singh, the then Maharaja of Kashmir, decided that it would remain as part of India and the state of Jammu & Kashmir was born.

Information
The Government of India Tourist Office (tel 5121) on Gulab Bhavan and the J&K Tourist Reception Centre (tel 5324) on Vir Marg are the standard reference centres. They're not the best tourist information points in India and obtaining information is difficult and requires patience. What information they do have is usually for people heading north into Kashmir. They've got little to tell you if you're travelling south. Both offices are open 9 am to 5 pm (closed for lunch) so for many visitors to Jammu, arriving late in the afternoon, they will be closed just

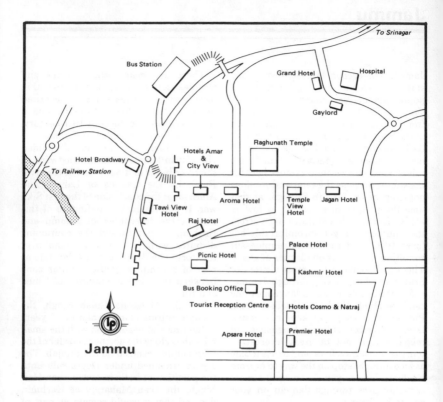

Jammu

when they are most needed! The tourist office has a branch at the railway station (tel 8803) which may be open when your train from Delhi arrives in the early morning.

The GPO is on Pacca Danga.

Raghunath Temple
Situated in the centre of the city, only a short stroll from the Tourist Reception Centre, this is the largest temple complex in northern India. Construction of the temple started in 1835, under Maharaja Gulab Singh, the founder of the present city of Jammu. The Purani Mandi, like the main complex dedicated to Lord Rama, was built in 1888 by Maharaja Ranbir Singh's wife. The smaller temples sur-

rounding the courtyard are dedicated to various gods and goddesses who feature in the Ramayana. The Raghunath Sanskrit Library is a vast storehouse containing thousands of rare and ancient manuscripts.

Rambireswar Temple
Just across the road from the Dogra Art Gallery, this Shiva temple was built in 1883 by Maharaja Ranbir Singh and features a number of crystal Shiva lingams and 11 larger black stone ones as well as the tallest shikhar in the city.

Old Secretariat
The former palace of the Dogra rulers, the Old Secretariat is near the centre of town. It's a huge complex of mansions with

several styles of architecture incorporated in its overall structure. Its walls are adorned with intricate paintings of flowers, creepers, birds and other decorations, and interesting motifs on the ceilings and walls.

Dogra Art Gallery

The collection here includes over 500 paintings of the Basohli, Jammu and Kangra schools. The Basohli-style miniature paintings here are of particular importance and interest. There are numerous other charming items of the old Dogra arts, including hundreds of exotic and exquisite Bahara miniatures. The gallery also houses a collection of sculptures, terracotta pieces, murals, weapons and illustrated manuscripts.

The gallery is situated in the Gandhi Bhavan by the New Secretariat. It is open from 7.30 am to 1 pm in summer and from 11 am to 5 pm in winter, except on Mondays when it is closed. Admission is free.

Bahu Fort

Clinging to a rock face on the opposite bank of the Tawi River, the huge fort is about four km from the centre. Although it is said to date back to Jammu's legendary founder, Jamboo Loochen, the present structure was built by the Dogras. An old, and highly esteemed, temple to the Goddess Kali can be seen inside the fort. Crowds of worshippers go there on Tuesdays and Sundays.

Opposite Bahu Fort on another hilltop is the consecrated spot dedicated to Maha Maya, a Jammu heroine who died fighting invaders. A statue of Shri Hans Raj, another important personage in Jammu's history, is in a park just at the entrance to the shrine.

Amar Mahal Palace

Built in the last century for Raja Amar Singh, the palace is a curious example of French architecture. It's situated on a hillock overlooking the Tawi River and commands an excellent view of the city and its surroundings. The palace museum has a family portrait gallery, a rich library and an important collection of paintings of the Pahari school. It's worth a visit if you have the time.

The museum is open from 5 to 7 pm daily and from 8 am to noon on Sundays. It is just off the Srinagar road on the northern outskirts of town.

Canals

The Ramblr Canal is about two km from the city, it's a favourite stroll in Jammu. The canal leaves the Chenab at Akhnoor, 32 km from Jammu. It provides electricity and irrigation.

Places to Stay

If you're en route to Srinagar and arrive in Jammu by train (as most people do) then you have two choices. The first is not to overnight in Jammu but to take one of the buses which wait at the railway station for the arrival of the trains and go straight to Srinagar. Most of these buses stop overnight at Banihal, below the Jawahar Tunnel, and continue on to Srinagar the following day. Accommodation in Banihal is generally in the *Tourist Lodge* and is very basic – three large dormitories without beds, no hot water and frequently no electricity.

The second choice is to stay overnight in Jammu and take a bus to Srinagar the first thing next day. Since they start earlier in the day these buses complete the journey to Srinagar in one day. If you decide to stay overnight then it's important to first find yourself a room and then book a ticket on the bus. Don't hang about as competition for both can be fierce during the tourist season. If you're coming down from Srinagar it's even more necessary to rush to find a room as you arrive late in the day, when spare rooms may be at a premium.

Places to Stay – bottom end At the bottom of the market the *Tawi View Hotel* (tel

47301), Maheshi Gate is undoubtedly the best of the bunch and very popular with travellers. Doubles with bath are Rs 31.50 and the manager is friendly and helpful. Opposite the Tourist Reception Centre on Vir Marg the *Tourist Home Hotel* is similarly priced and equipped. It's a bit noisy but convenient.

Another simple but clean place is the *Hotel Kashmir*, Vir Marg, where bathless doubles are Rs 30. There are many other budget hotels but there's not much to choose between them, it's usually a question of which ones have rooms available. Reasonable places include the *Hotel Aroma*, Gumat Bazaar (doubles at Rs 25 or Rs 35 with attached bath); *Hotel Raj* (bathless doubles at Rs 22) or the *Hotel Aryabhat* (overpriced and grubby – doubles at Rs 25 or Rs 45 with bath). The *Hotel Broadway* (tel 43636) on Gumat Chowk has singles with attached bath at Rs 42 to 50, doubles at Rs 60 to 75. Bathless doubles are Rs 30 to 40. They also have larger rooms available.

At the railway station there's Jammu's second *Tourist Reception Centre* (tel 8803) with doubles from Rs 25 to Rs 50 with air-con. There are also dorm beds but the dormitory is totally bare and best avoided. The station also has *Retiring Rooms* at Rs 45 a double or Rs 75 with air-con, dorm beds at Rs 10. Remember that the railway station is across the Tawi River, several km from the centre. The bus station is close to the centre and has rather decrepit *Retiring Rooms* with doubles at Rs 30 and Rs 5 dorm beds.

In the middle range one of the best places is the fairly new *Hotel Jagan* (tel 42402), Raghunath Bazaar, which also has an air-con restaurant. It's spotlessly clean, pleasantly decorated and has rooms at Rs 45/60 or with air-con doubles are Rs 100 to 125. Another popular mid-range hotel is the 128 room *Tourist Reception Centre* (tel 5421) on Vir Marg. Doubles range from Rs 50 (D Block), Rs 55 (C and H Block) to Rs 60 (A Block). There are also some air-cooled doubles at

Rs 80. All the rooms have attached bathrooms and there is also a restaurant. There's also a grim dormitory which should be avoided no matter how tight your budget. You're generally restricted to a maximum of two nights' stay in the Tourist Reception Centre.

Across Vir Marg from the Tourist Reception Centre the *Premier Hotel* is much improved and now one of the best, cleanest and newest hotels near the downtown area. Singles/doubles are Rs 65/90 or Rs 120/150 with air-con.

Also on Vir Marg the *Natraj Hotel* (tel 7450) has rooms with attached bath at Rs 35/75. Down the road from the Raghunath Temple are a number of bottom and middle bracket hotels. In the middle category is the *Hotel Gagan*, Gumat Bazaar, which has clean doubles with bath for Rs 50. The *Hotel Amar* and the *Hotel City View* (tel 46120) also in Gumat Bazaar, both have doubles with attached bath for Rs 45 to 60 or with air-cooling for Rs 75. These two are both often full.

Places to Stay – top end

At the top end of the market is the *Hotel Jammu Ashok* (tel 46154, 42084) on the outskirts of town to the north, close to the Amar Mahal Palace. Rooms are Rs 100/150 or Rs 225/300 with air-con. The *Hotel Asia* (tel 6373-5) is in Nehru Market close to the Jammu Tawi railway station and the airport but a long way from the centre. Rooms are similarly priced to the Jammu Ashok.

Hotel Cosmo (tel 47561) on Vir Marg is cheaper and more convenient. Singles are Rs 50 to 80, doubles Rs 80 to 120 or with air-con doubles are Rs 150 to 200. All these upper bracket hotels have a bar and restaurant.

Places to Eat

The usual government tourist centre menu is available at the *Tourist Reception Centre*. Reasonable sort of food. The *Cosmo Hotel's* air-con restaurant is far superior to the hotel – good for a pleasant meal in cool surroundings and a cold beer. It's probably the best restaurant in town.

A few doors down the *Premier* has Chinese and Kashmiri food but is rather expensive. There is a collection of little kebab stalls between the two. The railway station and the bus station have the usual station restaurant facilities.

Getting There

Air The Indian Airlines office (tel 5935, 3088) is at the Tourist Reception Centre (tel 8). The airport is seven km out of town and the Indian Airlines phone numbers there are 8164 or 5794.

By air it's only half an hour to Srinagar (Rs 179) and there are flights three or four days a week New Delhi-Jammu-Srinagar.

Bus Srinagar buses depart from various locations: A class, de-luxe and air-con buses go from the Tourist Reception Centre. B class buses go from the bus station. Buses also run from the railway station where they meet in-coming trains – thus you can take an overnight train from Delhi and catch a bus to Srinagar as soon as you arrive. Normally the buses depart for Srinagar between 6 and 7 am in order to reach Srinagar by nightfall. It is most important that you book your bus on to Srinagar as soon as you arrive in Jammu. Bus fares between Jammu and Srinagar are Rs 27 (B class), Rs 40 (A class), Rs 65 (super de-luxe) and Rs 100 (air-con). Travelling from Jammu to Srinagar some feel that the right side of the bus offers the best view.

Travelling south (towards Delhi) the luxury overnight Rs 100 video coaches leave just before the buses from Srinagar arrive in the evening. Day buses are all B class, crowded and leave early in the morning.

There are frequent buses from Jammu to Amritsar (Rs 15), Pathankot (Rs 8, three hours) and other cities to the south. Pathankot is the jumping off point for Dharamsala, Dalhousie and the other Himachal Pradesh hill stations. Buses also operate to Akhnoor, Banihal, Bhadrooh, Katra, Kishtwar, Poonch, Riasi, Ramnagar, Udhampur, Kud and Batote.

A last minute note indicates that a section of the Jammu-Srinagar road is now one-way and buses now go one-way on one day, the other way on alternate days. This may only be a short term policy.

Taxi You can travel by taxi between Jammu and Srinagar for approximately Rs 130 per person or Rs 520 for the whole taxi.

Train Jammu Tawi is the end of the railway line up from Delhi, many travellers come here on the overnight trains, only the earliest of which arrives in time to take a bus straight through to Srinagar on the same day. Fares from Delhi are Rs 193 in 1st class, Rs 60 in 2nd. Travelling south there are three or four trains a day, leaving in the afternoon or evening. Delhi-Jammu is 591 km and trains take nine to 13 hours.

Getting Around

Jammu has metered taxis, auto-rickshaws, a minibus service and a tempo service between a number of points. From the railway station to the bus station costs Rs 1 by the new minibuses. The same trip by auto-rickshaw would be Rs 5 to 7. It's only a short distance from the Tourist Reception Centre in the town centre to the bus station, say Rs 2-3 by autorickshaw.

AROUND JAMMU

The countryside around Jammu is uninteresting, comprising a low belt of plains made up of sandy, alluvial fans of silt deposited by the streams flowing out from the foothills of the Himalaya. The rainfall is low – 380 to 500 mm a year – coming mainly as heavy but infrequent showers in the summer (June to September) when the monsoon winds blow. The land is almost bare of trees, thorn scrub and coarse grass are all that remain.

For those with more time, or their own vehicle, there are many places around Jammu or along the road to Srinagar. Prior to the completion of the Jawarhar Tunnel the trip from Jammu to Srinagar took two days with an overnight stop at Batote. Today you make the trip in one day but it's a long haul (10 to 12 hours) with only a couple of rest stops and one lunch stop along the way. Most unusual for an Indian bus trip! There's certainly no time for looking around if you're on the direct bus.

Jammu-Srinagar Road

The route between Jammu and Srinagar is 293 km (183 miles) long. From Jammu the road winds gently up and down to Udhampur (61 km) then climbs steeply to Patnitop (107 km). From here it drops just as steeply to Ramban (158 km); the road follows a picturesque but hazardous river route along this stretch. At Ramban it ascends again to Banihal (187 km) and on to the Jawarhar Tunnel (204 km). The road descends rapidly into the Kashmir Valley after the tunnel, and runs flat the remaining distance to Srinagar.

There are numerous places of interest on this route in Jammu. Places of interest along the road but within Kashmir are covered in the Kashmir section.

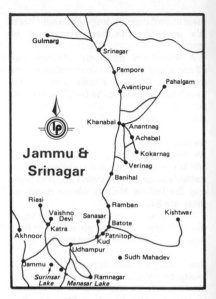

Akhnoor (32 km north-west)

A few km from Jhiri, this is a popular picnic spot where the Chenab River reaches the plains. The Rambir Canal branches off from the Chenab at this point. The massive ruins of an old fort stand beside the Chenab here. At nearby Ambran, sculptures and terra-cotta figures were discovered several decades ago. Two other important spots near here are the Kameshwar Shiva Shrine and the tomb of Babar Faiz Bux. Akhnoor is reached by a regular bus service.

This used to be the route to Srinagar from Jammu during the Moghul era. That road continues through Nawshera, Rajauri and Poonch, 246 km from Jammu.

Jehangir, who died en route to Kashmir, was buried at Chingas, 36 km before Rajauri. There is a huge Moghul sarai at Thana Mandi, near Poonch. The waterfall at Nuri Chham, a popular resting place for the Moghul queen Nur Jahan, is 16 km from here.

Basohli (125 km south-east, 53 km from Pathankot)

Situated fairly close to Dalhousie in Himachal Pradesh, Basohli is the birthplace of the Pahari miniature paintings which are so famous in this region. There are some palace ruins in Basohli and it is a good base for treks. Direct buses run here from Jammu.

Billawar & Sukrala

Billawar is on the road from Udhampur to Dhar, which is near Basohli. The majestic old temple in Billawar is now mostly ruined. There are many interesting ruins of old wells, known as *baulis* in this area. The temple of Sukrala Devi, with its fine old stone sculpture of the eight-armed Goddess Devi, is picturesquely situated on a hilltop, 10 km from Billawar.

Babor (72 km east)

This site is noted for its five partially ruined temples with carved figures of the Hindu gods. They are marked by exquisitely sculptured statues and statuettes, elaborate and minute carvings, huge fluted pillars with lion or elephant heads or ornamented capitals, gigantic decorated roof slabs and beams, all fixed without any binding material.

The statues include a particularly fine one of the goddess Ganga. The various temples at Babor include the richly and tastefully decorated temple of Devi with its numerous miniature medallions, depicting attractively carved gods and goddesses and celestial dancers and musicians. The Shiva temple has sculptured panels of geese, bulls and floral carvings, a frieze with two armed-cavaliers drawing their bows and another of the god Narasimha. Another frieze shows Krishna playing the flute with two attendants waving palm frond fans and Lord Vishnu reclining.

Purmandal & Uttar Behani (39 km southeast, off the Pathankot road)

The imposing rock temples of Purmandal nestle in the Siwalik range and are visible from a great distance. Maharaja Ranbir Singh, known for his patronage of art and learning, had planned to create a unique centre of pilgrimage. He named different spots between Purmandal and Uttar Behani, about 6½ km away, along the subterranean Dewak River, after the different Tirathas of the country. He started a grandiose project to build a stately shrine at each of these spots. Only a few were completed before he died and his ambitious dream – Purmandal – ended with him. The ruins of the half finished temples and the material that was collected for the construction are still scattered around the wilderness nearby.

Another attraction of Purmandal is the large number of wall paintings on the walls of the old buildings. A huge, white-marble bull and an outsize bronze bell beside some artifacts are among the attractions at Uttar Behani.

The temples at Purmandal have been built on a rock and a double basement has been cut out of the rock itself. The Dewak stream that flows at the base of this rock is considered to be very sacred by the Hindus. A hooded stone serpent jutting out of a cistern in the rock in the central shrine is an object of religious attraction, as it is believed to a unique manifestation of Lord Shiva.

As the Dewak is believed to flow underground, people dig pits in the bed and bathe in the water that comes out. Devotees also take this water away with them as a sacred treasure. Nearby are several palatial buildings constructed by Maharaja Rangit Singh, Maharaja Gulab Singh and Maharaja Ranbir Singh.

Purmandal is reached by a regular bus service and is also a popular picnic spot.

Surinsar Lake (45 km east)

This picturesque lake is surrounded by pine trees with a central tree-covered island which can be reached by boat. Situated at an altitude of over 700 metres the lake is about 2½ km in circumference. In summer the lake is covered in lotus flowers and makes a particularly beautiful sight.

Mansar Lake (80 km east)

Further, on the same road, beyond Surinsar this lake is also reached by a regular bus service from Jammu and accommodation is available there in the *Dak Bungalow*. The legendary hero of the Mahabharata, Anjuna, is said to have shot an arrow into the ground at Mansar. The arrow emerged at Surinsar and thus both lakes were created. The lake is about four km in circumference and surrounded by dense mangrove stands, backed by pine trees on the slopes of the hills. Like

Surinsar the lake is covered with lotus flowers in summer.

Beside the lake there is a small ruined palace with colourful frescoes on the walls and another ancient building is nearby. Often newly married couples can be seen walking around the edge of Mansar, as it is considered auspicious for their future well being.

Towards the end of May each year there is a major festival at Mansar in which the folk spirit of the Dogra people is reflected in exuberant singing and dancing. Later the Chhing festival features wrestling bouts with wrestlers invited from near and far to display their prowess. These festivities are repeated in a number of villages in the area, one after the other.

The mysterious ruins of Mahor Garh – nobody knows who built them or why – are reached from Mansar.

Vaishno Devi (60 km north-west)
This important cave is dedicated to the three mother goddesses of Hinduism. Thousands of pilgrims visit the cave, particularly during the four month pilgrimage season from March to July. The cave stands at 1700 metres, is 30 metres long and reached by a very narrow entrance. A small stream, Chara Dunga, flows from under the image in the cave and devotees pass through it to the shrine.

The road terminates at the beautiful town of Katra, 48 km from Jammu, and visitors have to make the final, steep, 12 km on foot. There is also a new road from Lower Sanjichat to the Dabba, by-passing Upper Sanjichat and the Bahairo Ghatti. This leaves you two km closer to the cave and with 300 metres less climb to be made.

The origin of the pilgrimage is shrouded in mystery. Various legends are, however, associated with the shrine. According to one, the goddess Vaishno Devi usually stayed at a place called Adkunwari (virgin since creation). The demon Bahairo wanted to marry her forcibly and chased the goddess, who ran all the way from Adkunwari to the cave where she took shelter after killing the demon. A big stone outside the cave is said to be the purified body of the demon. Pilgrims walking to the cave greet each other with the cry 'Jai Mataki' – 'Victory to the Mother Goddess'.

The pilgrimage route from Katra to the cave is now lit to allow pilgrims to travel at night. Adkunwari, half-way between Katra and the cave, is a holding stage with a temple of the goddess, two sarais, a water tank, tea stalls, halwai shops and a hotel. Pilgrims may spend the night at Adkunwari or rest and continue on.

Katra is at the foot of the Trikuta mountains and eight km from Katra is the village of Aghar Jito, site of the annual Kartik Purnima or Jhiri festival. This is held in memory of the hero Bawa Jito whose historic struggle against tyranny is admired today as a symbol of truth and personal courage.

From Katra at various walking stages there are *Chabils* where drinking water is available to pilgrims. There is a *Tourist Bungalow* at Katra, reservations for which can be made through the tourist officer at the Katra tourist bureau, the director of tourism in Srinagar, or the Tourist Reception Centre in Jammu. There are regular and de-luxe buses from Jammu to Katra. Taxis are also available from Jammu to Katra and return. Ponies, dandies and porters are available at Katra at fixed rates.

Riasi (80 km north-west, beyond Katra)
Three km from the town of Riasi is the ruined fort and palace of General Zorawar Singh, a controversial warrior best remembered in India for his clashes with the Chinese over Ladakh. The palace, situated on a ridge overlooking the mighty Chenab River, is considerably rundown although it is still inhabited by the descendants of General Singh.

There is a gurdwara, 15 km from Riasi, with some of the oldest known frescoes in the Pahari style. The 400 metre long Shiv Khori cave, another pilgrimage site, is 19 km from Riasi, the last five km must be completed on foot. The cave is difficult to negotiate but at its end there is a vast hall in which the Shiva lingam formation on the ground is just over a metre high and other symbolic figures are said to be naturally etched on the cave ceiling.

Ramnagar (102 km north-east, leaving the Srinagar road at Udhampur)
The Rangmahal, 'palace of colours', has a great number of very colourful and beautiful wall paintings in the Pahari style. The paintings of scenes from Krishna's life are particularly noteworthy. Buses go to Ramnagar from Jammu or Udhampur. The medieval style Hindu temples at Krimchi are 10 km from Udhampur. The temples are notable for their fine carvings and sculpture.

Krimchi (64 km north, leaving the Srinagar road at Udhampur)
There are four ancient stone shrines and a Shiva Dawala at Krimchi, 10 km by road from Udhampur. The lantern shaped structures are characteristic of early medieval Indian temple architecture. Three of the Krimchi shrines and the Shiva Dawala are located on the same plinth and the fourth shrine is a little below. The position of the temples indicates that there must have once been more temples to complete some votive pattern.

Kud (99 km north-east, on the Srinagar road)
Situated at an altitude of 1738 metres, this is a popular lunch stop on the Jammu-Srinagar highway. It's also popular in its own right as a hill resort and has a well known mountain spring, Swami Ki Bauli, 1.5 km from the road. Kud has a *Tourist Bungalow* and during the summer there is a festival with nightly dancing.

Patnitop (107 km north-east, on the Srinagar road)
Picturesquely situated at 2024 metres there are many pleasant walks around this popular hill station. It is intended that Patnitop will be the nucleus of tourist developments in this area which will include Sanasar, Kud, Batote and Sudh Mahadev. There are tourist huts, a *Rest House* and a *Youth Hostel* in Patnitop.

Patnitop is a good starting place for many short or longer treks into the nearby mountains. An attractive one-day walk is to Shive Garh, about 11 km from Patnitop at an altitude of almost 3500 metres. Good bridle paths passing through wooded lanes and fascinating scenery link Patnitop with Kud and Batote. There are three, gushing, ice-cold freshwater springs in the area which are said to have medicinal properties.

Batote (118 km north-east, on the Srinagar road)
Only 12 km further on and connected to Patnitop and Kud by a number of footpaths, the hill resort of Batote is at an altitude of 1560 metres. This was the overnight stop between Jammu and Srinagar before the opening of the Jawarhar tunnel. There is a *Tourist Bungalow*, tourist huts and several private hotels in Batote. As in Kud there is a famous spring close to the village – the Amrit Chasma is only 2.5 km away.

Sudh Mahadev (120 km north-east, off the Srinagar road at Kud)
Sudh Mahadev is well known for its archaeological importance, as a great pilgrimage centre and as a charming natural site.

The Shiva temple here attracts many pilgrims during the festival which takes place in mid-June each year. The Asad Purnima festival features three days of music, singing and dancing. The main shrine has a black marble carved figure of Shiva and Parvati and there is also an interesting inscribed iron trident known as the Shiva Triseshul; it is believed to have been used by a mahadeva to kill a demon.

Man Talai, five km from Sudh Mahadev, is of archaeological interest due to the red earthenware and terra-cotta figures discovered here. Gauri Kund, also five km distant, is a small cave associated with Parvati. Sculptures from Hindu mythology can be seen at the Pap Nashni Bauli springs. Shiv Garh is the highest mountain in the area.

Sudh Mahadev is only eight km, by a picturesque walk or jeep track, from Patnitop and Kud. There is also a regular daily bus service to Sudh Mahadev from Jammu. It stands on the banks of the holy Dewak River, held by some to be as sacred as the Ganges. The Dewak here hurtles down from the higher mountains and rushes out of dense jungle, cascading over rocks and boulders. There is a small pilgrim's rest house at Sudh Mahadev which is at an altitude of 1225 metres.

Sanasar (129 km north-east, off the Srinagar road at Patnitop)
At an altitude of 2079 metres the valley of Sanasar has a beautiful cup-shaped meadow where Gaddi and Gujar shepherds bring their cattle and sheep in the spring, on the way to the higher pastures for the warm summer months. All around are thick bands of lofty conifers on the mountain slopes. Accommodation is available in the *Tourist Bungalow*, in tourist huts and in several private hotels. Sanasar is just eight km from Patnitop.

Bhadarwah (204 km north-east, off the Srinagar road at Batote)
Every two years a procession of pilgrims starts from this beautiful, high altitude valley and walks to the 4400 metre high Kaplash Lake. The pilgrimage takes place two weeks after the Rakhi Purnima festival and is followed a week later by Mela Patt, a three-day festival in Bhadarwah.

There are bus services from Jammu to Bhadarwah, the road leaves the Srinagar highway at Batote and heads east towards Kishtwar. A road then branches south-east to Bhadarwah. There is a *Rest House* in this scenic location.

Kishtwar (216 km north-east, off the Srinagar road at Batote)
Well off the Jammu-Srinagar road, Kishtwar is connected to Srinagar by a trekking route which goes through Banderkot, Dadhpeth, Mughal Maidan, Chhatru, Sinthan and Daksum; crossing the 3797 metre Sinthan Pass. You can also trek from Kishtwar into Zanskar, as detailed in the Zanskar section. The town is noted for its natural beauty, history and art.

Kishtwar is sited on a plateau above the Chenab River and below the Nagin Sheer Glacier. It is noted for the fine saffron grown in the area and for the many waterfalls close by. A fall only three km from the town drops over 700 metres in a series of seven cascades. The falls are a marvellous sight, visible even from the town. Saffron, a very colourful sight in spring and summer, grows only in a limited area and the cultivation and harvesting is accompanied by merry festivals and ceremonies.

The pilgrimage site of Sarthal Devi, with its 18-armed goddess statue, is 19 km from the town. Kishtwar also has the tombs of two important Muslim saints.

Situated 115 km beyond Kishtwar at an altitude of over 4000 metres, are the blue sapphire mines of Paddar. There is a road leading up to this area from Kishtwar. Sapphire mines were only discovered in the 1880s and have been worked only intermittently since this time because of the difficult terrain and unscientific mining techniques. Now the mines are open regularly and are more productive.

Jawarhar Tunnel (200 km from Jammu, 93 km from Srinagar)
Until the completion of the tunnel, Srinagar and Kashmir were often totally cut off from the rest of India during the winter months. The tunnel has two separate passages, each over 2500 metres

long. It's at an altitude of 2500 metres and the condition of the road is terrible! Windscreen wipers are needed in the tunnel since it 'rains' inside.

The tunnel not only ensured that Kashmir was accessible year round but also took half a day off the trip between Jammu and Srinagar. From Banihal, 17 km before the tunnel, you are already

entering the Kashmiri region – many people speak Kashmiri as well as Dogri and many of the houses are of the traditional Kashmiri style. As soon as you pass through the tunnel you are in the Vale of Kashmir and its green lushness is strikingly different from the other side of the range.

Kashmir

Kashmir is one of India's most beautiful and touristically popular regions and has been since the time of the great Moghul emperors. It's probably most famous for the houseboats on picturesque Dal Lake – you've not really been to Kashmir until you've stayed on one – but there's a lot more to the Kashmir Valley than just lazing on board. Around the capital, Srinagar, there are a number of interesting mosques, temples and forts and, of course, the delightful Moghul gardens – laid out in formal patterns hundreds of years ago and every bit as beautiful today. But you have to get away from Srinagar, up to the hill stations around the valley, to really enjoy Kashmir. Pahalgam, Gulmarg and Sonamarg are all delightful in themselves, but they also serve as the jumping off points for Kashmir's many trekking possibilities.

HISTORY

Due to its isolation, in a high valley of the Himalaya, Kashmir has developed an independent cultural and historical tradition over the centuries. Until the arrival of Islam in the 14th century and the 1586 conquest of the region by the Moghul Emperor Akbar, Kashmir was ruled by local dynasties. Earlier still Buddhism had become established in Kashmir with, as in so many other places in India, Ashoka as its main promulgator. Around the time of the birth of Christ, the third Buddhist Congress took place in Kashmir and missionaries were sent out to neighbouring regions of Central Asia, Tibet and China.

In the following centuries Buddhism lost its influence and by the 7th century had almost been replaced by Hinduism. Hindu dynasties followed in rapid succession through the middle ages but they always exercised tolerance for Buddhism. The Kashmiris were gradually changing to the Islamic religion and a series of Muslim rulers commenced from the 1300s. One of the best known and most respected of these local rulers was Zain-ul-Abidin, whose tomb still stands by the Jhelum River in Srinagar and who was generally known as Badshah, 'the great king'. He ruled from 1421 to 1472 and was a considerable contrast to his father, Sultan Sikander, who, with the guidance of a fanatical prime minister, persecuted countless Hindus and virtually ended the historical religious tolerance of the valley.

With the conquest of the valley by the Moghuls, Kashmir entered into a period of stable political conditions and great cultural activity. The Moghuls chose Kashmir as their summer residence and built many fine gardens, particularly under Jehangir who took the art of designing Moghul gardens to its greatest heights.

As the Moghul period entered its time of decline the government of Kashmir became practically independent and in 1756 Kashmir fell to Afghanistan and then in 1819 was taken over by the Sikhs, who called upon the Kashmiris to aid them in their struggle against the brutal Afghan rule. The Sikh General Gulab Singh was given Kashmir in 1846 by the British as reward for his neutrality in the war between the British and the Sikhs.

Gilgit, Hunza, Nagar and Chitral were added to this region and, under the rule of the Hindu Dogra dynasty, the state of Jammu and Kashmir arrived at more-or-less its present shape. In 1947, with independence from Britain and the partition of India and Pakistan, Kashmir assumed the role as thorn-in-the-side of India-Pakistan relations which it has held ever since. Since Kashmir was a 'Princely State' and, theoretically, already independent the British could not simply grant it independence like most of India but had to persuade it to join one side or the other. Kashmir became one of the three states, the others were Hyderabad and the tiny principality of Junagadh, whose rulers could not or would not opt for India or Pakistan, but clutched at the feeble hope of remaining independent.

Hari Singh's decision not to join either country, or rather, some would say, indecision since he was far from being a strong or decisive ruler, was a fateful one. Kashmir was predominantly Muslim so on the basis of religion it should clearly have gone to Pakistan. Furthermore it was geographically more closely aligned to Pakistan than to India. When the Pakistanis realised that Hari Singh, who was a Hindu, may not have joined India but certainly did not intend to join Pakistan they organised an unofficial takeover bid. Pathan tribesmen from the North-West Frontier region moved into Kashmir and internal revolts soon had Hari Singh's army in tatters. He turned to India for assistance but the price was an obvious one – Hari Singh took Kashmir into the Indian union.

It might have been too late for Indian troops to save Kashmir but the tribesmen had been so busy looting along the way that they had still not arrived in Srinagar when the first Indian troops were flown in and confronted them in Baramulla. Nevertheless a full scale war between India and Pakistan was soon underway and was not halted until a UN cease-fire came into effect on 1 January 1949. A substantial part of Kashmir was in Pakistani hands but the Vale of Kashmir was firmly under Indian control.

The ceasefire line runs from Akhnoor northwards to near Keran on the Kishenganga – a rugged, dry, sparsely populated strip 25 km wide and 250 km long. From Keran the line turns east through Minimarg in the Gurais Valley and ends in the Karakoram Range. Gilit, Hunza and Baltistan are north of the line under Pakistan control.

At first Kashmir was run as an autonomous region with its own government and president. Karan Singh, son of the Maharaja, was the first to hold this office, but in 1957 Kashmir was formally made part of the Indian union, despite Pakistani protests. Pakistan has repeatedly requested that a referendum be held in Kashmir but although at one time India agreed they would eventually hold such a referendum there has always been some reason why it could not conducted. In 1965 India and Pakistan were again at war and again the Pakistanis nearly captured Srinagar, but although the cease-fire line was pushed back in several places the status quo remained essentially unchanged. In 1971, during the Bangladesh conflict, it was India that took the offensive and Pakistan that was pushed back.

In 1962 the Indians found themselves involved with a different foe, the Chinese. So neglected was the Ladakh region of the state that the Chinese actually managed to construct a high altitude road right across the area they now hold without India being aware of it. When the conflict had eventually ground to a halt another cease-fire line was drawn across the region. The Chinese hold a desolate, cold and bleak rolling plain nearly 5000 metres high and approximately east of a line joining Chusul with the Karakoram Pass.

Today Kashmir, which includes Ladakh, is divided between three countries and essentially-related people are artificially divided by enforced nationalities. There are no roads open across the borders of Kashmir and no official trade takes place between the Indian and other parts of Kashmir. Given freedom of choice the Kashmiris would probably opt for independence as a sort of 'buffer state' between India and Pakistan, with their borders open to both countries. Barring that choice some say they would prefer Pakistan to India but, given the impossibility of that dream today, they appear to make the most of life in India.

Recently Kashmir has suffered from some internal turmoil although this is unlikely to effect overseas visitors. The 1983 general state elections were bitterly contested and resulted in running clashes between members of the opposing Congress I party of Mrs Gandhi and the predominantly Muslim National Conference. While Congress I did not win enough seats to become the government of J&K it did make significant gains. This brought charges of ballot rigging by supporters of the National Conference and in the following weeks curfews and marshal law were enforced in parts of Kashmir.

PEOPLE

Kashmir has a population of about four million of whom about half a million live in Srinagar. The population is predominantly Muslim and more related to central Asia than to India in both appearance and temperament. They have a terrible reputation for trickiness, although in actual fact they're probably no worse (or better) than any other group of people in India (or Asia)! One less than entranced visitor summed them up as the only people he had seen to 'actually quiver with greed, outside of American television shows'.

Indians have many little proverbs about the Kashmiris – like: 'Kashmiris are so fond of the truth they'll rarely part with it'. In turn the Kashmiris think of India as quite a separate country – you 'return to India' when you head south to Jammu. Despite its Muslim majority Kashmir has a strong Hindu minority well known for their intellectual pursuits. Nehru, India's first prime minister, was a Kashmiri 'pandit' and many of the closest advisers of both Nehru and his daughter, Indira Gandhi, were Kashmiris.

The Aryan Kashmiris are not the only people of the region. The predominantly Muslim population that lives in the foothills and peaks surrounding the Vale are mostly Gujars, who do not speak Kashmiri. The Gujars, along with the Dards, are one of the few groups to maintain their tribal and nomadic identity. They speak a language akin to Punjabi. In summer, dressed in the robes of the Pathans, they live in stone and log huts among the giant deodars near the snow line. In winter they drive their large herds down to the plains.

RELIGION

As would be expected of a place where the trails and trading routes of Asia meet, most of the religions of the world have vied for the beliefs of the people of Kashmir. Buddhism and Hinduism reached Kashmir and Ladakh very early in their spread across Asia and from the 9th to 12th centuries AD Kashmir was a prominent centre of Hindu culture. There are still many Hindu holy sites and temples in Jammu and a lesser number in Kashmir.

Buddhism came to Kashmir as early as the 4th century BC and Ashoka built many Buddhist states throughout the Vale, a number of which were still standing at the time of the great Chinese traveller Hiuan Tsang in the 7th century AD. He recorded them in his diary – see *In the Footsteps of the Buddha* by Rene Grousset (Orion Press, New York, 1971). It is said that Nagarjuna, the monk who was credited with bringing Buddhism to Ladakh, resided at the monastery built near Harwan in Srinagar in the 2nd century AD.

By the 14th century Hinduism, after its period of major influence, had been supplanted by Islam which had come gradually to Kashmir. Sufi teachers began to spread the religion in the 12th century with their synthesis of Hindu thought in the form of Sufiism and the Bhakti movement. Due to Bulbul Shah, Shah Hamdan and other Sufi saints, Kashmir embraced Islam before any Muslim king invaded it. Muslims now constitute about 90% of the population of the valley and they are mostly of the Sunni sect, with a sprinkling of Shi'ite. Christian missionaries came to the Vale during the British period and their influence continues to this day.

SEASONS

Kashmir, with its lush vegetation and wide variety of fruits, presents a different face for every season. The almond trees blossom in March, when the thaw begins, but it's the chinars, which leaf in April, that really herald spring. Strawberries and cherries are on sale in May, followed by apricots in June and apples in July.

The sound of running water dominates the Vale in May and June as the snow melt rushes down from the high snows and is channelled onto terraces to irrigate the rice, barley and wheat crops. During these months, groups of colourfully dressed women sing as they stoop to plant the rice shoots in paddies right across the Vale. The chinar trees are in full leaf, while on the mountain slopes the villagers are cutting fir and cedar for building houses or repairing those damaged by the winter snow. The Gujars begin moving their herds of sheep and goats to the high pastures and ranunculus, anenome and impatiens begin to flower in the meadows and along the streams.

Srinagar in mid-summer is a noisy, busy and dirty city, much like the cities of the plains that many come north to escape. The only refuges are the houseboats on the quiet lakes and the hill stations like Gulmarg or Pahalgam.

The early autumn brings pears, pomegranates and walnuts. Waterbirds and swallows, heading south for the winter, pause in Kashmir in great numbers. Finally the leaves fall and by November or December the first snow can be expected around the valley. In January houseboat roofs must be shovelled clean to prevent them being pressed into the lake by the weight of snow. In winter the Kashmir Valley can be a bitterly cold place but the Dal Lake only freezes over on rare occasions. Kashmir becomes a quieter, more sedate place than during the hectic days of summer. Houseboat owners bring out their pot belly stoves and hang carpets at the doorways to keep in the warmth, and the valley, now stilled by a thick layer of snow, rests.

KASHMIRI FOOD

Kashmiri cuisine has some special variations from normal Indian food although it is basically of the north Indian type. Houseboat food tends to retain its early English influence – not a good sign! Some Kashmiri dishes you may come across include:

Gushtaba – pounded and spiced meat balls cooked in a yoghurt sauce. The meat is usually mutton or goat. *Rista* are rice balls and very similar to gushtaba but with less meat and less spice in the sauce.

Roghan josh – also fairly common elsewhere in north India, this is, in its most basic form, just curried mutton, but a good roghan josh will be cooked in yoghurt (curd) with a careful blend of exotic spices and added ingredients. *Yaknee* is similar to roghan josh.

Tabak maz is fried meat, not spiced at all. *Marchwangan kurma* is a hot mutton curry, usually served with rice and nan. *Methi kurma* is vegetables with chopped intestines – it tastes much better than it sounds. *Karma sag* is made from the popular Dal Lake vegetable known as lak – it's a bit like giant spinach. *Nadru yekni* is a very tasty dish made from lotus roots, cooked with curd or yoghurt.

Kashmiri nan is the usual flat Indian bread but with sultanas and nuts baked into it. Kashmiri nan is really delicious but Kashmiri bread is very good to start with. The Kashmiris also make a fruit and nut pillau – a bit like fried fruit salad! Popular vegetables in Kashmir include *bartha* – minced aubergines – and *brindi* – lady fingers.

Drinks Kashmir tea is a fragrant, delicate blend flavoured with cardamom and ginger – a delightfully thirst quenching drink. Quite possibly the best tea in India?

A really good cup of this *kahwa* tea will be brewed in a samovar and have grated almonds in it. It's usually drunk without milk. The Kashmiris also make a good blend of camomile and cardamom tea, which is very good for settling stomach upsets.

Soft drinks, freighted up from the plains, tend to be expensive but there's a delicious local brand of apple juice known as *Apco*. It's a great change from the sickly Indian soft drinks and costs Rs 4 or 5, about the same as regular soft drinks in Kashmir. Take care with Kashmiri water, especially if you suspect it may have come straight from Dal Lake!

Being good Muslims, the Kashmiris do not drink alcohol – at least publicly. Liquor is available, but at a high price and often of very low quality. You would be well advised to bring in your quota of duty free liquor. There's a ready black market demand for it. Beer, however, is readily available.

Trout Fishing

To the keen angler, nothing is more satisfying than landing a glistening trout after a brief battle and even the not so keen fisherman will probably enjoy a just-cooked trout from the clean and clear rivers of Kashmir.

Fishing is big business in Kashmir through spring and summer. The British introduced the brown and rainbow trout to the streams of Kashmir, where they have thrived. At the same time they introduced the system of anglers reserving 'beats' on their favourite river. Reservations for beats should be made before you arrive in Kashmir, through an Indian Government Tourist Office or directly to the Tourist Reception Centre in Srinagar.

The season runs from April to October. Only artificial flies are allowed and each licence entitles the angler to keep six fish a day, none being shorter than 7.5 cm. Beats may be reserved for a day or a week at a time in one of the three basic types of streams.

Larger rivers like the Sindh (Indus) or Lidder are full with snow melt from May to July, with an occasional pool under boulders. Spinning is allowed here, but the wet fly and weighted cast tests the skill of the angler and will produce good results. In April, August and September these rivers are quieter, and the bigger fish are said to lie in the stiller waters.

Tributaries and water channels near these main stream beats provide another type of fishing throughout the season. These are the smaller streams where only flies are allowed, with wet fly fishing good all season. The third type are the small spring-fed streams and high altitude lakes suitable for both dry and wet fly tackle.

It is not necessary to take tackle unless you are fussy, as everything can be bought or hired in Srinagar. A light two to three metre rod (fishing rods cannot be carried as hand luggage on aircraft for security reasons) with an eight cm reel will suffice. Common flies in use in Kashmir include Peacock, March Brown, Butcher, Jinger Quill, Coachman, Woodcock & Green and Watson's Fancy.

There are 61 beats open for reservation throughout the season, ranging from the turbulence of the Sindh and Wangat rivers to the tranquility of the high altitude lakes Krishanshar, Vishanshar, Gangabal and Nun Khol. On arrival at the beat, hand your permit to the watcher for that beat and the ghillie will be waiting to offer advice and service, such as netting the fish when it is brought to shore and gutting and cleaning. With licence, transportation, tips for the guides and the ghillie, a day's fishing could cost more than Rs 500!

THINGS TO BUY

Kashmir is famous for its wide variety of often very beautiful handicrafts. The Kashmiris are not only poets and philosophers but also artists and artisans producing exquisite carpets, embroidered shawls, silverware, gold ornaments, finely chiselled woodwork of walnut and oak, brilliantly coloured and painted papier mache and leather and fur garments. They are also great salesmen, even enterprising small Kashmiri girls, crouched precariously on the prow of their shikara, will adroitly paddle up to you on the lake and offer you a lotus blossom for a rupee or two, that they have picked from the water not 10 metres away. You'll have a hard heart and tight wallet if something doesn't convince you to take it home! Some of the better known items include:

Carpets One of the best known, and most expensive, Kashmiri handicrafts is carpet weaving. The art of weaving carpets first came from Samarkand in central Asia and was later modified by artisans from Iran. Zain-ul-Abidin is credited with first introducing the skill to Kashmir. Late in the 14th century, as a young prince, he was kept hostage by the scourge of Asia, Timur the Lame (Tamerlane) at his court in Samarkand. When Tamerlane died, the young prince returned to Kashmir, taking with him many of the artisans and craftsmen whom Tamerlane had collected from many parts of Asia. The carpet industry was given a new direction during the reign of Jehangir when a Kashmiri craftsman brought the Persian knot style of weaving back from Persia.

Present day carpets come in a variety of sizes – three by five foot, four by six foot, and so on. They are either made of pure wool, wool with a small percentage of silk to give a sheen (known as 'silk touch'), or pure silk. The latter are more decorative than intended for hard wear. To see just how decorative Kashmiri carpets can be as a wall hanging pay a visit to the restaurant in the Broadway Hotel where carpets are hung around the walls, like paintings.

Kashmiri carpets are not cheap – expect to pay from Rs 5000 for a good quality four by six carpet and don't be surprised if the price is more than twice that level. Beware of cheap imitations from Amritsar and of false knotting. The present situation in Iran has resulted in oriental carpets becoming rather cheaper in the last few years. So if you are thinking of buying a carpet in Kashmir it is important to investigate prices at home for comparison. There are many carpet importers in Europe, Australia and north America and their prices are often very competitive. Studying one of the many books on oriental carpets will also help you to avoid making a disappointing purchase.

Carpets are very easy to come by – in fact it is almost impossible to avoid them.

Someone on your houseboat will be either selling carpets, have a brother who owns a carpet factory, or will want to take you to a carpet factory. Do go and visit one, most of the weaving is done on hand looms by young boys and working in winter, in darkened rooms with the very fine threads ruins their eyes by their early twenties.

The carpet showrooms provide the greatest entertainment with beautifully patterned wool rugs or shiny silk ones piled high in the corner or rolled in racks around the edge of the room. You will be seated at the far edge of the room, away from the door, and offered Kashmiri tea and biscuits. Every imaginable pattern and colour of carpet will be shown to you and you will be made to feel that if you do not buy one you will have missed the bargain of the century. The salesmen have an impressive array of techniques.

Most carpet dealers will now take all types of credit cards as well as travellers' cheques and, of course, cash. If you cannot pay in full, you will be offered the facility of leaving a deposit and having the money transferred from your bank when you reach home. At this time the carpet or carpets will be sent to you. Most of the time you will indeed get a carpet. Most of the time you will indeed get the right carpet! Some of the time something will go astray – usually caused by the Indian postal system. You can, of course, buy a carpet and mail it or carry it home yourself. To avoid import duty if mailed, the carpet must be addressed to you and labelled as a gift.

The Kashmiris will show you all manner of testimonials from satisfied customers around the world – 'my friends'. They will not admit to having dissatisfied customers. Don't hesitate to bargain with the carpet salesman. For a start, whoever brought you here, either the brother who lives on the houseboat or works in your hotel, or the boy who picked you up in the street, or the taxi driver, will get a commission on the sale – sometimes up to 20%. Many of the boys and young men you will meet on the streets earn their living this way, over the school or university summer holidays. If you have done your homework you will know how much you can afford and how much the carpet is worth.

The Kashmiris' powers of persuasion are immense. If you refuse to buy, it will be taken as a personal insult to all in the room, and you will feel that you have to sneak out. This is why you have been seated so far from the door. If you can't afford it or you don't like it, don't be afraid to get up and walk out. They have not yet resorted to mugging tourists who don't buy.

Kashmir also has some cheaper, more country-crafted rugs such as the embroidered *numdas* and the applique-like *gabbas*. You can compare the different types in the Srinagar handicrafts emporiums.

Papier Mache Instantly recognisable as a product of Kashmir are the papier mache items. They're usually cheap, well made, light and easy to carry. The basic papier mache article, made in a mould, is painted and polished in successive layers until the final intricate design is produced. Prices are generally dependent upon the complexity and quality of the painted design and on the amount of gold leaf used. The gold leaf is applied in tiny pieces to produce a leaf design or other pattern.

Papier mache is made into bowls, cups, containers, jewellery boxes, letter holders, tables, lamps, coasters, trays and so on. Prices can be as low as Rs 10 for a cheap bowl to several hundred for some large, fine quality piece. Production is very much a cottage industry with the moulded 'rough' form being made in one place, the painting and polishing being done in another, adding the intricate and colourful designs in still another. It's very easy to arrange to go to a papier mache 'factory' to see how it's done.

Leather & Fur You can have shoes or boots or leather coats made to measure in just a few days in Srinagar. The beautifully embroidered suede coats are particularly interesting, but you have to put your conscience in the back seat when it comes to the fur trim. The same goes for the many fur coats – fur should be left on the backs of its original owners. Wolf, fox, jackal, brown and black bear, marmot, leopard and lynx are all being driven from the slopes of the Himalaya by hunters. And in any case the best furs are exported immediately.

You can, however, find sheepskin lined or trimmed coats. Although Kashmiri leather, suede or sheepskin may look very fine the quality is often abysmally low – look carefully before buying. Expect to pay Rs 400 to Rs 1000 for a coat, good boots can be made for Rs 200 to Rs 400.

Tailoring Srinagar's hordes of tailors ('I am just like Saville Row, only cheaper') search you out on your houseboats if you don't go to them. They'll make anything from a shirt to a suit and, depending on the time of year, often very quickly. Late in the tourist season, however, tailors often have far more orders than they can satisfy and these orders lay partly completed until the slack winter time. Resident Srinagar tailors are generally more reliable than summer visitors from Delhi or the Punjab. If you are having something made, insist on having several fittings and give clear instructions each time.

Wood Carvings Intricately carved designs are a hallmark of Kashmiri woodcraft. You can see the complex relief work on every houseboat. Look for tables, chests, boxes and screens. Wood carving is relatively cheap. Inlaid ivory is often incorporated into the design; it may or may not be genuine, but if it is it does the world's elephant population no good.

Shawls & Embroidery Kashmiri shawls are noted for the extreme fineness of the cream coloured goats' wool known as pashmina and for the intricate embroidery work. Pashmina wool comes from goats that live above 4000 metres. The wool is expensive, light and extremely warm but it's not easy to tell pashmina wool from ordinary goat's wool. Expect to pay from Rs 100 to Rs 200 for a low quality (raffal) shawl although a genuine pashmina shawl could cost Rs 400 to 1000 for a middle quality, even more for a really good one.

Shawl-making has been a Kashmiri speciality for over 500 years. The word 'shawl' was not used until 1533 when Nagz Beg of Khokand in central Asia came to Kashmir with his master, Mirza Haider Dughlat. Nagz Beg presented his master with a piece of pashmina, and he asked Beg what it was. Beg replied 'a shawl', the name used by the people of Khokand for a blanket. Since then this type of weaving has been termed a shawl. The embroidered shawl or *amilkar* was started by an artisan, Ala Baba, who covered up some footprints made by a fowl on his white material with coloured thread.

In 1796 a blind man, Sayyid Yehyah, from Baghdad, visited Kashmir and received a shawl from the Afghan governor. Sayyid presented it to the Khedive of Egypt, who in turn presented it to Napoleon. In France it caught the eye of the French court, which through history had set the fashion in Europe. The subsequent demand was enormous, and in those days the shawls sold for amounts varying from Rs 60 to Rs 7000. More than 40,000 looms worked day and night in the Vale to satisfy the unprecedented demand from Europe. In 1820, the English explorer Moorcroft learnt the art and sent instructions to England. The English weave shawls are not equal to the originals from Kashmir.

Embroidery of all types is a Kashmiri craft – embroidered suede coats or bags, embroidered shirts or dress material, they're all popular items.

Antiques There are many shops around Kashmir which sell statuary and antiques.

Much of this material is said to come from Ladakh or Tibet but the majority of it is likely to be 'instant antiques'. You should be aware that there is a prohibition of the export of any item from India that is more than 100 years old. At the very least it could be confiscated from your luggage at the airport – all baggage is searched when you are leaving India. Kashmir is certainly not unaffected by the world trade in counterfeit antiques – ivory or bone will often turn out to be plastic and all but worthless.

Honey The cardinal rule when buying honey in Kashmir is taste it first. Kashmiri substitutes for the real thing include sugar dissolved in water or alcohol! Do not, however, be put off by the packaging – Kashmiri honey can be very good although the best honey will be found at small stalls reached only by shikara. You may also find lotus blossom honey as well as the normal variety. Although honey is very good in Kashmir it is also very expensive.

Other Dried fruit may be a Kashmiri speciality but it's another expensive one. Dried apricots and apples are from Ladakh and better to get there, walnuts are a genuine Kashmir product. Much jewellery is really from Rajasthan but there's also a thriving business in Tibetan jewellery and other artifacts. Nice, coarsely hand-knitted sweaters in grey or dark brown wool are available from Rs 75, from Rs 100 for cardigans. Some of them are made in Ladakh. Saffron, the highly fragrant orange-coloured spice and dye is a Kashmiri speciality. Pure saffron is very expensive and it's an easy product to adulterate so take care.

Kashmir Dress

For many years Kashmiri men and women have worn the same style of dress. The *pheran* and *poots* consist of two gowns, one on top of the other, falling to the feet in the case of a Hindu, worn up to the knees by a Muslim. Muslims wear the sleves wide and open; Hindus wear them narrow with turned up ends.

The garments are made of cotton, wool or embroidered silk with the necks closed by a gaily coloured string or jewelled button. A pashmina belt goes around the waist. A Moghul-type turban, sometimes 20 metres long, completes the costume for men. Most Muslims wear skull caps, especially the farmers. The headdress of a Kashmiri woman is a brightly coloured scarf.

The traditional way of coping with the bitter cold of a Kashmiri winter is with a *kangri*. A *kangri* is an earthenware bowl which, fitted in a wicker container, is carried in front of you under your enveloping *pheran*. Red hot coals from the pot belly stoves used in houses or houseboats are placed in the *kangri* and you have personal, portable central-heating! The *pheran* channels the heat up to the neck. Kashmiri's often squat to talk or smoke with the *kangri* between their feet and the *pheran* spread over it. Beware of burning embers falling out of the bowl; long term *kangri* carriers usually have the burns to prove it.

An equally vital part of a Kashmiri's existence is the hookah (hubble-bubble) pipe – they're in every shop, in every shikara. In winter coals from the *kangri* are used to light the pipe.

Srinagar

The capital of Jammu and Kashmir and the largest city in the state, Srinagar is famous for its canals, houseboats and Moghul gardens. The city itself is quite unlike most other large Indian cities for here you are much more in central Asia than on the sub-continent. It's a city full of intriguing alleyways and curious buildings. A place where it's very easy to spend a few hours simply wandering – particularly along the old city streets near the Jhelum River.

The city has long been a centre of the arts and learning – it has had a university or for hundreds of years and is a centre of Sanskrit study 'Sri' means beauty or wealth of knowledge and 'nagar' means city. The city was originally founded by the great Buddhist emperor Ashoka – his old city is marked by the present village of Pandrethan. The present city was founded by Pravarasena II (79-139 AD) who named it Praparapura and built it practically contiguous with the old capital, which was called Srinagari.

Praparapura is recorded in Chinese annals by Hiuan Tsang who visited the city in about 630 AD and described it as extending about four km from north to south and about two km from east to west along the right bank of the Jhelum. King Ananta (1028-63) was the first to transfer his royal residence to the left bank of the river.

Legend has it that when Pravarasena decided to build himself a new capital, to choose the location he started walking at midnight and was confronted by a demon on the other side of the Mahasarit River. The demon spread his bent leg across the stream and dared the king to cross over it to the other side. The king cut off the leg with one stroke of his sword and calmly crossed. The demon was delighted with the king's boldness and told him to build the city where he would find the beginnings of a plan laid out for him. The next morning the king found the boundary lines drawn at the foot of Hari Parbat and built his city there. To this day the waters of the Dal Lake are separated from the Tsont-i-Kul by a *sathu* or bund that is shaped like a bent leg.

Information

Srinagar stands at an altitude of 1768 metres and has a population of about 450,000. There are a number of banks in Srinagar and money changing facilities are also available at the airport and in several of the larger hotels. The GPO, with efficient poste restante facilities, is on the Bund, quite near the Tourist Reception Centre. The telegraph office and the telephone office are on Maulana Azad Rd (Hotel Rd).

Non-commonwealth citizens wanting to renew their visas beyond three months should go to the Foreigners' Registration Centre in the park between the post office and the Tourist Reception Centre. They get mixed reports on their helpfulness, however. Some people say they're OK, others say they found Delhi a better place for visa renewals. Indian Airline's office is in the TRC (tel 3538, 32370 & 6242) and is open from 10 am to 5 pm. The J&K Road Transport Corporation is also located at the TRC. There are some good bookshops around Srinagar, one of the best is under the Indian Coffee House, another is the Kashmir Bookshop on the Bund.

Tourist Office The Srinagar office of the J&K Department of Tourism is at the Tourist Reception Centre – a large complex which houses the various tourist departments, Indian Airlines, a restaurant/cafeteria, an accommodation block, hotel and houseboat booking counters and is the departure and arrival point for J&K Road Transport Corporation tour buses and buses to Jammu and Leh. The tourist office here has not, to be frank, enjoyed a reputation for efficiency or helpfulness. However, a new Director of Tourism has recently taken over the reins and insists that great improvements have been made.

The tourist office attempts to steer all tourists through the Tourist Reception Centre initially. All the buses to Kashmir arrive and depart from the centre and if you come by bus from the airport you will also arrive there although you can ask to be dropped off earlier. Although the tourist office may say that you should book accommodation through them this is not necessary and is likely to be more expensive or offer less choice than if you dealt with houseboats or hotels directly.

The tourist department staff, of which there are a great number, have little or no printed information and are not always very knowledgeable. An exception is the Ladakh tourist officer, Urgain Goba. He has gone to a lot of trouble to collect the type of information visitors ask for and has had it typed and printed to hand to tourists. He is also very knowledgeable about most areas of Ladakh and willing to talk and answer questions. He also makes a point of knowing the state of the Srinagar-Leh road – a very important matter for visitors arriving in Kashmir in May and early June when the road is just about to open.

The Taxi Drivers' Union office and one of the major taxi stands for up-country routes is directly across the road from the Tourist Reception Centre, as is the Houseboat Owners Association office.

Around Srinagar

All the distances to the places of interest described below are from the Tourist Reception Centre in town. Note that admission to all the Moghul gardens is free, except for the Chasma Shahi which costs 50p. The gardens are all open from sunrise to sunset.

The art of designing formal gardens, which the Moghul emperors expended

such time and energy upon, reached its zenith in Kashmir. The Moghul gardens in Agra or Lahore may be very fine but only in Kashmir is the formal beauty of the gardens matched by the natural beauty of the surrounding countryside. The gardens follow a standard pattern with a central channel carrying water through the descending terraces in a delightful series of cascades, falls and pools.

Dal Lake

Dal Lake is, initially, one of the most confusing parts of Srinagar for it's not really one lake at all, but three. Furthermore much of it is hardly what you would expect a lake to be like – it's a maze of intricate waterways and channels, floating islands of vegetation, houseboats that look so firmly moored they could almost be islands and hotels on islands which look like they could simply float away.

Dal Lake lies immediately to the east and north of Srinagar and stretches over five km. The lake is divided into Gagribal, Lokut Dal and Bod Dal by a series of causeways. Nagin Lake, which is usually thought of as a separate lake, is also divided from Dal Lake only by a causeway. The causeways are mostly suitable for walkers and bicycles only so they make a very pleasant way of seeing the lake without having to worry about traffic or shikaras. The main causeway across the lake carries the water pipeline for Srinagar's mains water supply. Dal Gate, at the city end of Dal Lake, controls the flow of the lake into the Jhelum River canal. It's the steady flow of water through the lake, combined with its relatively cold temperature, which keeps it so clear looking.

The largest group of houseboats lies along the western edge of the lake near the lakeside Boulevard, towards Dal Gate. They are lined in looping rows and around small islands. Several hotels can also be found on flat islands in the lake. Beyond the houseboats to the northwest are the floating gardens.

Top: Jhelum River in Srinigar (TW)
Left: Shah Hamdan Mosque on the Jhelum River, Srinagar (TW)
Right: Pari Mahal, looking out over Dal Lake (TW)

Top: Shikaras assembled at a ghat on Dal Lake (TW)
Left: Vegetable shikara on a Srinagar canal (TW)
Right: Nishat Bagh by Dal Lake (TW)

There are three islands in the lake; three real islands anyway, there are other 'sort of' islands joined by causeways. Around the lake are many of Srinagar's most interesting sights, in particular the pleasant Moghul gardens. It's also flanked by hills, particularly along its east bank. The Shankaracharya Hill provides a very fine view over the lake.

The waters of Dal Lake are amazingly clear, considering what must get poured into it from the hundreds of houseboats! Nevertheless you're well advised not to go swimming in the lake although the swimming houseboats, equipped with diving boards and chutes, are moored in a deeper part of the lake, 'upstream' from the concentration of houseboats. Swimming here can be quite refreshing, especially on a hot afternoon. You will undoubtedly be joined by a number of Indians, including Hindu women who swim in their saris.

There are many tours around the lake but by far the best way to see it is to take a shikara for a day and do a circuit of the Moghul gardens. The cost will range from about Rs 50 (say Rs 5 to 20 an hour depending on the season) and there's hardly a lazier and more pleasurable way of getting into the swing of Srinagar. If one of the home-made chocolate merchants comes by and sells you a luxurious quarter kilo of his wares you're set for the day. You'll have to ignore the steady stream of floating merchants who pass by. You can also approach the gardens by road, the Boulevard runs along the eastern edge of the lake, providing fine views all the way.

The lake is probably at its most beautiful when the lotus flowers bloom in July and August. The floating gardens, known as *rad* in Kashmiri, are one of the stranger aspects of Dal Lake. They're composed of matted vegetation and earth which are cut away from the lake bottom and towed to a convenient location where they are moored. Tomatoes, cucumbers and melons all grow amazingly well in these gardens, if you look underneath you can see that they do literally float on the lake. Of course one

problem with a floating garden is that a lazy and dishonest gardener can steal it!

You will often see weeds being pulled up out of the lake – this serves a double purpose. The lake waterways are kept clear and the weeds are rotted until they form an excellent compost for the gardens. The shallowness of the lake and it's heavy growth of waterweeds is probably the main reason there are so very few powered boats on the water. Dal Lake would be nowhere near as pleasant if there were powerboats rushing back and forth across its tranquil surface.

Islands

There are three main islands in the lake, each popular excursion points. Silver Island (Sona Lank) is at the northern end of Dal Lake and is also known as Char Chinar after the four (char) chinar trees which grow on it. There's a small snack bar on the Island as there is also on Gold Island (Rupa Lank) at the south end of the lake. It is also known as Char Chinar for it too has four chinar trees.

The third island is Nehru Park, at the end of the main stretch of the Boulevard and only a short distance from the shore. It too has a restaurant although it's a very run down, miserable affair. The children's playground here has also seen better days. Often in summer there are evening shows, dances and festivals at Nehru Park.

North of Nehru Island a long causeway leads out into the lake from the Boulevard. Just off its end is Kotar Khana, the 'house of pigeons', which was once a royal summer house.

The Bund

From above Zero Bridge to below Badshah Bridge you can walk along the banks of the Jhelum River on the popular footpath known as the Bund. It's a pleasant relaxing place to stroll along and many doonga houseboats can be seen beside it. The GPO, the Government Handicrafts Emporium (in the old British Residency) and a string of handicraft shops are all close beside the Bund.

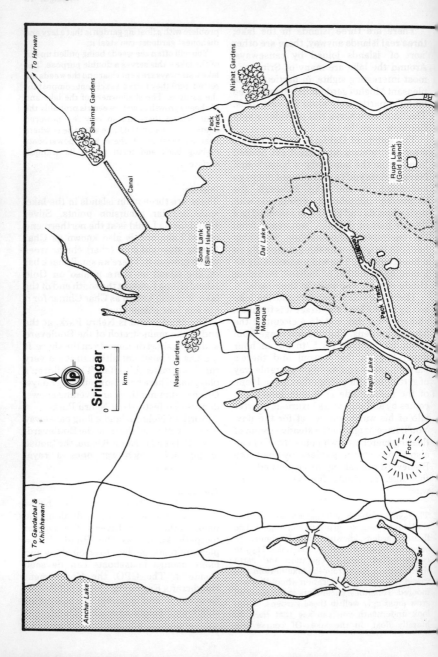

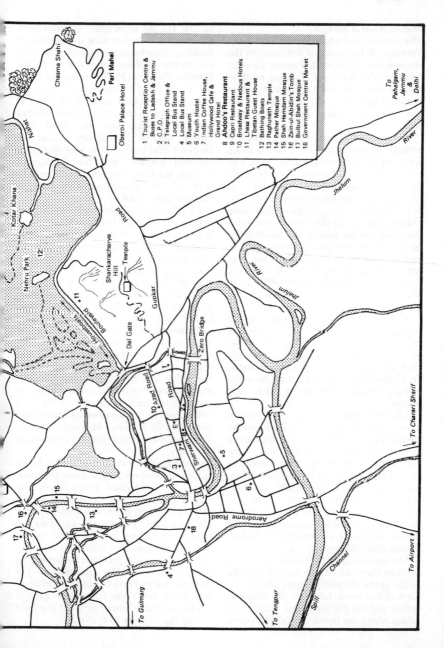

1 Tourist Reception Centre &
   Buses to Ladakh & Jammu
2 G.P.O.
3 Telegraph Office &
   Local Bus Stand
4 Local Bus Stand
5 Museum
6 Youth Hostel
7 Indian Coffee House,
   Hollywood Cafe &
   Grand Hotel
8 **Ahdoo's Restaurant**
9 Capri Restaurant
10 Broadway & Nedous Hotels
11 Lhasa Restaurant &
   Tibetan Guest House
12 Bathing Boats
13 Raghunath Temple
14 Pather Mosque
15 Shah Hamdam Mosque
16 Zain-ul-Abidin's Tomb
17 Bulbul Shah Mosque
18 Government Central Market

Jhelum River & Bridges

The Jhelum (Vetasta in Hindi) flows from Verinag, 80 km south of Srinagar, to the Wular Lake in the north. Passing through Srinagar it's a wide, swift flowing, muddy-looking river. The river draws water from the lakes around the city and many canals and rivers meander through the city area.

The Jhelum is famed for its nine old bridges although some of them are being replaced by more modern structures. The stretch north of the city is particularly picturesque with many fine views of Srinagar's old buildings on the riverbanks. You'll also find Srinagar's most interesting old mosques along this stretch and since the roads are too narrow and winding for most vehicles it's an interesting area to explore on foot or bicycle. You can also take a shikara along the river from Dal Gate; the cost should be around Rs 40 to 50 for two people, up to Rs 100 for larger groups.

Starting from Dal Gate in a boat you first go south along the canal connecting Dal Lake to the river. On the right is the golf course and on the left the Srinagar Club where tourist visitors are welcome. Just beyond the club the canal enters the bridge immediately above the first bridge.

The first Jhelum bridge, close to the Tourist Reception Centre, is Zero Bridge. Thus the next bridge is commonly known as the first bridge as it's the first of the 'old' bridges. Built by Amir Khan it's named the Amira Kadal. Between Zero Bridge and the Amira Kadal you drift along beside the Bund, past the Government Handicrafts Emporium and the Government Silk Weaving Factory on the opposite bank. Beyond that is the Shri Pratap Singh Museum.

The next bridge is the heavily trafficked modern Badshah Bridge and the Habba Kadal in the old part of town. On the left bank of the river, between the Badshah Bridge and the Habba Kadal, is the royal palace where the previous Maharaja used

to live. It's set back some distance from the riverbank and is now a government building. Nearby you will also find the new secretariat building and the Mahatma Gandhi Memorial Park. On the right side the Tsont-i-Kul or 'apple canal' joins the Jhelum. This canal starts from the Dal Gate and with a loop of the Jhelum makes part of Srinagar into an island. The busiest part of the old city is near the Habba Kadal bridge, in an area where the national hospital and the Raghunath Mandir, Kashmir's biggest temple and the twin of the golden-spired temple in Jammu, also stand.

The Fateh Kadal, the third old bridge, is just before the Shah Hamdan Mosque and a new bridge has recently been built just upstream from it. The Zaina Kadal is the next bridge and crosses the river close to the tomb of its builder, the famous Kashmiri ruler Zain-ul-Abidin.

The fifth bridge, the Ali Kadal, is named after his son. Finally there's the Nawa Kadal and the Saffa Kadal. Lesser mosques close to the river include the Mosque of Bulbul Shah, close to the Ali Kadal. Bulbul Shah was a Kashmiri mystic and the first Muslim fakir to visit the valley. The ruined Badshah Mosque, close to the tomb of Zain-ul-Abidin, is enclosed by an old stone wall and there is a belief that the bricks of this mosque could cure smallpox. The Maharaja Ranbir Gang Bazaar, an important trade centre, is also here.

Just below the sixth bridge, the Nawa Kadal, you can see a canal enter the river, this is the Kota canal which diverts the river's flow at times of flood. It leaves the Jhelum between the Amira Kadal and the Habba Kadal. There's the old Yarkand Sarai, a travellers' resting place, by the seventh bridge, the Saffa Kadal. The Jhelum weir is just past this bridge and on the left bank are the graineries of the Kashmir Valley Food Control Department. Also close by is the large open ground known as Idgah where prayers are held during the Muslim Id festival.

At the Taski Kadal you can again leave the river on the Tsont-i-Kul canal and pass under the floodgate back to the Dal Gate.

Museum

The Shri Pratap Singh Museum is in Lal Mandi, just south of the river between Zero Bridge and Amira Kadal. It has an interesting collection of exhibits relevant to Kashmir including illustrated tiles excavated near Harwan.

The museum is open from 10 am to 5 pm except on Wednesdays when it is closed. Admission is free.

Shah Hamdan Mosque (3 km)

One of the oldest mosques in Srinagar, the wooden Shah Hamdan Mosque stands right beside the Jhelum and is noted for the papier mache work on its walls and ceilings. No nails or screws were used in the construction of this all wooden mosque. Originally built in 1395 it has been destroyed by fire in 1479 and again in 1731. The roof is covered with turf in which flowers are planted in the spring. The mosque is shaped like a cube with a pyramidal roof rising to a 38 metre high spire. Arcades, verandahs and porticos surround the large, central, wooden hall. Non-believers are not allowed inside.

Nearby there is a market for curios, wood carving, papier mache, embroidery, silverwork and precious and semi-precious stones amongst other articles.

Pather Masjid (3 km)

Almost directly opposite the Shah Hamdan Mosque, on the other bank of the Jhelum, the Pather Masjid is a fine stone mosque built by Nur Jahan in 1623. It is not, however, in everyday use today and is consequently rather run down. Reach it by crossing Zaina Kadal, the fourth bridge.

Tomb of Zain-ul-Abidin (4 km)

On the east (right) bank of the river, between the Zaina Kadal and the Ali Kadal, is the slightly decrepit tomb of King Zain-ul-Abidin, the highly regarded son of Sultan Sikander, who built the Jami Masjid. The tomb, built on the foundations of an earlier temple, shows a clear Persian influence in its domed construction and glazed tiles. Moulded bricks can also be found at intervals in the exterior walls. In the enclosures are fragments of inscriptions, the oldest in Kashmir in Pali characters. Over the posterior gate is an inscription in Persian.

Jami Masjid (5 km)

Srinagar's most important mosque is an impressive wooden structure, notable for the more than 300 soaring pillars supporting the roof; each made of a single deodar tree trunk. The main gate is to the south and the outer cloisters surround a spacious, green and peaceful inner courtyard. The roughly square building is 117 metres on each side, topped by four minars in the centre of each side and three pagoda-shaped minarets from which the faithful are called to prayer.

The mosque has had a chequered history – first constructed by Sultan Sikander in 1385, it was enlarged in 1402 by his son Zain-ul-Abidin but in 1479 it was destroyed by a fire. The mosque was rebuilt by 1503 but was destroyed in another fire during the reign of the Moghul emperor Jehangir. It was rebuilt by the Kashmiri architect and historian Malik Haider Chaudara but burnt down yet again in 1674 during the reign of Aurangzeb. The present mosque dates from that time but was rebuilt, on the last occasion, to the original Indo-Saracenic design.

Shankaracharya Hill

Rising up behind the Boulevard, beside Dal Lake, the hill was once known as Takht-i-Sulaiman, the Throne of Solomon. It is thought that a temple was originally built on top of the hill by Jaluka, Ashoka's son, around 200 BC. The present Hindu temple was built during the reign of the Emperor Jehangir and its enclosing wall and plinth is thought to date from the earlier temple.

There's a road running up the hill to the TV transmitting station, just below the temple, but it's a very pleasant stroll to the top. Go up early, when the sky is clear, and you'll be rewarded with fine views over the houseboats, on the lake directly below, and out, across Srinagar to the mountains in the distance. There are paths leading up from the Nehru Park end of the Boulevard (look for the small pavilion half way up the hill) or from the hospital at the Tourist Reception Centre end of the Boulevard. There's also a steep trail to the top from directly behind the hotels and bazaar at Dal Gate.

Moghul Gardens

The Moghul emperors built gardens from Tehran to Agra but it is in Kashmir, complemented by the lake and the mountains, that they reach their perfection. Indeed after houseboats and the mountains it is these gardens for which Kashmir is most famous. The gardens all follow the same rectangular layout with a series of terraces rising one above the other up the hillside. Down the centre flows a stone channel carrying water through a series of pools and cascades. This system of carrying running water through the artificial cascades, and the layout of the fountains, was introduced to India by the artisans employed by the Emperor Akbar. 'Bagh' means garden. You can enjoy some of Srinagar's better gardens in a leisurely bike ride around the shores of the lake.

Chasma Shahi (9 km)

Smallest of the Srinagar Moghul gardens, measuring just 108 metres by 38 metres, the Chasma Shahi, or 'royal spring', are well up the hillside, above the Nehru Memorial Park. The fresh water spring in these pleasant, quieter gardens is reputed to have medicinal properties. The gardens were laid out in 1632 by Ali Mardan Khan and include three terraces, an aqueduct, waterfalls and fountains. The water from the spring supplies the fountains and then goes through the floor of the pavilion and falls to the lower terrace in a fine cascade

of five metres, over a polished black stone chute.

Some extensions have recently been made to the gardens. Like all the gardens the Chasma Shahi is open from sunrise to sunset but unlike the other gardens this is the only one which charges admission. There is a small shrine, the Chasma Sahibi, near the gardens which also has a fresh water spring.

Pari Mahal (10 km)

The old Sufi college of Pari Mahal, the 'palace of the fairies', is only a short distance above the Chasma Shahi gardens. You can easily walk from the gardens up to the Pari Mahal then follow a footpath directly down the hill to the road that runs by the Oberoi Palace Hotel. The Pari Mahal consists of a series of ruined, arched terraces and had, over the years, become considerably overgrown and neglected. Recently it has been turned into a very pleasant and well kept garden with fine views over Dal Lake. It's attractively sited on a spur of the Zabarwan mountains.

The college was built by Prince Dara Shikah, who had a keen interest in Sufiism and Hindu philosophy. The eldest son of Shah Jahan, his right to the throne was usurped by his younger brother who became the Emperor Aurangzeb and was noted for his fanatical Muslim beliefs. There is a shrine to the Goddess Parvati near the foot of the Pari Mahal hill. It's popular on Thursdays in May-June, the Kashmiri month of Jeth. Near the spring is a large chinar with groves of fruit trees, poplars and willows all around.

Nishat Bagh (11 km)

Sandwiched between the lake and the mountains, the Nishat gardens or 'garden of pleasure' have a particularly fine view across the lake to the Pir Panjal mountain range to the west. The gardens were designed in 1633 by Asaf Khan, brother of Nur Jahan, and follow the same pattern as the Shalimar gardens with a polished stone channel running down the centre and a series of terraces.

It's the largest of the Moghul gardens, measuring 548 metres by 338 metres, and often the most crowded. The walks beside the channel are bordered with lines of cypresses and chinars. The garden has 10 terraces and the remains of some Moghul period buildings including a double-storey pavilion enclosed on two sides by latticed windows.

Directly behind the garden is the Gopi Tirth, a small spring gushing forth crystal clear water which feeds the garden water channel.

Shalimar Bagh (15 km)

Set some distance back from the lake, but reached by a small canal, the Shalimar gardens were built by Emperor Jehangir for his wife Nur Jahan, 'light of the world', in 1616. Although it is known today as the 'garden of love' it was originally named the Farah Bakhsh or 'delightful garden'.

The garden is built in four terraces with the traditional water channel running down the middle. The gardens measure 540 by 183 metres. During the Moghul period the top terrace was reserved for the emperor and the ladies of the court and was the most magnificent. It included a pavilion made of black stone in the middle of the tank. Black marble fluted pillars supported the pavilion which was used as a banquet hall.

The gardens are beautifully kept even today and a son et lumiere (sound and light) show is put on here every evening during the May to October tourist season. The English performance takes place at 9 pm and tickets cost Rs 3 or Rs 7.50. The gardens tend to be very crowded on Sundays.

Hazratbal Mosque (7 km)

If you were doing a clockwise tour of the lake by shikara after winding your way through the floating gardens and the channels and waterways you'd eventually come out on the open lake and find yourself at the Hazratbal Mosque. The fairly new and shiny mosque, the name means Majestic Palace, enshrines a hair of the prophet but is probably more interesting, to non-Muslims, for its simply stunning situation on the banks of the beautiful lake with the mountains unfolding as a backdrop behind it. The mosque bazaar is fantastically busy on Fridays.

The sacred hair was brought to India in 1634 by Syyid Abdullah and acquired by a Kashmiri trader, Noor-ud-Din, in 1692, It eventually made its way to Kashmir, in the care of another Kashmiri, in 1700. The mosque is a blend of Moghul and Kashmiri architecture with a three-tiered roof topping walls and porticos of brick masonry on a base of dressed stone.

The Kashmir University campus stands just 200 metres from the mosque. The campus was a grant from Dr Karan Singh.

Nasim Bagh (8 km)

Only a short distance beyond the Hazratbal Mosque, the Nasim gardens, the 'garden of tepid airs' or 'garden of the morning breeze', were built by the Moghul Emperor Akbar after his conquest of Kashmir in 1586. He had 1200 chinar trees planted in the garden, which is the oldest of Kashmir's Moghul gardens. Today it's used by an engineering college and is not kept up for the public like the other Moghul gardens in Srinagar. It is possible to camp in this garden, but permission has to be obtained from the Tourist Reception Centre.

Nagin Lake (8 km)

Known as the 'jewel in the ring', Nagin is generally held to be the most beautiful of the Dal Lakes. Its name comes from the many trees which encircle the small, deep blue lake. Nagin is only separated from the larger Dal Lakes by a narrow causeway and it also has a number of houseboats moored around its perimeter. If you want to really get away from it all then Nagin is a good place to find a houseboat and do it,

the surroundings are much more serene
and isolated than on Dal Lake. You can
rent rowboats from the camping site here
– either to simply row around the lake or to
look around for a houseboat.

Since the water in Nagin is deeper (up to
12 metres deep) and less polluted it's also
good for swimming and there are
fibreglass sailing boats available for hire
and water-skiing facilities. The noisy and
smelly motor boats are rather low-
powered for skiing although they make a
valiant attempt. If you try water-skiing,
keep a wary eye out for swimmers.
Likewise if you are swimming watch out
for the boat drivers.

The Nagin Club, on the bank of the lake,
has a bar and a tea pavilion. It is a branch
of the Srinagar Club and temporary
membership is available to visitors.

Hari Parbat Fort (5 km)

The 18th century fort tops the Sharika
hill, which is clearly visible, rising to the
west of Dal Lake. The fort was constructed
by Atta Mohammed Khan from 1776 but
the surrounding wall is much older, it was
built between 1592 and 1598 during the
rule of Akbar. The wall stretches for five
km and is 10 metres high and has two
gates, the Kathi and Sangin Darwaza. The
Kathi is the main entrance with Persian
commemorative inscriptions surrounding
it. The Sangin, however, is more ornate
with sculptured windows on either side.

Visits to the fort, now used as an
arsenal, are only possible with written
permission from the Director of Tourism
so for most visitors the fort will remain just
a pleasant backdrop. The fort contains a
temple revered for its image of the
Goddess Sharika. Outside the fort's
southern gate there is a shrine to the sixth
Sikh Guru. It's known as the Chati Pad
Shaki. The hill, which rises 122 metres
from the valley floor, is surrounded by
orchards of almond trees where many
Kashmiris come for picnics in the spring
and summer.

Pandrethan Temple (5 km)

A small, beautifully proportioned Shiva
temple built around 900 AD, the
Pandrethan Temple is in the military
cantonment area on the Jammu road out
of Srinagar.

Shadaharwan (22 km)

Five km beyond the Shalimar Gardens,
this place is said to have been the site of a
monastery in which the Fourth International Council of Buddhism was held in
the year 300 AD. At this time Kashmir was
part of the Kushan Empire under the rule
of the Buddhist emperor Kanishka. The
monastery is said to have contained a
stupa, some chapels and other buildings.
Excavations in the area recently have
brought to light some illustrated tiles on
the hillside south of the village of Harwan.
You can see examples of the tiles, with
their central Asian influence in the
peoples' dress and ornaments, in the
museum in Srinagar.

Nearby is the Harwan Lake, at the foot
of the 4267 metre Mahadev peak, a
popular climb for hikers during the
summer. The lake is actually the reservoir
which provides the water supply for
Srinagar and it is supplied by the run-off
from Marsar Lake. There is also a garden
and trout hatchery at the site.

Burzahom (24 km)

In the opposite direction from the
Shalimar Gardens, about five km to the
north-west, are the even older excavations
of Burzahom. The archaeological dig here
has provided evidence of people living in
the Vale up to 5000 years ago. The oldest
excavations have revealed implements,
pots, animal skeletons, arrowheads and
tools from the neolithic age. Much of the
material taken from this site is now in the
museum in Srinagar.

Jesus in Kashmir

Search out the Rauzabal or 'prophet's tomb' in
the oldest part of the city while you're in
Srinagar. You'll have found the final resting

place of Jesus Christ – or so the legend goes. Following his reappearance after the crucifixion (not so much rising from the dead as a narrow survival) Jesus fled from Palestine, the Kashmir story relates, accompanied by his mother Mary and the disciple Thomas. They paused in Damascus but eventually made their way east to the sub-continent where Mary died in Murree, near Rawalpindi in present day Pakistan. Supposedly you can locate her tomb there too.

Jesus and Thomas continued on to Kashmir where Jesus settled in Yusmarg while Thomas went to the south of India. Jesus is, of course, also one of the great prophets of the Islamic faith and in Kashmir his name translates as Yus Asaf. So Yusmarg is the 'meadow of Jesus'. After marrying a Kashmiri girl from Pahalgam Jesus lived out his life in Kashmir, eventually dying aged 85 or more. There are numerous texts and clues pointing, according to interested Kashmiris, to his life in Kashmir. Even the Hemis Gompa in Ladakh is said to have evidence of a visit. And if that's not enough you can also look for the tomb of Moses, he's buried in Kashmir too!

Places to Stay

Srinagar has a great number of hotels apart from its well known floating hostelries. If you want something at the very bottom of the price scale or, conversely, at the top end of the luxury scale, you may find it easier on dry land. Prices are very variable with the season and the number of tourists. Prices are higher than down on the Indian plains but like the tribe of merchants they truly are, the Kashmiri hotel keepers are only too willing to bargain with you, especially if tourists are not numerous or if you arrive early. You will always get a good price for being the first customer of the day.

As with houseboats the hotels are categorised. Official rates for double rooms are A class Rs 150-250, B class Rs 60-90 and C class Rs 30-40. Take these figures as bargaining guides only. The best approach is to know roughly what you expect of a hotel and what you are prepared to pay for it. If you find an acceptable room but at too high a price,

walking out the door may bring the price down.

Places to Stay – bottom end

There are cheap hotels scattered all around Srinagar although those around the Lal Chowk area can be very noisy. The best bargains in cheap hotels are probably to be found actually on Dal Lake, scattered amongst the houseboats. Not only are the prices pleasantly low but they're also much quieter than streetside hotels. Prices in these cheapies can be very variable depending on season and demand but can go as low as Rs 5 or 10 per person.

Some of these hotels in the lake can be fairly spartan but try the Green View Hotel with doubles from Rs 40, the Island Hotel with singles from Rs 25 and doubles from Rs 30 or the Hotel Leeward, behind Nehru Park, with singles from Rs 30 and doubles from Rs 40. The Latif Guest House or the Hotel Sundowna are even cheaper but the Sundowna has, reportedly, gone downhill of late. Right next door to the Sundowna is the Hotel Savoy with rooms from Rs 25 (spartan) through Rs 40 to Rs 50 and good food. A little up market from these places – and further up the channel towards Dal Gate – is Hotel Heaven Canal with doubles from Rs 50 to 80.

If you want your feet on solid ground, but cheaply, try the friendly Tibetan Guest House which you find through the Lhasa Restaurant, just off the Boulevard. The guest house itself is on Gagribal Rd, parallel to the Boulevard. Rooms cost from just Rs 30, doubles Rs 50. Zero Inn, by Zero Bridge, is also reasonably quiet but rather more expensive at Rs 50 or more for a double. They also have good value 'dorm' beds. Remember that Kashmir is not a cheap place for accommodation by Indian standards. In Raj Bagh, a reasonably quiet area of town, the Hotel Greenacre is a small hotel in a lovely garden, with singles from Rs 40, deluxe rooms from Rs 90.

Around Dal Gate there is the Hotel

Embassy with doubles from Rs 45, the *Metro Kashmir Hotel* with doubles from Rs 40 and the *New National Hotel* with doubles from Rs 45. *Hotel Hill Star* in Buchwara, close to Dal Gate, is another popular cheap hotel – 'lovely garden, clean, good breakfast'. Two other cheap hotels are the *Greenwood Hotel* near the bus stand and *Hotel Sailors* off Dal Lake.

The J&K tourist office operates four accommodation units in Srinagar. Right at the *Tourist Reception Centre* (tel 76107) there are retiring rooms, rooms and suites with prices ranging from Rs 60 for doubles, from Rs 90 for suites. They are intended only as short stay places (rates double after 48 hours) despite which they are generally full up during the season. The two J&K operated hotels are the *Lalla Rukh Hotel* (tel 76590) in Lal Chowk and the *Badshah Hotel* (tel 76063 & 76599) in Badshah Chowk. There are many cheap hotels in Lal Chowk but this is a noisy part of town. At the Lalla Rukh doubles cost from Rs 55. At the Badshah singles cost from Rs 35, doubles from Rs 55. Finally there are the *Tourist Huts* near the Chasma Shahi gardens. These come complete with kitchens and cooking equipment but are only really usable if you have your own transport. They cost around Rs 200 a night for a double and are booked through the Tourist Reception Centre.

The Srinagar *Youth Hostel* (tel 75414) on the Wazir Bagh, is across the river from the town centre, near the museum. Nightly charges are just Rs 1 on the floor, Rs 1.50 for a cot with bedding in one of the 14 bed dormitories. They also have doubles for Rs 8 per person, Rs 2 each for a third or fourth person. Reservations must be made through the Education Department. To get in you must be a student, teacher, scout, social worker or YHA member.

There is a campsite just beyond the Nagin Lake causeway, only a short distance before the Hazratbal Mosque. A good place if you've come to Kashmir with your own vehicle or have camping gear for trekking. You can also find rooms in private houses – such as at the village of Supta Ganga near the Nishat Bagh. These rooms are often well kept and excellent value.

Places to Stay – top end

Prices in Srinagar's top end hotels have been fairly static or even fallen over the past couple of years. In any case the prices are likely to be very variable with demand. Srinagar's top of the list establishment is the *Oberoi Palace Hotel*, the one-time palace of Maharaja Hari Singh. It's situated off the Boulevard, several km around the lake from Dal Gate. The actual building is rather uninspired, particularly if you've seen the sumptuous palace hotels of Rajasthan, but the gardens in front of the hotel provide superb views out over the lake. The rooms are still decorated with the original Bokhara carpets and there's also a private golf course. The hotel is only open from April to November. The Oberoi Palace (tel 75641-3) has 110 rooms with singles/ doubles at Rs 615/875 including all meals.

Much more central is *Nedou's Hotel* (tel 73015-16) on Hotel Rd, also known as Maulana Azad Rd. It's only a short stroll from the Tourist Reception Centre or the central shopping area. Nedou's is a little decrepit looking and has 79 rooms with singles/doubles from Rs 200/260. Almost next door, and looking as new as Nedou's is old, you'll find the *Broadway* (tel 71211-3). The 97 rooms in this pleasant, modern hotel cost Rs 290/425 for singles/doubles and it has a popular restaurant. The *Hotel Jehangir* (tel 73013-14) is just across Badshah Bridge from the centre. Here singles/doubles cost Rs 100/175.

Srinagar has many other hotels in the upper class bracket – some in the central part of town but most along the Boulevard looking out on Dal Lake. For example the *Hotel Boulevard* (tel 74964, 76195) has singles/doubles from Rs 120/150 and the

Hotel Shahanshah (tel 75856) at Rs 150/
225.

Other hotels along the Boulevard
include the pleasant *Hotel Paradise*, the
air-conditioned and centrally heated
Shah Abbas (tel 74158, 77789) and the
Gulmarg. The Shah Abbas overlooks the
lake and has good, modern, well appointed,
clean rooms at Rs 275 for a double.
They're a bit smaller than rooms at the
Broadway but the view more than
compensates. The Gulmarg is: 'good value
at around Rs 300 a double, very plush and
in terrible taste'! The *Mazda Hotel* is on
the Boulevard with rooms at Rs 100/150
while *Hotel Green View* is down by Nehru
Park. The *Nehru Guest House* is opposite
Nehru Park while *Hotel Holy Night* is
actually on Dal Lake.

Srinagar's largest hotel is the brand new
Center Lake View Hotel, Chasma Shahi
which has 281 rooms. There's also a more
expensive hotel right out on the lake. The
small (just 11 rooms) *Lake-Isle Resort* (tel
78446) is on an island in the lake and has
singles including breakfast for Rs 150,
doubles from Rs 175 to 225.

Houseboats & How to Find Them

Staying in a houseboat is one of the prime
attractions of a visit to Kashmir. They are
lined up in colourful ranks in Dal Lake,
across from the Boulevard, or along the
Jhelum River. Those who want a little
more isolation and peace can also find
them at Nagin Lake.

Houseboats originated in the Victorian
era as a superbly British solution to a
tricky political problem. The British liked
Kashmir but the Maharaja wouldn't allow
them to buy land to build houses on. So
they had houseboats built and the style
has hardly changed from the first boat in
1888 right down to boats being built
today. They're a great escape from the
noise and hassle which any Indian city,
and Srinagar is no exception, seems to
have an over-ample supply of. As soon as
you get out on the lake the traffic and
confusion simply fades away.

Houseboats are also highly entertaining
– you just sit out on the verandah on the
front of your boat or laze on the roof and
life passes by in front of you. A flock of
ducks, children barely old enough to walk
(but quite adept at paddling), hookah
smoking shikara men, fat ladies in saris,
travellers and freaks (often paddling
themselves in circles); they all pass by
you. You don't have to go to the shops –
the shops come to you. Jewellers, papier
mache dealers, incredibly persuasive
tailors, even the local supermarket will
turn up – 'you want beer, soap, cold drinks,
toilet paper?' And if none of those appeal –
'hashish?' Remember that it has been said
that houseboat owners make their profit
not from the room charges but from the
kickbacks on what their visitors buy!

In the early morning you can see ravens
and hawks swooping on the lake to catch
insects and fish. Late in the afternoon the
garden boats, laden with produce from the
floating gardens, will glide by. Or the weed
collector, with his boat that seems always
ready to sink, laden with the heavy and wet
weeds of the lake.

The view also changes with the season
although the magnificent mountains of the
Pir Panjal, with glimpses of the great
Himalaya, are a constant backdrop. In
winter the whole of this scene is covered
with snow, with the exception of the clear
waters of the lake itself. And even the lake
freezes over in exceptionally cold winters.

Officially houseboats come in five
categories with official prices (singles/
doubles) for each category. These are
lodging only or for board and lodging –
including all meals:

	full board	lodging only
De-luxe or 5-star	Rs 220/325	Rs 150/225
A class	Rs 150/220	Rs 90/140
B class	Rs 100/170	Rs 60/100
C class	Rs 65/115	Rs 30/40
D class*	Rs 45/60	Rs 20/30

*doonga boats

There are different costs for children or for sole occupancy of an entire boat.

First of all what is a houseboat and what do you get for your money? Basically it's a flat bottomed, very stationary boat, something between 20 and 40 metres long and three to six metres wide. Construction is of pine, lined with cedar. They follow a very standard pattern in their design – you board the boat by a small verandah, furnished with padded seats, and then enter the living room/lounge area. It's inevitably furnished in a style you could describe as 'English 1930s chintz'. From the lounge you enter the dining room followed by the small kitchen area – although food is generally prepared in a nearby kitchen boat. Stairs lead up from here to the rooftop sundeck. Finally a corridor leads back along one side of the boat to two or three bedrooms, each with its own bathroom and toilet.

The 'all-inclusive' price will include your room, all meals (breakfast, lunch and dinner), tea at least a couple of times a day, and transport back and forth between your boat and the shore in the houseboat's shikara. Of course getting back is only possible if your shikara man happens to be waiting at the landing. Generally you'll have to take, and pay for, one of the shikaras waiting there. Houseboats are usually owned in groups of two, three or more with one shikara to serve them all and also one kitchen boat (or land-based equivalent) to feed them all.

The top 5-star boats will be very luxurious indeed with new furniture and fittings, chandeliers in the dining room, radio or even TV, running hot water and so on. This technological luxury can be a little too much of a good thing – when the electrical goodies blow the fuses with regularity or when a neighbour plays the TV loud!

Moving down the scale the drop in standards is usually a matter of age rather than facilities – houseboats all look remarkably alike, just younger or older.

Doonga boats are, however, usually much smaller, often just one-roomed and with primitive sanitation facilities. The working doonga boats, which are usually inhabited year round, are usually found along the banks of the Jhelum River.

The tourist office 'official' prices are actually nowhere near as rigid as their neat categorisation might indicate. For a start the boats vary within their categories – there's 5-star and **5-STAR**! Similarly some run-down A class boats are no better than some well kept C class boats. Secondly there's competition – even at the height of the season there are a lot more houseboat berths than visitors and out of season the competition is intense to try and lure you aboard! End result is prices are generally subject to negotiation. At the worst you should be able to get away with paying the level that applies in the category one step down.

When enquiring about houseboats remember that this is Kashmir. It's necessary to pin them down on every little detail or be prepared for arguments when it comes to departure time. Find out what you can expect for the meals (how many eggs for breakfast?); if you opt not to have dinners some nights check what the reduction will be. Most people decide to have lunch off the boat every day. Make certain the shikara trips to shore are included – if not remember that it's only Rs 0.50 to get across from boat to shore, so don't pay too much for a few ferry rides. If you're in a lower class boat without hot water check that they'll supply buckets of water in the morning – Srinagar is a little chilly for washing in cold water. Check if your boat is hooked up to the mains water supply or not, water pumped straight from the lake is definitely not drinkable.

It's virtually impossible to recommend particular boats. Since you're much more 'contained' in a boat than in a hotel little things can make all the difference. If the regular cook goes on holidays and the food standards fall you're stuck with it since you can't walk to the restaurant at the corner! Similarly a friendly shikara man can make all the difference to an otherwise unexceptional boat – he has to bring you washing water, make the tea and bring it across, shuttle you back and forth from boat to shore. Hopefully with a smile. Food even in the best boats can get monotonous and since a C class boat may well be sharing the same kitchen boat as a 5-star boat there is not likely to be a great difference between categories.

Finally, how to find a houseboat. Don't do it through the tourist office – you're likely to end up paying the maximum price and your choice of boats is probably restricted to the friends of the man behind the counter. It's much easier just to drift down to one of the landing 'ghats' and either let somebody grab you or take a shikara and go looking for a suitable berth. The kids at the ghats always know which boats have vacancies and by the time you've looked into half a dozen you'll have a pretty good idea what your money buys you. There are hundreds and hundreds of houseboats so you can always shift to another if you find yours isn't such a bargain after all, or if the food is not to your taste.

Houseboat touts, incidentally, are energetic and ingenious. They don't even wait for you to appear by the lakeside, at the Tourist Reception Centre or even at Srinagar airport. You'll actually find them lying in wait at Delhi airport if you're flying from there to Srinagar! Naturally being talked into a houseboat at this point, sight unseen, is likely to have some drawbacks. Touts at Srinagar airport may, however, provide free transport out to the lake to see their houseboat and you're not obliged to accept it if you don't like it.

Marriage in Kashmir

If you spend a long time in Kashmir you may get an opportunity to see a large Islamic wedding. The ceremonies often take place over several days and because of the huge cost involved it is not unusual for several sisters to be married on the same day.

The festivities take place not in houses but in lavish tents which are erected in gardens. Men and women are kept strictly separate during the festivities. Before the wedding day the bridegroom is occupied with the monetary gifts of friends and relatives. On the evening before the actual ceremony he goes, with the entire wedding company, to the house of the bride to sign the *nika* or marriage contract. Only men take part in this ceremony and the bride is represented by her father. The contract is sealed in the presence of a mullah and a small sugarball or *shirien* is distributed to each guest. Late into the night a feast is held to celebrate the union

The next morning the bride, in a draped litter or in a car with draped windows, and the bridegroom, on a horse, are accompanied by the whole wedding party to the bridegroom's house. The bridegroom generally gives his future wife a very valuable item of jewellery as a wedding present, often a massive golden necklace and armband.

Places to Eat

Because so many people eat on board their houseboats Srinagar is not a very exciting place for eating out. Surprisingly nobody has yet come up with a floating restaurant on Dal Lake – a logical follow on to all those houseboats. Supposedly there are such restaurants on Nagin Lake – such as *Mama Mia*.

The *Oberoi Palace Hotel* does a very superior buffet dinner for Rs 60 and at lunch-time you can dine, or simply have a snack, on their sweeping lawn. A la carte, most dishes are in the Rs 20 to Rs 35 bracket. The *Broadway* also has a slightly cheaper buffet in their pleasantly carpet-decorated restaurant. Food here (on the non-buffet nights) is quite reasonably priced and you can sample quite possibly the best kahwa tea in Srinagar – an expensive treat.

Ahdoo's, which fronts on to the Bund and backs on to Residency Rd, has been said to have some of the best Kashmiri food in Srinagar but generally fails to live up to its reputation. Most dishes are under Rs 15. Across the road the *Grand* has a similar menu. Others include the *Capri Bar & Restaurant* and the *Premier*.

Just off the Boulevard the Tibetan run *Lhasa Restaurant* with its 'candle-lit garden' does quite good Chinese-Tibetan food. Most dishes are Rs 10 to 25, a complete meal for two will cost Rs 50 to 75. This friendly place is very popular with travellers. Further back towards Dal Gate, on the Boulevard, there's the *Shamyana* with a nice outside garden area, good vegetarian food and reasonable prices. The *Punjab Hotel & Restaurant*, on Lal Chowk opposite the Palladium Cinema, has cheap, tasty food at Rs 3 to 6 per dish plus more expensive tandoori food. Near Dal Gate the *Glocken Bakery* has good fresh brown bread and other baked goodies such as apple pie or cheese cake. In the same area there's a place doing good south Indian masala dosas, across the road from the Indian Overseas Bank.

Right in the central area the *Indian Coffee House* is a good place for a coffee and a chat – the food line here is rather limited: quite good vegetable cutlets and rather so-so masala dosas. Or at least it was a good place, it was burnt out recently and may not yet be re-opened. Right across the road the *Hollywood Cafe* has much, much better food than its plain appearance would suggest. Seekh kebab or kanti roast make an excellent lunch here and their french fries are superb by any standards. Plus good cakes or snacks at other times of day.

Ice cream is not bad at *Dimples*, either in the centre (opposite the Hollywood) or by Zero Bridge. The latter is known as the *Little Hut* and also has good milkshakes and iced coffee. There's a good selection of Indian sweets at *Shakti Sweets* also by the Hollywood. You'll find a variety of restaurants and snack bars along the Boulevard or at Dal Gate, such as the cheap *Vegetarian Paradise*. The cafe at the *Tourist Reception Centre* is terrible but you can get early morning snacks from the stalls which set up opposite the TRC for the early bus departures.

Getting There

Air Indian Airlines fly to Srinagar from New Delhi (Rs 549), Chandigarh (Rs 464), Amritsar (Rs 314), Jammu (Rs 179) and there are flights operating from Srinagar to Leh and back. Flights are more frequent during the summer tourist season, at that time there will probably be several flights a day between Delhi and Srinagar using 737s and Airbuses. Some will be direct, others will operate via Chandigarh, Amritsar or Jammu. Flight time from Delhi on the direct flights is about an hour and ten minutes. As usual in India you should book your flight as early as possible.

At Srinagar airport, which is about 13 km out of the city, there is a fairly chaotic scene as the Tourist Office tries to register every incoming foreigner and insists that you book any accommodation through the Tourist Reception Centre. They're generally happy if they get the names and passport numbers of a dozen or so and in any case it's a harmless procedure although you'll get better prices for houseboats if you negotiate yourself with the houseboats.

Taxi drivers and houseboat touts are not allowed into the arrival area so this is a last chance for a little peace and privacy. There's an airport bus to the Tourist Reception Centre in Srinagar which costs Rs 10. You can ask to get off before then if you want. Buses leave for all the outgoing flights. By taxi it officially costs Rs 40 although you can usually do better than that.

In Srinagar the Indian Airlines office is at the Tourist Reception Centre (tel 73538 & 73270) and is open from 10 am to 5 pm. It's also at the Tourist Reception Centre in Jammu (tel 2735 & 7088).

Train & Bus It's 880 km from Delhi to Srinagar although almost everybody coming up from Delhi, or other Indian cities, by land will come through Jammu (591 km from Delhi) from where the buses run daily to Srinagar. By train there are about four services a day from Delhi or New Delhi to Jammu Tawi, across the river from Jammu. The trip takes nine to 13 hours, usually overnight, and costs about Rs 193 in 1st class, Rs 60 in 2nd class. There are also buses from Delhi but people making the trip by road will most probably be coming via Chandigarh, Amritsar or the Himachal Pradesh hill stations.

Buses leave Jammu early in the morning (between 6.30 and 7 am) for the 10 to 12 hour trip to Srinagar in the Kashmir Valley. Bus fares are Rs 27 (B class), Rs 40 (A class), Rs 65 (super de-luxe) and Rs 100 (air-con). B class buses seat two and three, A class two and two, super de-luxe two and two in individual seats with headrests. Although there are many buses (a veritable armada leaves Jammu each morning) you should book a seat as soon as you arrive in Jammu. The same applies from Srinagar as the day before departure all seats may be sold out. Srinagar-Jammu the left side of the bus has the best view, some say. A recent report indicates that certain stretches of the road are now one-way on alternate days so on one day buses only go Srinagar-Jammu, on the next Jammu-Srinagar. This may be only a temporary policy.

Buses also go from here to Leh – B class Rs 58, A class Rs 78, de-luxe Rs 153. To Kargil the fare is Rs 29 on A or B class buses. See the Ladakh section for more details.

The buses all arrive and depart in Srinagar from the Tourist Reception Centre bus compound. From here's it's about a 10 to 15 minute walk to Dal Lake and the houseboat ghats and you will be pestered by taxi and auto-rickshaw drivers, houseboat touts and various other salesmen every step of the way. If you want to go straight to the houseboat area or to one of the upmarket hotels by the lake ask for the Boulevard

For information about booking trains from Jammu while in Srinagar enquire at the railways office in the Tourist Reception

Centre or at N D Radha Kishen & Sons, Railway Out Agency, Badshah Chowk, Srinagar (tel 2146). Bus booking are made at the Tourist Reception Centre (tel 2698), allow plenty of time as the booking system is archaic.

Taxis & Jeeps Taxis can be hired for long distance trips as well as within the Vale. A taxi to Jammu costs Rs 130 per seat or Rs 520 for the whole vehicle. See the Ladakh section for taxis and jeeps to Leh.

Getting Around

There is a wide choice of transport available either on the lake or out and around it, plus a variety of tours. The tour buses are generally much more com-fortable than the usual run of over-crowded buses and, since many of them offer one-way fares, they can be used for getting out to hill stations in the valley.

Srinagar lends itself to human-power transport – either feet, bicycles or shikaras. Many of the interesting parts of town are within walking distance wherever you stay. If you are on a houseboat, walking along the Boulevard into the area of Residency Rd, the Tourist Reception Centre, the polo ground and the Bund, will provide you with the opportunity for plenty of sightseeing and shopping.

The best known Kashmiri transport is, of course, the shikara:

Shikaras These are the graceful, long boats which crowd the Srinagar lakes. They're used for getting back and forth from the houseboats or for longer tours. Officially there is a standard fare for every trip around the lake and these are prominently posted at the main landings (ghats); in practice the fares can be quite variable. To be shuttled across to your houseboat should cost Rs 2 in a covered ('full spring seats') shikara but the kids who are always out for a little pocket money will happily paddle you across to the closer houseboats for 50p in a basic, open shikara. Of course late at night, particularly if it is raining, the tables are turned and getting back to your houseboat at a reasonable price may require a little ingenuity! If you hire a shikara by the day or for a longer trip, count on about Rs 7 or Rs 8 per hour, up to Rs 20 at the height of the season.

Try paddling a shikara yourself sometime – it's nowhere near as easy as it looks. You'll spend lots of time going round in circles trying to master that single, heart-shaped paddle. Even if you do start to travel in a straight line you'll find it requires a good amount of stamina to maintain the pace. If your houseboat hasn't got one to spare some children passing by will find you a boat although you may have to pay Rs 4 or Rs 5 per hour. You can rent rowboats on Nagin Lake.

Taxis & Autorickshaws There are stands for these at the Tourist Reception Centre and other strategic locations in town. Srinagar's taxi-wallahs are extremely reluctant to use their meters so you'll have to bargain hard. Count on about Rs 10 to 15 for a taxi from the Tourist Reception Centre to Dal Gate or the houseboat ghats (Rs 5 to 10 by auto-rickshaw) or Rs 40 to the airport. Large items of baggage may cost extra.

For longer trips the official fares (one-way/return) are all posted by the stands:

Moghul Gardens	Rs 75/90
Gulmarg	Rs 170/220
Pahalgam	Rs 220/270
Sonamarg	Rs –/280
Wular Lake	Rs –/225
Ladakh*	Rs 3500

*one week, round trip

Buses The Jammu & Kashmir Road Transport Corporation buses go from the Tourist Reception Centre while private buses operate from a variety of stands in Srinagar. Taxi or auto-rickshaw drivers will usually know which stand you need. Certain major long distance routes are reserved for the J&K buses (Jammu, Leh,

etc) but others are open for competition and there will be a great number of buses operating. Fares are set for all routes and the drivers or conductors are usually very helpful. Take a number 12 bus to Nagin Lake or the Hazratbal Mosque. See the relevant sections for costs.

Tours The J&K Road Transport Corporation operate a number of daily tours from the Tourist Reception Centre. Private bus companies, particularly the KMDA (Kashmir Motor Drivers' Ass.), also have a number of tours. The J&K RTC tours are:

Pahalgam	daily	Rs 36 **, Rs 18 *
Daksum	daily	Rs 36 **, Rs 18 *
Gulmarg	daily	Rs 40 **, Rs 20 *
Aharbal	Tues, Thur, Sun	Rs 25
Verinag	Wed, Sun	Rs 25
Wular Lake	Mon, Wed, Fri	Rs 30
Yusmarg	Tues, Thur, Sun	Rs 28 **, Rs 15 *
Sonamarg	daily	Rs 28 **, Rs 15 *
Moghul Gardens	twice daily	Rs 16

* one-way
** round trip

KMDA tours include Pahalgam (Rs 28 round trip, Rs 20 one way), Aharbal (Rs 21), Verinag (Rs 18), Wular Lake (Rs 18), Sonamarg (Rs 24) and Moghul Gardens and Shankaracharya Hill (Rs 10).

Bicycles Seeing Srinagar by bicycle is a surprisingly pleasant way of getting around. Although the mountains soar up all around the valley, Srinagar itself is surprisingly flat. Bicycles are economical too. You can hire bikes for Rs 6 per day from bicycle shops. There are several along the Boulevard close to Dal Gate. Be careful of the traffic; like all Asian drivers the Kashmiris rely on their horns more than their brakes. Pleasant trips to be made include:

Top: Hazratbal Mosque by Dal Lake (TW)
Bottom: Houseboats on Dal Lake (TW)

Top: Fruit vendor on a Srinagar street (TW)
Left: Srinagar houses (TW)
Right: Jami Masjid Mosque, Srinagar (TW)

Round Dal Lake – an all day trip going by the Moghul gardens. It's particularly pleasant around the north of the lake where the villages are still relatively untouched.

Across the lake – you can ride right across the lake on the causeway, a nice trip since there are no problems with vehicle traffic and there is plenty of opportunity to observe the lake life without being in a boat.

Nagin Lake – you can ride out to the Hazratbal Mosque via Nagin Lake and then make a complete loop around the lake on the way back. This trip can easily be combined with a trip along the Jhelum, taking in the various mosques close to the river. The streets here are very narrow so vehicles keep away and bike riding is pleasant.

Places to Shop
There are a whole string of Government Handicraft Emporiums scattered around Srinagar but the main one is housed in the fine old British Residency buildings by the Bund. Here you'll find a representative selection of reasonably good quality items at reasonable prices. Even if you don't buy there, and take advantage of the government's quality guarantee, it's a good idea to familiarise yourself with what's available here.

Other good shopping areas include along the Boulevard by Dal Lake where some of the flashiest shops can be found. The Bund also has an interesting selection of shops including *Suffering Moses*, where you'll find some particularly high quality items. The Government Central Market, across Badshah Bridge, has a variety of stalls and again some government quality and price control is exercised. Hari Singh St, near the Amira Kadal Bridge, is a popular older shopping area, as are Polo View Rd and Lambert Lane in the centre.

There are literally hundreds of other shops scattered all over Srinagar and if you don't fall prey to those persuasive salesmen they'll pursue you all the way back to your houseboat – countless shikaras patrol Dal Lake like shoals of sharks, loaded down with the same items you'll find in the shops.

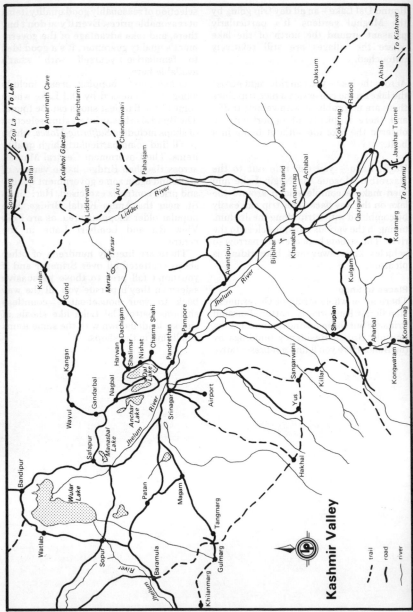

Kashmir Valley

- - - trail
—— road
∼ river

Kashmir Valley

There are many interesting places around the Kashmir Valley. Some of these make good day trips, others are pleasant to stay at in their own right or make good bases for day walks or longer trekking trips. The J&K Road Transport Corporation operates a variety of day tours around the valley, backed up by privately operated bus company tours. You can also get out and about in local buses or taxis. The two main valley resorts are Pahalgam and Gulmarg. Other places of interest are covered along the route to Pahalgam, the Sindh Valley route, and other places to the south of Srinagar.

ON THE ROAD TO PAHALGAM

The road to Pahalgam starts out towards Jammu but later branches off to the east at Anantnag. There are a number of points of interest along this route including several Moghul gardens – indeed if you take a bus tour to Pahalgam you'll be thoroughly saturated with Moghul gardens by the time you arrive.

Pampore (16 km)

Only 16 km out of Srinagar on the main highway south, Pampore is the centre of Kashmir's saffron industry. Highly prized for its flavouring and colouring properties, and rather expensive, saffron is gathered from flowers which are harvested in October.

Avantipur (29 km)

This popular stop on Pahalgam excursions is noted for its two ruined Hindu temples. The temples were both constructed by King Avantivarman, after whom this ancient centre was named, between 855 and 883 AD. The larger of the two is dedicated to Vishnu and known as the Avantiswami Temple. The central shrine is enclosed by a huge wall with four smaller shrines around the centre. The courtyard is paved and enclosed and measures 52 by 45 metres. The entrance still bears some fine relief sculptures and the columns, richly covered in carvings and sculptures, give the temple an almost Grecian appearance.

The other temple, dedicated to Shiva and known as the Avantishvara, is about a km before the Vishnu temple, but also close to the main road. It is situated in a courtyard, enclosed by a massive stone wall with a gateway on the western side.

The nearby village of Bijbihara has a huge chinar tree, claimed to be the largest in Kashmir.

Sangam (35 km)

A little further down the road, Sangam is interesting for its strong local industry of (believe it or not) cricket bat manufacturing! You'll see thousands of cricket bats displayed by the roadside and thousands more roughly-cut lengths of wood being seasoned.

Anantnag (56 km)

At this point the road forks, one route turning north-east to Pahalgam and two others south-east to Achabal and Kokarnag or to Verinag. The Jammu road leaves this route just before Anantnag at Khanabal.

Anantnag has a number of sulphur springs, esteemed for their curative properties. The largest spring is believed to be the home of Ananta, the serpent on which Vishnu reclines and from which the town takes its name – 'Abode of Ananta'. Ananta means 'endless' and the water issues from the base of a small hillock and rushes into another spring in the middle of which is a natural mineral deposit column which the locals revere as a lingam. On the 14th day of a full moon fortnight in September/October, there is a festival where the people fast and pour rice and milk into the spring to feed the goldfish.

At one time Anantnag was known as Islamabad but this name is no longer used, due to the confusion it would cause with the not-too-far distant capital of Pakistan, also named Islamabad.

Achabal (58 km)
The Moghul gardens in this small town were begun by Nur Jahan and completed by Jahanara, daughter of Shah Jahan, in 1640. It's one of the most carefully designed of the Kashmir gardens and was said to be a favourite retreat of Nur Jahan. Water from a copious spring flows from the garden in three stone-lined canals, over three terraces and three cascades, with several fountains in the main canal. There are three pavilions on the upper terrace, shaded by chinar trees.

There's a *Tourist Bungalow, Tourist Huts* and a camping ground at Achabal.

Kokarnag (77 km)
You may be suffering garden overload by the time you get there but Kokarnag has yet another one, noted for its roses. Like Achabal there is a *Tourist Bungalow, Tourist Huts* and a camping ground.

Daksum (90 km)
Somewhat above Kokarnag, along the Bring River valley, there's the small hill resort of Daksum at 2438 metres. It's on the trekking route to Kishtwar and has a *Rest House, Tourist Bungalow* and plenty of camping spots. From Daksum the trail rises fairly steeply to the Sinthan Pass at 3748 metres. The pass is open from April to September. See the Trekking in Kashmir section for more details.

Mattan & Martand (61 & 64 km)
Only a few km beyond Anantnag, on the Pahalgam road, Mattan is an important Hindu pilgrimage point due to its fish-filled springs. A complicated legend relates that the springs were created when Shiva broke open an egg which had been thrown there, the egg being the reincarnated form of a forgetful boy, who had

been cursed by a wandering sage . . . . and that's only half the story!

On a plateau above Mattan and three km to the south, stands the huge ruined temple of Martand. Built by Lalitaditya Mukhtapida (699-736 AD) it is the most impressive ancient ruin in Kashmir and beautifully sited. The ruins are 67 metres by 43 metres and consists of a portico with a small detached shrine on either side and a quadrangular courtyard. The courtyard was surrounded by 84 columns – the multiple of the number of days in the week by the number of signs in the zodiac.

From here to Pahalgam the road follows the course of the Lidder River, past some good trout-fishing stretches.

Verinag (80 km)
Close to the foot of the Pir Panjal range, the spring at Verinag is said to be the source of the Jhelum River, which flows north through Srinagar. Jehangir built an octagonal stone basin at the spring in 1612 and in 1620 his son, Shah Jahan, laid out a garden around it. The spring is said to be over 15 metres deep and is reputed never to dry up or overflow. There is a *Tourist Bungalow* at Verinag.

PAHALGAM
At an altitude of 2130 metres and about 95 km from Srinagar, Pahalgam is probably the most popular hill resort in the Kashmir Valley. Since it is rather lower than Gulmarg the night time temperatures do not drop so low and it has the further advantage of the beautiful Lidder River running right through the town. Pahalgam is situated at the junction of the Aru (or West Lidder) and Sheshnag (or East Lidder) Rivers and surrounded by soaring, fir covered mountains with bare, snow capped peaks rising behind them. The Aru flows down from the Kolahoi Glacier beyond Lidderwat while the Sheshnag originates from glaciers along the Great Himalaya.

There are many short walks available from Pahalgam and in addition it is an

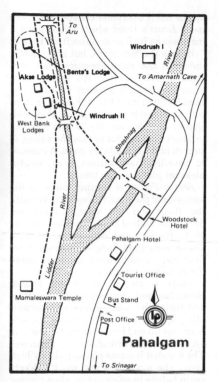

Pahalgam

To Aru

Windrush I

River

Akse Lodge | Bente's Lodge

To Amarnath Cave

West Bank Lodges

Windrush II

Sheshnag

River

Lidder River

Woodstock Hotel

Pahalgam Hotel

Tourist Office

Mamaleswara Temple

Bus Stand

Post Office

To Srinagar

excellent base for longer treks such as those to the Kolahoi Glacier or to the Amarnath Cave. Pahalgam can also be used as a starting point for treks out of the region – see the Trekking in Kashmir section for more details. Pahalgam is particularly famed for its many shepherds and they're a common sight, driving their flocks of sheep along the paths all around the town.

Information
The Tourist Office (tel 24) is just around the corner from the bus halt, on the main road. They may be able to help with hiring porters or ponies but otherwise are not much use. Fishing permits have to be obtained in Srinagar. There is a bank in

Pahalgam and a post office during the tourist season. If you're planning on trekking from Pahalgam there are plenty of shops selling food supplies although it's cheaper and more plentiful in Srinagar. If trekking is altogether too strenuous Pahalgam also offers the Pahalgam Club with tennis courts, badminton courts, a golf course and card evenings!

Pahalgam Walks
Mamaleswara Only a km or so downstream from Pahalgam, and on the opposite side of the Lidder, is this small Shiva temple with its square, stone tank. It is thought to date from the reign of King Jayasima in the 12th century, even earlier.

Baisaran This meadow, about five km from Pahalgam and 150 metres higher, provides excellent views over the town and the Lidder Valley. The grassy glen is surrounded by pine forests and the snow-clad mountains. You can hire ponies for this trek from near the centre of town.

Tulian Lake If you continue 11 km on beyond Baisaran you reach the Tulian Lake at 3353 metres, 1200 metres higher up. It is covered in ice for much of the year and surrounded by peaks which rise more than 300 metres above its shores. It also can be reached by pony trek.

Aru The little village of Aru is actually the first stage from Pahalgam on the trek to Lidderwat and the Kolahoi Glacier. It makes an interesting day walk from Pahalgam, following the Lidder River for 11 km upstream. The main track, which also unfortunately takes cars, is on the left bank of the river. There is a less used, and more difficult path, on the right bank.

At Aru you will often find the Gujars, living in their log huts with their flocks of sheep and goats, en route to the higher pastures for the summer. Aru has two very nice *PWD Tourist Rest Houses*, two small tea houses (the *Travellers Lodge* and the *Paradise Lodge*) with rooms, the *Green*

View Guest House, near the river just before you reach the village, and a new deluxe hotel. The *PWD* accommodation costs Rs 20 for one or two people, Rs 26 for three.

Fishing

Pahalgam is one of Kashmir's popular trout fishing beats. Kashmir is famous for its trout although they tend to be rather small. Additionally, fishing licences are hard to get and rather expensive. They only allow so many rods on each stretch of the river so there is often a queue for licences. The cost, in Pahalgam, is Rs 50 per day for the licence. Add to that Rs 20 for rod and equipment rental and Rs 20 for the compulsory guide and you've spent Rs 90 before you start – rather a lot for the six fish which is the daily limit. It's not surprising that trout rarely feature on Kashmiri menus!

Places to Stay

Pahalgam has a curious mixture of old and somewhat rundown hotels and guesthouses together with more modern establishments. There are many hotels along the main street of Pahalgam including the expensive *Pahalgam Hotel* (tel 26) or the equally pricey *Woodstock* (tel 27) which costs Rs 350/400 for singles/doubles. Other hotels around the town centre and close to the bus stand include the *Mount View Hotel*, the *New Pine Hotel* and the *Hotel Natraj*. The Natraj has regular rooms and also three-bedroom huts with kitchen, baths, verandah and a private garden for Rs 200 a day, or a five-bedroom hut with drawing/dining room, pantry, kitchen and private garden for Rs 400 a day. Food is extra.

Most budget travellers head across the river to one of the lodges on the other (western) bank. The once very popular riverside *Windrush* (not to be confused with another Windrush on the town side) burnt down and has relocated up the hill from the river. Singles start as low as Rs 10, doubles from Rs 20 to 30. It may be renamed *Woodlands* now, to avoid confusion with the other 'Windrush', on the town side of the river. A little further

up the hill is the rather cheaper and more basic *Bente's Hotel* where you can get a mattress at Rs 5 or doubles from Rs 20.

Before the Windrush, but also slightly uphill, is the more expensive, but very popular, *Aksa Lodge*. It's rather more luxurious (even hot water) with doubles from Rs 50 to Rs 100 (lower out of season) with attached bath. Cheaper doubles with shared facilities are Rs 30 and 35. The location, looking out across the valley, is superb and the food very good. A number of travellers have written to say what a pleasant place to stay this is.

Brown Palace is another lodge on the west side of the river. Prices here vary with the floor and the view – there are dormitory beds at Rs 10, doubles from Rs 40 to Rs 110 and cottages at Rs 200. These west bank lodges generally have fires and pot-bellied stoves, which make the evenings particularly pleasant.

There is also a *Government Tourist Bungalow* and *Government Tourist Huts* and during the summer season the tourist office operates a number of tent sites with ready set up and furnished tents. The *Dar Camp* has been particularly recommended. The wooded Rajavas plateau, sitting high above the town, is where most trekkers camp before heading out or when coming back to Pahalgam. It is a magical campsite, where one can taste the real flavour of mountain life in Kashmir. The tall firs and cedars on the plateau shelter tents from the warm afternoon sun, while the rushing streams bound over the rocks down into the valley below. There are brown bears in the nearby woods, but they are said to be vegetarian, although you should keep your distance.

Getting There

Local buses from Srinagar cost Rs 7.50 and take 2½ to four hours, there are six to 10 departures a day. J&K Road Transport have tour buses which cost Rs 18 one way or Rs 36 return. They leave the Srinagar Tourist Reception Centre around 7 am and by the time you arrive in Pahalgam around 1 pm you'll have had a thorough surfeit of Moghul gardens. The KMDA tour buses also take a long time with many stops on the way.

Taxis cost over Rs 250 return although you can sometimes find a taxi going back from Pahalgam empty and willing to bargain. If you want to get a return ticket on one of the more comfortable J&K tour buses you have to catch them when they come in around noon in order to get tickets. Get someone from your hotel to do it for you. You can get buses direct from Pahalgam to Jammu.

Ponies can easily be hired in Pahalgam for trekking trips. The fixed costs to popular destinations are all clearly posted but they're basically bargaining guidelines.

GULMARG

The valley of Gulmarg, a large meadow about three square km in area, stands at 2730 metres, 52 km from Srinagar. The name means 'meadow of flowers' and in the spring it's just that, a rolling meadow dotted with countless colourful bluebells, daisies, forget-me-nots and buttercups. The valley itself is about three km long and up to a km wide.

It's a popular day trip from Srinagar although many people extend their stay or use it as a base for trekking. The road from Srinagar rises gently towards the lower slopes of the range, passing through rice and maize fields. From Tangmarg, at the foot of the range, there are two paths to Gulmarg – a steep footpath (also suitable for ponies) or a winding sealed road.

In the winter Gulmarg is the skiing centre of India, there are four ski-lifts on the slopes – a two km long aerial ropeway from Gulmarg to Khilanmarg, a rope tow on the training slope and two other ski lifts on the higher slopes.

In summer Gulmarg boasts one of the highest altitude golf courses in the world – the Gulmarg Golf Club stands at 2652 metres. Tournaments are held in June and September. There are many huts and hotels scattered around the fields.

Skiing in Kashmir

We had a ski-bearer for the first day – he was very helpful in finding accommodation, ski-hire places, lifts, etc. It almost broke his heart when we told him we didn't need him the second day. He charged Rs 30 a day for the two of us, a bit out of our budget. The standard was from nursery to easy intermediate but the ski slopes were deserted. You can also walk up to 14,000 ft and ski down to 9000 ft – if you're good. Some Aussies staying in our place would mess about on the slopes and the local instructors would go away and hide, 'cos they couldn't compete! Lessons weren't really recommended. The equipment was reasonable, perhaps two or three years older than stuff one would find in Europe. Skis, boots and poles cost Rs 160 for five days and you can also hire parkas. Lift passes were Rs 20 for a half day on four drag lifts or Rs 55 for 20 goes on the chain lift. There was no queueing for lifts; often they would stop the chair lift when we got to the top and wait for us to ski down. The snow was excellent for us, but the day we left some of the slopes were wearing a bit thin.

M L Bridge

Information

The Tourist Office is the green/blue-coloured building complex with three patches of new wooden roof, on the valley bottom about a half km beyond the golf course. Gulmarg can get pretty cold at times, even compared to Pahalgam. Come prepared with plenty of warm clothes; sleeping bags are essential. Gulmarg has a bank but it can be a bit hit and miss – they obviously aren't used to changing money there.

Gulmarg Walks

Outer Circular Walk A circular road, 11 km in length, runs right round Gulmarg through pleasant pine forests with excellent views over the Kashmir Valley. Nanga Parbat is clearly visible 137 km to the north, Haramukh 60 km to the east, while to the south you can see the Ferozpore and Sunset Peaks (Romesh Thong) and the Apharwat ridge. Nanga Parbat, the 'lord of the mountains', is the fourth highest peak on earth at 8500 metres.

Khilanmarg This smaller valley is about a six km walk from the Gulmarg bus stop and car park. The meadow, carpeted with flowers in the spring, is the site for Gulmarg's winter ski-runs and offers a fine view of the surrounding peaks and over the Kashmir Valley.

It's a 600 metre ascent from Gulmarg to Khilanmarg and during the early spring, as the snow melts, it can be a very muddy hour's climb up the hill. The effort is rewarded, if it's clear, with a sweeping view of the great Himalaya from Nanga Parbat to the twin 7100 metre peaks of Nun and Kun to the south-east.

Alpather Beyond Khilanmarg, 13 km from Gulmarg at the foot of the twin 4511 metre Apharwat peaks, this lake is frozen until mid-June and even later in the year you can see lumps of ice floating in its cold waters. The walk from Gulmarg follows a well graded pony track over the 3810 metre Apharwat Ridge, separating it from Khilanmarg, and then up the valley to the lake at 3843 metres. The more adventurous trekkers can climb straight up the boulder strewn slope of the ridge and descend the other side to the path.

Ningle Nallah Flowing from the melting snow and ice on Apharwat and the Alpather Lake, this pretty mountain stream is 10 km from Gulmarg. The stream continues down into the valley below and joins the Jhelum River near Sopur. This long, grassy valley is a popular picnic spot and the walking path carries on, crossing the Ningle Nallah by a bridge and continues on to the Lienmarg, another grassy meadow and a good spot for camping. In early summer you will probably share the campsites with Gujars moving their herds up to the high meadows.

Ferozpore Nallah Reached from the

Tangmarg road, or from the outer circular walk, this mountain stream meets the Bahan River at a popular picnic spot known as 'waters meet'. The stream is reputed to be particularly good for trout fishing; it's about five km down the valley from Gulmarg but quite close to Tangmarg. The river can be reached by walking three km down the path from the gap near Tangmarg and then heading south through the forest, down a slope towards the stream.

Near here there is a bridge which leads to the small waters meet picnic spot on the right bank. Looking south from Tangmarg the river can be traced up to its source, close to the rugged peak known as Ferozpore or Shinmahinyu. On the right bank the stream branches, the left path leading to Tosa Maidan, while the right bends away towards the Gogaldara road at a second bridge, about 32 km upstream, and then leads away to the Ferozpore pass, Poonch and Kantar Nag.

You can continue on from here to Tosa Maidan, a three day, 50 km walk to one of Kashmir's most beautiful margs, crossing the Basmai Gali pass at about 4000 metres. The track here is very close to the ceasefire line with Pakistan and on the right you will pass the Jamainwali Gali, the pass at 4000 metres is one of the easiest and safest routes into the Punjab.

Ziarat of Baba Reshi This Muslim shrine is on the slopes below Gulmarg and can be reached from either Gulmarg or Tangmarg. The Ziarat, or tomb, is of a well known Muslim saint who died here in 1480. Before renouncing worldly ways he was a courtier of the Kashmir king Zain-ul-Abidin.

Places to Stay

Hotel Highland Park (tel 30, 50) costs from Rs 330/450 for singles/doubles. All rooms have attached bath and hot and cold running water. There's a beautiful lounge/bar with colonial trophies and the restaurant offers English, Chinese, Indian

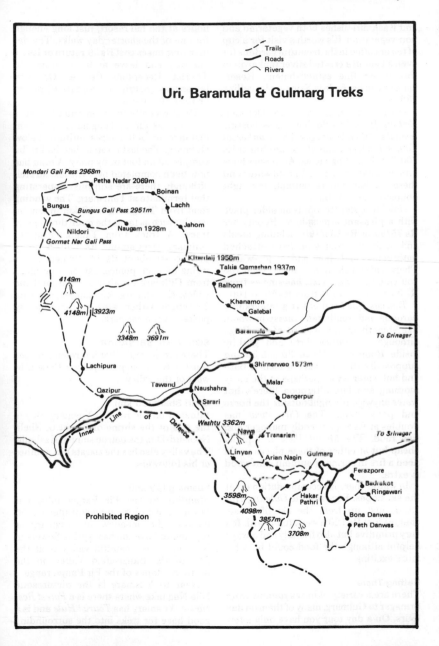

Uri, Baramula & Gulmarg Treks

Trails
Roads
Rivers

Mondari Gali Pass 2968m
Petha Nadar 2069m
Boinan
Lachh
Bungus
Bungus Gali Pass 2951m
Jahom
Nildori
Naugam 1928m
Gormat Nar Gali Pass

Khardaij 1950m
Takia Qamashan 1937m
Balhom
Khanamon
Galebal
4149m
Baramula
4148m 3923m
To Srinagar
3348m 3691m

Lachipura
Shirnarwao 1573m
Tawand
Malar
Qazipur
Naushahra
Dangerpur
Sarari
Line of Defence
Washtu 3362m
Nawa
Tranarian
To Srinagar
Inner
Linyan
Gulmarg
Arian Nagin
Ferazpore
Badrakot
Ringawari
3598m
Hakar
Pathri
4098m
Bona Danwas
3857m
Peth Danwas
3708m

Prohibited Region

and Kashmiri dishes both vegetarian and non-vegetarian. It's worth a visit for a cup of tea or coffee in the beautiful gardens (or even a beer in a crested silver tankard!) in this rather fine establishment. Reservations can be made in Srinagar by calling 73328.

Open only from May to October. *Nedous Hotel* has double rooms costing from Rs 250 and cottages. The *Yamberzal Tourist Inn* has rooms at Rs 125/200 or Rs 200/350 including meals. All rooms have attached bath and hot and cold water and there's a bar and restaurant. It's right opposite the bus stand.

Hotel Kingsley (tel 55) is an older place with a pleasant atmosphere. Rooms are Rs 75/90 or Rs 135/190 including meals and again the rooms all have attached bathrooms and hot and cold water. There's also a cheap dormitory. Near the golf club the *Snow View* has singles from Rs 30 to 70, doubles from Rs 50 to 100.

Tourists Hotel (tel 53) is a remarkably baroque and weathered fantasy in wood, like something out of *Lord of the Rings* although it's rather dirty and grubby inside. Rooms cost Rs 20, 30 and 50 and supposedly they all have attached bath and hot water – well perhaps in the early morning and late afternoon there's hot water anyway. It's right outside the horse and pony stand. The *City View* has doubles at Rs 25, a friendly manager and fine food. The *Mount View* is equally cheap but at either of these places you'll need a fire in spring or autumn, and wood is extra.

In winter there is accommodation up at the ski slopes. For example *Gulmarg Hut 197A*, just up from the ski lift base, charges just Rs 120 a week full board. It's very primitive but also friendly and always helpful although the food could be a bit more exciting.

Getting There
There are a variety of buses running from Srinagar to Gulmarg, many of them on day tours. On a day tour you have only a few hours at the hill resort, just long enough for one of the shorter day walks. The deluxe tour buses cost Rs 39 return or Rs 21 one-way and leave at 9 am from the Tourist Reception Centre. Ordinary buses leave hourly and cost Rs 12 return or Rs 7.50 one-way.

Until recently the road from Srinagar only ran as far as Tangmarg, seven km distance or 500 metres altitude below Gulmarg. The last stretch then had to be completed on foot or by pony. A road has now been completed over the last stretch although, there are still buses operating that terminate at Tangmarg. The winding road from Tangmarg is 13 km in length, nearly twice as far as the more direct pony track. A truck from Tangmarg up to Gulmarg costs around Rs 3.50. A riding pony costs about Rs 14. Ponies, either riding or pack ponies, can also be hired from Gulmarg to other sites around the valley. Khilanmarg, for example, costs Rs 25 return. Other rates are prominently posted at the car park.

SOUTH OF SRINAGAR
There are several other interesting places south of Srinagar, principally to the south-west of the valley.

Chari Sharif (30 km)
Situated on the road to Yusmarg, this is the site of the shrine or Ziarat of Sheik Noor-ud-Din, the patron saint of Kashmir. The valley also has the ziarats of a number of his followers.

Yusmarg (40 km)
Standing in the Pir Panjal hills, out beyond the airport, at an altitude of 2700 metres, the meadow of Yusmarg is reputed to have the best spring flowers in Kashmir. The beautiful valley is at the foot of the Sangisafaid Valley on the northern slopes of the Pir Panjal range.

Near to Yusmarg is the picturesque Nila Nag lake where there is a *Forest Rest House*. Yusmarg has *Tourist Huts* and is a good base for treks into the surrounding

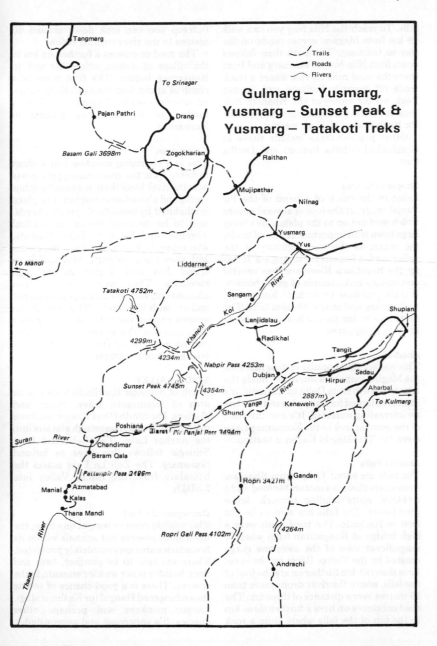

hills. To reach the Nila Nag you can walk 19 km from Magam, across roads on the way to Gulmarg. The path then follows down from Nila Nag to Yusmarg and from there the road runs to Yus, where a track leads off towards Sangam and Sunset Peak, up the valley of the Khanchi Kol. Sunset Peak is the highest mountain in the Pir Panjal range at 4746 metres.

Other popular treks include those to Sangisafaid (Chitta Pathar) and Dodha Patri.

Shupian (50 km)

Lying in the crook of a bend of the Pir Panjal range, at the foot of several passes which lead out on to the plains, this fairly large town is an important centre of trade, the centre of the wool industry of the valley, and is famous for its apples. It lies on the Rembiara River and has several rest houses and a couple of guest houses. It is also the base for treks to Konsarnag, to Yusmarg and to the Aharbal falls. The first stage on the trek to Konsarnag is the drive to Kongwatan.

Aharbal

This was another popular resting place for the Moghul emperors when they made the long trip north from Delhi to Kashmir. It's in an area famed for its apples and also has an interesting waterfall. It's also the start of the popular trek to the Konsarnag Lake – see the Trekking in Kashmir section.

Aharbal Falls

The falls are about 13 km from Shupian, from where there is a motorable road and a trekkers' route leading through dense pine forest. The falls are said to be the best in Kashmir. The road leads over a high bridge at Kongwatan from where a magnificent view of the awesome gorge created by the Vishav River can be seen. Less than two km further on are the foot of the falls, where the river drops more than 15 metres over a distance of three km. The road continues on here a further three km to the top of the falls where from a rock

outcrop you can look down around 60 metres to the river rushing below.

The road continues a further six km to the village of Sedau, where the trek to Konsarnag begins. The first stage is a climb of about four hours to Kongwatan, an upland meadow. From here it is a further 10 to 15 hours walking to Konsarnag.

Kongwatan

This is a charming meadow just a short distance from the river. Among the pines near the river bank there is a small sulphur spring and also a forest rest hut. The place is inhabited by nomadic Gujar shepherds, said to be descendants of the biblical Abraham and Isaac, or Gujar Rajputs, who come each summer from the plains with their flocks of cattle and buffalo to spend July and August in the high meadows. They wear black clothes adorned only with a small cap, embroidered and set with kari shells. The caps of the women project over the neck to protect from sunburn. the women are very agile and seem to do all the work as well as taking care of the children.

SINDH VALLEY

North of Srinagar the Sindh Valley is an area of mountains, lakes, rivers and glaciers. The Sindh River flows down from the Amarnath and Haramukh glaciers into the Anchar Lake. The Leh road from Srinagar follows this river to beyond Sonamarg. The Zoji La Pass marks the boundary from the Sindh Valley into Ladakh.

Dachigam (21 km)

This wildlife reserve was, at one time, the royal game reserve but animals within its boundaries are now completely protected. There are said to be panther, bear and deer, besides other smaller animals, in the reserve. There is a good chance of seeing the endangered Hangul (or Kashmir stag), Langur monkeys and perhaps other species. It's very quiet and uncrowded.

Permits to enter the reserve cost Rs 20 and are simply and quickly obtained from the Wildlife Warden at the Tourist Reception Centre. The reserve is quite close to Shadaharwan – see the Srinagar section. Camping is not generally possible at the reserve – overnight trips are only allowed by special arrangement for studying snow leopard or bear which exist in the remoter regions of the park.

This is a good starting point for the climb to the top of Mahadev. The walk begins from the upper end of the reservoir.

Getting There Take a bus to Harwan (Rs 1) from the local bus stand. The trip takes nearly an hour and from the Harwan bus terminal it's five minutes to the park gates where, for a tip, a guide will show you around.

Anchar Lake (11 km)
Although this large lake (5½ by four km) is no great distance from Srinagar and easily reached by bus, it is rarely visited. A daily bus leaves Srinagar for the lake at 8.30 am and returns late in the afternoon. In winter it is home for a wide variety of water birds including mallard, pochard, gadwall, snipe and teal.

Gandarbal (19 km)
Just beyond the Wular and Manasbal Lakes turn-off from the Leh road, this pleasant little town marks the point where the icy Sindh River leaves the mountains and enters the plains. Gandarbal is the official headquarters of the Sindh Valley and was originally called Doderhom. It has a bazaar, a post office and two hospitals.

About five km from Gandarbal, in the village of Tullamulla, is the shrine of Khirbhawani, the Goddess Ragni, the Hindu guardian goddess of Kashmir. The marble temple, built by Maharaja Pratap Singh, stands in a small spring. It is an irregular, seven-sided structure and is said to be surrounded by 360 springs, most of which have run dry or been silted

up. The village is a floating garden surrounded by swamps. Its many islands are covered with willows, poplars and wildflowers, while the island on which the spring stands is covered with chinar, mulberry and elm trees. The nearby village named after Khirbhawani has almond groves where the best quality almonds in Kashmir are said to grow.

Gandarbal can be reached from Srinagar by road or you can go there by boat along the Mar Canal, or take a six hour round trip via the Jhelum River and Anchar Lake. There are many excellent camping places along these routes.

Manasbal Lake (28 km)
Situated in the Jhelum Valley on the route to the Wular Lake via Safapur, the lake can be reached from Srinagar via Shadipur or via Nasim and Gandarbal. The secluded, crystal clear sheet of green water was named after the sacred lake of Mansarowar, that skirts the equally sacred Mt Kailas.

In summer the lake, which averages 12 metres deep, is covered with lotus flowers and in winter it is a bird watchers' paradise as it is one of the largest natural haunts of aquatic birds in Kashmir. The Baladar mountain overlooks the lake's eastern bank while on its northern bank are the ruins of Darogabagh.

There is a Moghul garden, built by Nur Jahan, by the lake. It's called Caroka, meaning bay window, due to its view out over the lake. A grove of chinar trees at the nearby village of Safapur is known as Badshah Boni, Royal Chinar, and was planted in imitation of the Nasim Bagh in Srinagar. Safapur is irrigated by a canal taken from the Sindh River, constructed by Badshah in the 15th century. Nearby is a cave dug by a mystic, with his grave lying next to a small shrine. Near this is a *Tourist Hut*.

Camping is possible at another lakeside chinar grove known as Qoz Bagh. There is also a government *Rest House* by the lake.

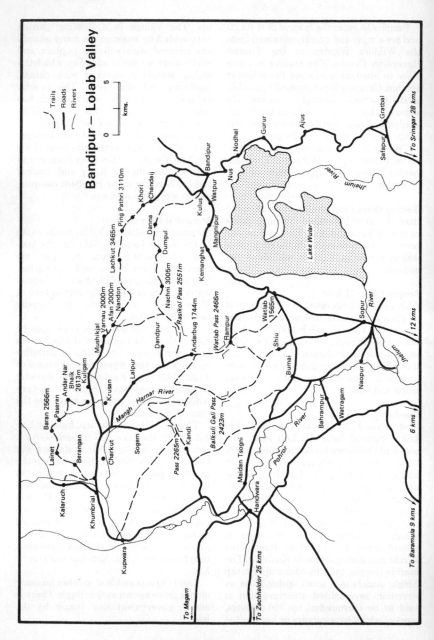

Bandipur – Lolab Valley

Trails
Roads
Rivers

0 — 5
kms.

Wular Lake (50 km)
Claimed to be the largest freshwater lake in India, the Wular Lake can spread over nearly 200 square km but its actual surface area tends to vary during the year. The Jhelum River flows into the lake, 40 km downstream from Srinagar, and then out again. The lake, calm though it may appear, is noted for the fierce winds that sometimes blow up. The deepest part of the lake is known as Mota Khon, the 'Gulf of Corpses', since the bodies of people drowned in the lake were all supposed to be washed to this place. At one time there was an artificial island on the lake, where boatmen could shelter if the weather turned bad, but silting on that side of the lake has joined the island to the lakeside. It's now a popular picnic spot.

There are several large towns or other places of interest around the shore of the lake. Sopur, at the south end of the lake where the Jhelum leaves it, is noted for its fruit growing – particularly apples and walnuts. The main resort town for the lake is Ningal Nullah, five km from Sopur. From here you can hire sailing boats to cruise on the lake or for fishing. Beyond Sopur is the Lolab Valley, reached either by a road from Sopur or by following the bridal path from Kiuhnus. To the west of the Lolab Valley there is an extensive flat meadow called Bungas, at 2896 metres above sea level and 114 km from Srinagar. It's like an undeveloped Gulmarg.

Kiuhnus Bay is a small valley 20 km from Sopur and 12 km from Bandipur. Further up this valley of the Madumati River there are several waterfalls. The important town of Bandipur, famous for its woven blankets, is on the eastern shore of the lake, at the foot of the 3355 metre Tragbal pass. On the north-west side of the lake, near Ashtiung, there is a ziarat or shrine to Baba Shukur-ud-Din, a disciple of the saint Nur-ud-Din.

Houseboats, doongas and sailing boats can be hired on the lake. The three main mooring places are at Ningal Nullah, Kiuhnus Bay and at Ajus Spur on the south-east side. Around the lake there are various canals which lead through the silt at the river mouths up into the rivers themselves. One of the best is to the Erin Valley which starts from Nodhal and winds 6½ km up to two high altitude lakes.

Baramula, to the south-west of the lake, was on the main route to Rawalpindi, the chief route from Kashmir to the Indian plains prior to independence. Roads also run from here to Gilgit and Hunza, into what is now the restricted zone controlled by Pakistan. Baramula is the legendary place from which Vishnu is said to have drained the waters which once filled the Kashmir Valley.

Close to Shadipur, where the Sindh River flows into the Jhelum, there are the ruins of a number of Hindu and Buddhist shrines. Shadipur has a camping site and is noted for the abundant fish in the waters around it. Narmarg, above the lake, is a popular trekking centre.

Getting There Buses leave the Tourist Reception Centre in Srinagar in the morning for a day trip around Wular Lake and back. The bus first stops at Anchar Lake, then on to Safapur, to stop at Manasbal Lake, thence to Bandipur, 56 km away. This is followed by lunch at Watlab where there is a government *Rest House*, and a tour of the mosque of Baba Sakar-ud-Din, then on to Sopur. The lake can be reached by river as well as road.

Sonamarg (83 km)
At a height of 2740 metres, Sonamarg is the last major point in the Kashmir Valley before the Zoji La pass into Ladakh. At the pass the green, lush Kashmiri landscape abruptly switches to the barren, dry landscape of Ladakh. Sonamarg is thus not only a good base for treks but also a jumping off point for trips into Ladakh. The name means 'Meadow of Gold' and although this could be due to the profusion of flowers that carpet the meadow in the spring it is also possible

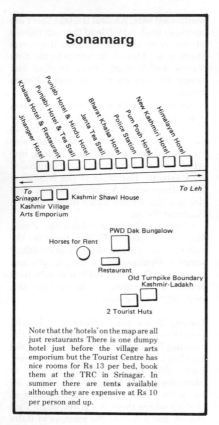

Sonamarg

Jhanger Hotel
Khalasa Hotel & Restaurant
Punjabi Hotel & Tea Stall
Punjabi Hotel & Hindu Hotel
Janta Tea Stall
Bharat Khalsa Hotel
Police Station
Purn Posh Hotel
New Kashmiri Hotel
Himalayan Hotel

To Srinagar
To Leh

Kashmir Shawl House

Kashmir Village
Arts Emporium

PWD Dak Bungalow

Horses for Rent

Restaurant

Old Turnpike Boundary
Kashmir-Ladakh

2 Tourist Huts

Note that the 'hotels' on the map are all just restaurants There is one dumpy hotel just before the village arts emporium but the Tourist Centre has nice rooms for Rs 13 per bed, book them at the TRC in Srinagar. In summer there are tents available although they are expensive at Rs 10 per person and up.

that the name derives from Sonamarg's strategic trading position in the days when this was a major route into central Asia.

One of the most popular short walks from Sonamarg is the four km route to Thajiwas, a small valley at the foot of the Sonamarg glacier. A path leads up to the Shakhdar Hill, overlooking the glacier from the north-east. It is dangerous to climb the steep slope leading up to the

glacier. Often in early summer you will meet groups of Gujar passing through Sonamarg on their way to the alpine meadows for the summer. See the Trekking section for details of treks from Sonamarg.

Places to Stay There are *Tourist Huts*, a *Rest House*, a *Tourist Bungalow* and some extremely basic and rather dirty small hotels at Sonamarg. The Rest House is midway between Sonamarg and Thajiwas and has rooms at Rs 15, but officials have preference. The Tourist Bungalow is extremely beautifully situated about 25 minutes walk from Sonamarg. Rooms here are Rs 20 and the food is cheap and very good.

Sonamarg is a very pleasant and relaxing place to stay. Except in summer, there is no real town to speak of, just a row of huts that serve as businesses for the many tourists who come here. The traders here sometimes have colourful things to sell if you ask.

Baltal (98 km)

This beautiful meadow is right at the foot of the Zoji La pass and thus is the final place in Kashmir. The river from the foot of the Amarnath glacier meets the Indus near Baltal. It stands at a height of 2743 metres and during the Amarnath pilgrimage there are tents set up here, they cost around Rs 6. Food is also available at that time but it's not very good.

It is possible to walk to the Amarnath Cave, more usually approached from Pahalgam, in one day. Check about conditions before departing, though. The the weather can be treacherous and at other times melting snow and ice make the route very dangerous. There's now a jeep road most of the way to the cave. The turn-off to Baltal is at 94 km on the Leh road, then it's three km or so downhill.

Top: Gangabal Sar, one of two glacial lakes at the foot of Mt Harmukh, Kashmir (BP)
Bottom: Gulmarg (TW)

Top: Main street in the hill resort of Pahalgam (TW)
Left: The Lidder River between Pahalgam and Aru (TW)
Right: En route between

Trekking in Kashmir

There are numerous beautiful treks in and around the Kashmir valley. They vary from short day walks from valley hill stations, to longer walks in the valley and across the surrounding ranges, to hard treks out of the Kashmir region to Zanskar or Ladakh. Many of these routes follow the trails used by the Gujar shepherds to take their flocks to high altitude pastures during the summer months.

SONAMARG-WANGAT

This 81 km trek can take up to six days, or even longer in early June or late October when there may be snow or heavy thunderstorms. It reaches a maximum altitude of 4191 metres. The first few days the route follows the Sogput Dhar, a ridge of the western Himalaya, crossing and recrossing it at convenient points. The first part of the trek as far as Nichinai is straight forward, but from here there are several routes to Narannag and Wangat. There is also a route beyond on the longer trek to Erin and Bandipur.

Day 1: Srinagar-Sonamarg

The 84 km journey from Srinagar to Sonamarg takes three to four hours by bus or car. The route goes through the villages of Gandarbal, Kangan, Gund and Kulan en route to Sonamarg, which is the last large village in the Kashmir Valley on the way to Leh. Kangan is the point at which you will rejoin the Srinagar road if you come down through Wangat. It is also the best (and last) town at which to buy supplies – good vegetables and fruit, biscuits and bread, matches, etc – or get your stove repaired or buy a second cooking pot. Sonamarg is at an altitude of 2740 metres and has tourist huts as well as wood and water if you are camping. Ponies can be rented in Sonamarg.

Day 2: Sonamarg-Nichinai

Half a km past the Shitkari bridge, over the Sindh River on the road toward the Zoji La and Ladakh, the trail leaves the bank of the Sindh and climbs towards the stone water mill, up the left side of the mountain. If you have started late in the day you can stay the night at the small village of Lashimarg where there are good camping sites.

From here it's a steep climb up the Galwanbal, a forest covered mountain to the top at an altitude of 3109 metres. From here the trail climbs gently through the Hirampathri meadows, to an altitude of 3658 metres, and the Nichinai Nar stream. The trail then follows the narrow, steep valley of the Nichinai to the Nichinai Bar pass at 4080 metres. There is a glacier on either side of the valley here, and to the east lies the Bushkapathri Range, while to the west lies the Sahnai Range, covered in glaciers and snow beds. Nichinai is at 3620 metres, 900 metres above Sonamarg and 15 km distance. Wood and water are on hand in the camp.

Day 3: Nichinai-Krishansar

The 13 km trek starts by crossing the 4080 metres Nichinai ridge then follows the river before crossing it at Hirampathri. You pass by Vishansar Lake at 3680 metres and reach the camp at Krishansar at 3819 metres. The lake lies in the widest part of the valley at the foot of the glacier and the slopes on the south-eastern side of the mountain are ideal for camping. The lake is just over a km long and about a half km wide. It's stocked with trout, but it is within a national park and fishing permits are required. There is a good site for camping with water available and if there are Gujars here, herding their sheep, they may sell you wood, but at rather high prices.

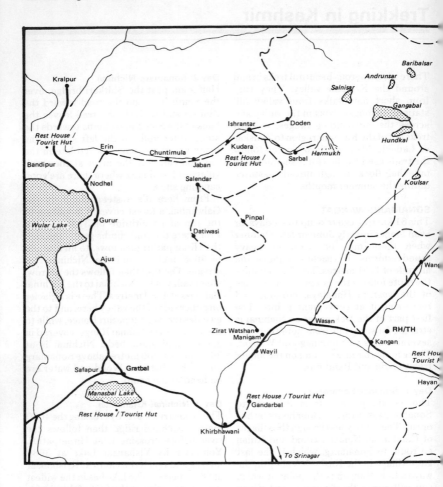

Day 4: Krishansar-Dubta Pani

You cross the stream that flows out of Vishansar and the path climbs a further 150 metres to the small tarn Krishansar, at a height of 3818 metres. Huddled within the small, narrow valley, Krishansar usually has icebergs floating in it even as late as August. From here the trek to Gadsar is about 23 km and begins with a steep climb to the Razbal Gali, at 4191 metres, followed by a rapid descent over snow to Yemsar, the 'Lake of Death',

about 200 metres below. During the descent there is a string of tarns, which in spring and early summer will be surrounded by blossoming wildflowers.

Around a bend in the trail the beautiful Gadsar Lake at 3900 metres suddenly appears. Glaciers from the surrounding peaks come almost down to the lake, which is circular and surrounded by mountains on three sides. The fourth side is a grassy slope, covered with flowers, a good spot for camping. From here the

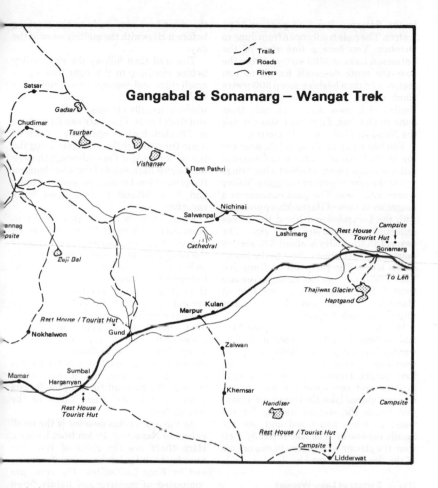

Gangabal & Sonamarg – Wangat Trek

Trails
Roads
Rivers

Satsar
Gadsar
Chudimar
Tsurbar
Vishansar
Nam Pathri
Nichinai
Salwanpal
 annag
psite
Cathedral
Lashimarg
Rest House /
Tourist Hut
Campsite
Sonamarg
Gaji Dal
To Leh
Thajiwas Glacier
Haptgand
Rest House / Tourist Hut
Nokhalwon
Marpur
Kulan
Gund
Zaiwan
Mamar
Sumbal
Harganyan
Khemsar
Rest House /
Tourist Hut
Handisar
Campsite
Rest House / Tourist Hut
Campsite
Lidderwat

track descends gradually along the bank of the Gadsar to the mouth of the gorge at the foot of the Kasturgand Mountain, the home of the Kastura or musk deer.

The path through the gorge leads on a three day trek to Gurai, a beautiful series of rolling valleys. The route to Gangabal avoids the gorge, but crosses the stream and zig zags up the flowery mountain slopes of Kasturgand, a steep climb through clumps of birch and pine. The path follows the mountain ridge until it

reaches Dubta Pani, where the stream goes underground to reappear at the foot of a gorge about a km below. There is no wood at Dubta Pani, you should collect fuel on the final ascent to the camp at 3280 metres.

Day 5: Dubta Pani-Gangabal Lake The day's 17 km trek starts with a short walk to the Satsarsan Lake, another place with good campsites. The path continues across the rocky valley floor and ascends to the Satsaran Bar Gali pass at 3680 metres. The pass is only open from June to October. You have a fine view of the Satsarsan Lake at 3600 metres. From the pass the route descends for about 100 metres and then begins a steep 500 metre climb on the right to the 4081 metres Zajibal Gali pass, also open only from June to October. From here you can see the Nund Kol Lake at 3501 metres.

You can camp at Mengandub, near the top of the pass, or continue to Gangabal Lake. A sharp ascent of about a km brings you to the spot where the Gangabal Valley comes into view. The pass commands a magnificent view of Harmukh, opposite it, with the Gangabal and Nund Kol Lakes reflecting the glaciers and sky. The descent to the valley is about 600 metres down a gradual, grassy slope to the banks of the lakes. The camp site at Gangabal Lake (3570 metres) has wood, water and trout fishing. The lake, at the foot of Harmukh, is the site for a major pilgrimage each August.

Wardens patrol the national park here and fishing is totally controlled. The warden will more than likely confiscate your fishing gear and any fish you may have caught. However, if you arrive early in June and can stand the pain of the freezing glacial lake, the trout lie dormant just below the surface waiting for the water to warm and a rod and line are hardly necessary. The lake is fed by melt from the glacier which splits in two on one of the flanks of Harmukh.

Day 6: Gangabal Lake-Wangat

The 19 km trek descends 1500 metres to Wangat at 2050 metres. Leaving Nund Kol there is a primitive stone and wood bridge which crosses the swiftly flowing and painfully cold Mungshungun Nullah. Thoughtless trekkers have, from time to time, broken off parts of the wooden planks of the bridge to use for firewood, as there is no wood available at the campsite here. As a result the bridge is becoming less and less reliable. It is possible to ford

the river here very early in the morning before it rises with the melting snow of the day.

The trail then follows the river valley before climbing to the right, crossing a small ridge and coming out at Trunkul, or Field of Grass. This is a beautiful meadow which is usually crowded with the Gujar and their herds. There are two forest huts at Trunkul, both of which have suffered again from thoughtless trekkers using the timber for cooking fires. Although the tree line begins here, most of the wood lying on the ground has been scavenged by Gujars and it is difficult to find wood for a campfire.

From here there are two routes to Narannag, each about 17 km; one a steep and sometimes slippery descent following the river, and the second more interesting trek across the ridges above the river, followed by a sharp descent to Narannag through a pine and deodar forest. This second path leads to Poshi Matun, where there is a spring near the top of the peak. This small meadow looks down into the valley of the Sindh. From here there is a steep descent over sedimentary slate of almost 1200 metres. Some of the path is rocky and slippery, but it also winds through the fragrant fir and pine forests down towards the green valley of the Kranki Nadi.

At the foot of this descent is the small village of Narannag, 10 km from Kangan. Here there are the ruins of Buddhist temples built by Jaluka, a son of Ashoka, and by King Lalitaditya. The ruins are composed of massive and tightly fitted stone blocks, formed into a large temple complex. There is a huge bath about five metres long and two metres broad and almost two metres deep, carved from a single block of stone. Nearby there is a large pool with a spring issuing from beneath the mountain slope, which is said to have magical healing powers. There is a well maintained forest hut here with a dormitory and six beds, and a kitchen plus hot water for showers and washing.

From here it is a further five km along the sealed road to Wangat at 2050 metres. Here there is a *Rest House* as well as camping facilities, with wood and water. The bus leaves Wangat for Srinagar at 1.30 pm and the trip takes 2½ hours.

Gangabal-Wular Lake

As an alternative to turning south from Gangabal to Kangan it is possible to continue west to the Wular Lake. From Gangabal take the track towards the Loolgul Gali. The 4052 metre pass is open from June to October. The five km trek to the top passes on the way, with short detours, the spectacular lakes of Andansar and Loolgul. The descent from the pass is over a boulder-scattered slope down a track which leads to Sulanaisar, a small lake in a small valley on the right. From here it is 10 km to the open meadows and two small lakes of the Sarbal Valley. For those wanting to climb Harmukh the valley is an ideal place to set up base camp.

The path gradually descends from here through forests along the valley of the Chitrasur Nullah, to its junction with the Erin Nullah Valley, 13 km away, and the village of Kudor. This village is 24 km from Nadihal, a pleasant walk through rice and corn fields. Nadihal is 50 km from Srinagar on the way to Bandipur. Ponies may be hired at either Bandipur or Nadihal. From here you can take a pleasant boat trip along the Wular Lake and up the Jhelum River to Srinagar.

WULAR-GANGABAL (via Poshpathri)

This is an alternative route on the reverse trek from around the Wular Lake to Gangabal and then either down to Wangat or on all the way to Sonamarg.

Day 1: Srinagar-Erin

It is about 80 km from Srinagar to Erin via Bandipur. Get off the bus at the small village of Nadihal from where you walk to Erin. There is a *Rest House* and riverbank camping sites at Erin, (1983 metres).

Day 2: Erin-Chuntimula-Poshpathri

The ll km trek starts by crossing the Erin River near the Rest House. The first three or four km of the route, which ascends in stages, is in good condition as it is maintained by the forest small-holders. The route passes the village of Kudara, where there is a *Rest House*, and reaches Poshpathri at 2440 metres.

Day 3: Poshpathri-Sarbal

A difficult 8½ km ascent takes you to Minimarg after which the rest of the ll km route to Sarbal is not so difficult. There is a good campsite on the banks of the Sarbal Lake at the foot of Harmukh, but you will have to bring firewood with you. The Shirsar Lake stands above Sarbal.

Day 4: Sarbal-Kundsar Lake

The day's nine km trek starts off from the left of the Gujar huts. It follows a steep ascent for about 2½ km then climbs more gradually the rest of the way to the lake at 3800 metres.

Day 5: Kundsar Lake-Gangabal Lake

The ll km trek first follows the bank of the Kundsar then, after about 1½ km, climbs over a glacier and dips into a depression for nearly three km. After a further three km the route turns left and drops 150 metres then climbs about 150 metres to the top of the ridge before descending to the lake. You need rope, ice-axes and U-bolts for this day's trek because of the crevices in the glacier. You can camp at the lake (3572 metres) or at Nund Col about 1½ km away. There are many fish in the lake. There is a *Rest House* at Trunkul.

Day 6 onwards

From day 6 onwards you can either turn south to Wangat, as on day 6 of the Sonamarg-Wangat trek, or continue east to Sonamarg, as on day 1 to 5 of that same trek.

PAHALGAM-KOLAHOI GLACIER

This short trek from Pahalgam is one of the most popular in Kashmir. From June through September the route can be quite crowded.

Day I: Srinagar-Pahalgam

It is about 90 km from Srinagar to Pahalgam and only takes two hours by car, rather longer by bus. The route follows the Jammu road out of Srinagar then turns up the Lidder Valley through a number of villages to Pahalgam. There are fine views of rice paddies and snow-capped peaks all along the road. The Lidder has many fish but a trout fishing licence is rather expensive. Pahalgam is at 2130 metres and has a wide variety of accommodation.

Day 2: Pahalgam-Aru

It is only about 12 km from Pahalgam (the 'village of shepherds') to Aru and cars can also follow this part of the route, which runs along the right bank of the Lidder River through pine forest. Riding and load carrying ponies can easily be obtained in Pahalgam, either directly from the pony owners or through the Tourist Office. Aru is a picturesque little village at the confluence of two smaller rivers. It is also spelt Arau. There are several places to stay in Aru – see the Pahalgam section in the Kashmir Valley chapter.

There are two routes from Aru to the Kolahoi Glacier. The first leads straight through the forest to Lidderwat; starting with a steep ascent then following the Lidder River for the rest of the way. The other route is much harder, particularly for ponies, and goes right to Armiun then over the Hari Gali pass, (3800 metres).

Day 3: Aru-Lidderwat

It is about 12 km from Aru to Lidderwat where there is a magnificent camping location at the meeting point of the Kolahoi Glacier's stream and the stream from the Tarsar Lake. Lidderwat also has a two-room *PWD Rest House* and the pleasant *Paradise Guest House*.

Day 4: Lidderwat-Kolahoi Glacier-Lidderwat

It's a day trip from Lidderwat to the glacier (13 km) or to the Tarsar Lake. The stretch to the glacier leads east through a pine forest until Satlanjan where the landscape opens out. The glacier begins at 3400 metres and extends to over 4000 metres. To the north-west of Kolahoi, beneath the glacier, is the Dudh Nag Lake at 4267 metres. The Kolahoi mountain, from which the glacier descends, is 5485 metres high.

Day 5: Lidderwat-Pahalgam

It's an easy walk back to Pahalgam or an extra day may be spent going to the Tarsar Lake. From the lake at 3962 metres you can climb over a 250 metre ridge which separates Tarsar from the Marsar Lake. It is also possible to continue on from Lidderwat to the Sindh Valley, meeting the road from Srinagar to Leh near Sonamarg. This trek is detailed below:

PAHALGAM-SONAMARG
Day 1-2: Pahalgam-Aru-Lidderwat

The first two days are as for the Kolahoi Glacier trek from Pahalgam. An additional day can be added here to actually visit the glacier before continuing on from Lidderwat.

Day 3: Lidderwat-Sekiwas

The 10 km walk ascends the Sekiwas Nullah to Sekiwas at 3430 metres.

Day 4: Sekiwas-Khemsar

The 11 km trek takes you over the 4115 metre Yemhar Pass to Khemsar at 3659 metres. The descent from the pass is fairly easy during July and August. There is no firewood available at Khemsar.

Day 5: Khemsar-Kulan

The trail descends through forests to the Sindh River where you cross the Kulan bridge at 2226 metres. Sonamarg is only 16 km from Kulan and can be reached either by a good track up the Sindh Valley or by bus.

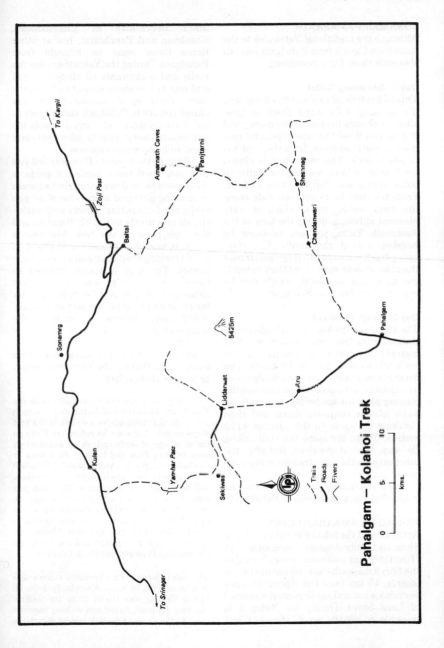

Pahalgam – Kolahoi Trek

SONAMARG-AMARNATH

Although the traditional Yatra trek to the Amarnath Cave is from Pahalgam you can also walk there from Sonamarg.

Day 1: Sonamarg-Baltal

This 15 km trek takes about five hours and it's an easy walk since there is little altitude change between Sonamarag and Baltal. You should be able to get a lift on a truck to the road block, from there on it is better to walk. The road block is closed until noon or later, waiting for traffic to come across the Zoji La from Ladakh. From the road block you can walk along the river valley track which is very pleasant although, during the time of the Amarnath Yatra, you are pestered by begging nomad shepherds. The river valley track is also two to three km shorter than the vehicle road. A military camp is the first sign of Baltal, which can be reached in a day from Srinagar.

Day 2: Baltal-Amarnath

The 15 km trail to Amarnath climbs over a thousand metres from Baltal at 2743 metres to the cave at 4175 metres and the walk takes about nine to 10 hours. The route crosses one major snow bridge over a river and climbs steadily up, crossing the Satsing pass, 3½ km before Amarnath, at 4115 metres dropping down and then climbing up again to the cave at 4175 metres. There are some tea stalls along the way, even at the river, and after the junction with the main trail there are even more.

From Amarnath you can follow the traditional Yatra trail down to Pahalgam.

PAHALGAM-AMARNATH CAVE

At the time of the full moon in the month of Shravan (July-August) thousands of Hindu pilgrims make the annual 'Yatra' to the Shri Amarnath Cave. Situated at 4175 metres, 45 km from Pahalgam, the cave contains a natural ice lingam, the symbol of Lord Shiva. During the Yatra it is possible to obtain wood, kerosene and other necessities at Chandanwari, Sheshnag and Panchtarni, but at other times these must be brought from Pahalgam. During the Yatra there are tea stalls and restaurants all along the trail and tent hotels about every five km at the most. Food is, of course, cheaper the closer you are to Pahalgam and it tends to be very simple so you'll probably appreciate some snacks like chocolate bars, so bring some with you.

Although the tourist office may tell you that you need tents, ponies, a guide, a cook, porters, 'and everything but a harem of dancing girls and a brass band' all you really need is a porter to carry your pack – the air gets pretty thin at 3000 metres and the high point of the trek, Mahagunas Peak, is nearly 4500 metres. If you're in good trekking shape you don't even need a porter. The trail is clearly defined so there's no problem with getting lost although a sharp pointed stick is necessary for crossing the many ice and snowfields. Bring warm clothing, at Amarnath the temperature at night will be below freezing.

There are different opinions on whether to go to Amarnath at the Yatra time or not, as two trekkers relate:

It's really more fun to trek at other than the Yatra time when the trail becomes a real mob scene. At that time prices escalate in the rest stops as well. A few weeks before the Yatra an entire village of tents springs up at each rest stop, offering food and lodging. So a week or two before or after the Yatra these facilities will be set up and the Sikhs (usually) who run them will be hungry for customers. This way you don't have to carry food or bedding. The ice lingam is not likely to be much of an attraction, except for Shiva freaks, but the terrain is spectacular. Once you get over Mahagunas Peak it's a real moonscape and you'll run into old snowfields as you approach the cave.

This has to be one of my favourite experiences in nine months in India. Everybody, from all Hindu castes, was there; from the sadhus smoking chillums, naked and walking barefoot through the snow, to the rich and fat decadents being carried along by coolies. Kashmiris were there for the business, renting horses and tents, putting up tea stalls all along the 100 km trek. The police, well organised and friendly, were walking as well – taking care of the most hysterical pilgrims or those nearest to death! In other words, the atmosphere and the scenery together make this not so much a hard trek as a mass migration by a happy band of nomads. In fact it was sad to see it end after a week and we stayed in Pahalgam for a good week afterwards, saying goodbye to friends we made along the way. The organisation of the Yatra is amazingly well done and it's an experience highly recommended, giving you a glimpse of a wide variety of Indian characters and a better understanding of their culture.

Day 1: Pahalgam-Chandanwari
The route follows a jeepable road for 13 km to Chandanwari at 2900 metres. This is a colourful place during the Yatra with many sadhus. Since it is the first stop from Pahalgam there is a much wider variety of food available and at lower prices than further along the trek. There is a *PWD Rest House* at Chandanwari where the Sheshnag and Astanmarg rivers meet. Chandanwari is famous for its snow bridge.

Day 2: Chandanwari-Sheshnag
There is a choice of routes for this 14 km trek. One goes past the Pisu hill while the other goes via the Pisu gali, this is the pilgrim route where, during the Yatra season, there will also be numerous beggars. The walk climbs steadily from Chandanwari with one particularly steep ascent near a waterfall.

The Sheshnag Lake is at 3700 metres and there are camping facilities at Zojipal while at Wavjan, just above Sheshnag, there is a wonderfully situated *PWD Rest House* with doubles for Rs 20. The view down to the lake is superb. In season there are also tent hotels for the pilgrims.

Day 3: Sheshnag-Panchtarni
It is 11 km from Wavjan, at 3950 metres overlooking Sheshnag, to Panchtarni at 3500 metres.

This is the hardest day on the trek since you have to cross many snowfields and the snowbound Mahagunas pass at nearly 4500 metres. From there it is eight km down to Panchtarni, a beautiful place whose name means 'five streams', since it is the meeting point of five small rivers. It is possible to walk from Chandanwari to Panchtarni in one day. The simple, but pleasant, *PWD Rest House*, has doubles for Rs 20.

Day 4: Panchtarni-Amarnath Cave
The final stretch to the cave is just eight km, climbing from 3500 metres at Panchtarni to 4175 metres at the cave. The tent accommodation here is rather bad and there are only a few places to camp. Outside the peak of the Yatra season you can sleep in the cave although it's very cold. A km before the cave there are good camping grounds along the river and concrete shelters.

It is possible to continue from the Amarnath Cave to Baltal, on the Srinagar-Leh road about 15 km from Sonamarg. This is an alternative to returning from the cave to Pahalgam. See the Sonamarg-Amarnath trek report above.

PAHALGAM-PANNIKAR (Suru Valley)
This is quite a hard trek best made between June and September. Porters can be hired in Pahalgam but you must reckon on Rs 40 or more per day. You should carry a tent and all necessities must be brought from Pahalgam, including food and kerosene for cooking. The only places with lodging available are Chandnwari and Sheshnag, as on the Amarnath Cave trek. After that you're on your own and for some stretches it's necessary to carry water. 'Places' on the map along this route are often just meadows.

Day 1 & 2: Pahalgam-Chandanwari-Sheshnag
As on Amarnath Cave trek.

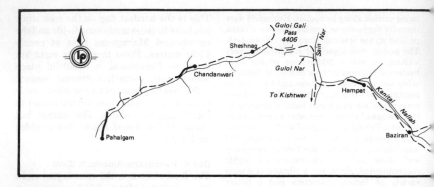

Day 3: Sheshnag-Rangmarg

The route ascends the 4406 metre Gulol Gali Pass then descends on the left bank of the Gulol Nar down to the mouth of the Sain Nar. Here you take the right bank (definitely not the left!) and complete the 7.5 km walk to Rangmarg.

Day 4: Rangmarg-Hampet

The trail follows the Sain Nar until it joins the Kanital Nullah on the left then follows on the left bank to Hampet, a total distance of 5.5 km.

Day 5 & 6: Hampet-foot of the Lonvilad Gali

From Hampet the track continues on the left bank of the Kanital Nullah to Baziran. Here the trail divides with a long route leading straight ahead to to Pannikar. Follow the Kanital on its right bank to the foot of the Lonvilad Gali, a total of 22 km.

Day 7: Lonvilad Gali-Chalong Glacier

The 4660 metre high Lonvilad Gali has to be ascended and the descent is then made over a glacier which comes from the Chalong Nullah. The overnight halt is made at the foot of the glacier.

Day 8: Chalong Glacier-Pannikar

The 15 km walk starts with the descent into the valley of the Chalong Nullah, which is then followed to Pannikar. From Pannikar there is a road leading north to Kargil or east to the Zanskar Valley.

KONSARNAG TREK

This four or five day trek in the Pir Panjal range reaches a maximum altitude of 3700 metres.

Day 1: Srinagar-Aharbal It takes three to four hours to reach Aharbal by road from Srinagar. The journey leads through a number of picturesque villages standing in the rice paddies. On the last part of this stretch the road ascends gradually. There is a government *Rest House* and a good camping site (with water and wood) at Aharbal. The waterfall, about 10 km from Aharbal, and the conifer forest past the Rest House are of interest. Aharbal is at 2460 metres.

Day 2: Aharbal-Kongwatan

The nine km trek to Kongwatan only takes about three hours. The route follows the Vishav River to the 1½ square km Kongwatan meadow at 2559 metres. There is a *Rest House* at Kongwatan with two rooms. With an early start from Srinagar you can reach Kongwatan on the first day.

Day 3: Kongwatan-Mahinag The day's walk starts through thick forest then climbs slowly beside the Vishav River. The ascent from Kongwatan to the Yechini is a distance of 16 km. The path, which is in good condition, goes along the right bank to Mahinag, and after some

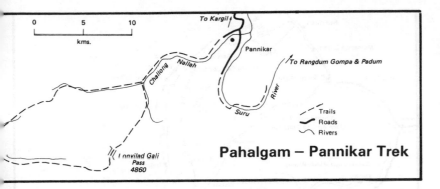

Pahalgam – Pannikar Trek

time crosses over to the other bank and becomes rougher. The plateau of Mahinag is surrounded by lovely mountains and has a group of glass-clear, ice-cold springs. Mountaineers can find a number of climbing opportunities in this area. It is possible to continue straight on to the mountain lake of Konsarnag in the same day but it is better to camp for the night at Mahinag which is at 2989 metres.

Day 4: Mahinag-Konsarnag-Kongwatan

The ascent to the pass overlooking Konsarnag Lake is 305 metres. The last 60 to 70 meters will be covered with snow and very steep, a slip would mean a fall to the snowfield below. From the top of the pass one can see the stream that flows out of the lake and has dug a deep gorge about 12 km long.

The way down to the lake is not difficult and can be accomplished by sliding over the snow. Across the lake and over to the left is a snowfield at the foot of the Brahma Shakri peaks, at the head of a snowbound valley. It is possible to climb to the lake at 4419 metres and return to camp after rounding the lake. The walk takes around 12 hours.

Konsarnag Lake is below the three towering peaks of the Panjal range, some 25 km from Shupian, and is said to be shaped exactly like a right foot with five toes and a heel – hence its name of Vishnu Pad. It is surrounded by the Bharma Shakri peaks, up to 4800 metres high and with steep slopes which are permanently snow covered. Lying from north-east to south-west it is about three km long and up to a km wide, reaching an estimated depth of 50 metres. The deep, dark blue waters are excellent for swimming.

The lake is fed by streams on the north-eastern shore, thence becoming progressively narrower until it ends in a point towards the south-west. On the northern side there is a subterranean passage through which water is seen and heard, gurgling down towards Kashmir.

Day 5: Kongwatan-Srinagar

From Kongwatan you return to Aharbal and then to Srinagar by road.

SRINAGAR-DAKSUM-KISHTWAR

This five day trek out of the Kashmir Valley into the Jammu region reaches a maximum altitude of 3700 metres and is best made between June and September.

Day 1: Srinagar-Daksum

The 100 km trip can be made by bus or taxi and takes about three hours. There are camping facilities with wood and water in Daksum and ponies can be hired there or in Wagil. Overnight accommodation in Daksum must be booked beforehand in Srinagar.

Daksum – Kishtwar

Day 2: Daksum-Sinthan Pass
This 16 km trek takes about five to six hours and reaches the maximum altitude of the trek. There are wooden huts in Sinthan; wood and water are on hand.

Day 3: Sinthan-Chhatru
The day's eight km trek only takes two or three hours. Wood and water are available at the camping area and there is a small shop for provisions in the village.

Day 4: Chhatru-Mughal Maidan
There are again some shops in the village which is reached after a nine km trek.

Day 5: Mughal Maidan-Dadhpeth
There are daily buses at 10 am and 4 pm from Dadhpeth to Kishtwar. Dadhpeth is only eight km from Mughal Maidan. Kishtwar has a *Dak Bungalow* and other accommodation or camping possibilities. Kishtwar has some notable waterfalls and is also a centre of saffron cultivation. It's a popular jumping off point for other treks (including one into Zanskar) and mountain climbing. From Kishtwar you can reach either Jammu or Srinagar by bus in one day.

Ladakh

It has been called 'the moonland', 'little Tibet' or 'the last Shangri La'. Those romantic definitions hold more than a slight degree of truth. Ladakh is the most remote region of India, a barren, virtually rainless area which lies north of the Himalaya, an area known geographically as the Tibetan plateau. The Himalaya serve as a barrier to clouds carrying rain from the south, virtually none of it gets across to fall on Ladakh which, in consequence, has only a few cm of rain per year – as little as the Sahara. The result is the 'moonland' label – much of Ladakh looks much like the moon, a barren, grey-brown landscape utterly devoid of vegetation. Only where rivers, running from far-away glaciers or melting snow, carry water to habitation do you find plant life.

Ladakh really is a 'little Tibet'. Although Tibet is politically part of China today, Ladakh, like parts of Nepal, is situated on the Tibetan plateau. The people of Ladakh are related to the Tibetans and follow similar cultural and religious practices. Ladakh also has many Tibetan refugees who fled Tibet with the invasion from China. Ladakh today is probably far more Tibetan than Tibet itself, where the Tibetan culture has, no doubt, been considerably changed by the Chinese.

Finally Ladakh could well be 'the last Shangri La'. Due to its strategic location – the area is disputed by the Indians, Pakistanis and Chinese – it has been virtually closed to outsiders from the end of WW II right up to 1974. The daunting height of the Himalaya added to this isolation, even today the main route into Ladakh is open for less than six months of each year. Until 1979 there was no regular civilian flight into Ladakh so from October to June the region was completely cut off. Because of this relatively recent exposure

to the outside world, and the rapid growth in tourism to the region, it is especially important to treat Ladakh, its people and their culture with respect and care. It's a gentle, crime-free, peaceful and religious society and visitors have a duty to keep it that way.

Today Ladakh is open to outsiders, or at least as open as its geography permits. No special permission is needed to enter Ladakh and within the region you can travel around with relative freedom. Ladakh is full of amazing sights – strange gompas perched on soaring hilltops, dwarfed by snow-capped mountains; the barren, shattered looking landscapes splashed with small but brilliant patches of green; ancient palaces clinging to sheer rock walls. But most of all it is notable for its delightful people – friendly as only Tibetans can be and immensely colourful. It's an amazing place.

HISTORY
The early history of Ladakh was succinctly summed up by Moorcroft, the English explorer who lived in Ladakh from 1820 to 1822: 'The earlier history of Ladakh is that of Tibet in general, as it originally formed one of the provinces of that kingdom, governed as to temporal matters by an independent prince, and in spiritual affairs by the Guru Lama, or chief pontiff of Lhasa'. Earlier still rock carvings scattered around the countryside indicate that the region has been used for thousands of years by nomadic tribes, blended from the Mons of north India, the Dards of Baltistan and the Mongols of central Asia. Over the centuries Ladakh has also had a variety of names – Hiuan Tsang the 7th century Chinese traveller referred to it as Ma-lo-pho, the 'red land'. It has also been known as Kachanpa, the 'land of snow', or Ripul, the 'land of mountains'. Finally Ladwak, the 'land

93

under the passes' evolved into the current name Ladakh.

Early rulers of Ladakh were the Thi dynasty, followed by the Che-lik and Uto-ylde kings. In 842 AD, according to the written history of Ladakh, the Lha-chen dynasty was founded by Skyid-Lde-dyimagon. His grandson, Nima-gon, ruled from 975 to 990 and extended the kingdom far and wide by defeating invading tribes from central Asia. The victorious king built a new capital at Shey, near Leh, as well as constructing many forts and reorganising the army.

In 1150 Naglug came to power and built many palaces. He was followed by Tishi-gon in 1230, who was a patron of Buddhism. In 1290 Norub-gon was a strong king and another promoter of religious activities. It was during his reign that the famous Buddhist scriptures, the 100 volume *Kandshur* of Ladakh, were compiled. His son, Gyalpo Rinchen, extended his rule to Kashmir and at the same time accepted Islam. He ruled under the name Sultan Sadar-ud-Din from 1324-27 and was Kashmir's first Muslim king.

In 1531 Ladakh was invaded by Mirza Haider Dughlat who marched through the Nubra Valley, defeating the local chief and his nobles, took Leh without resistance and pressed on to Kashmir. Ladakh's golden age started in 1533 when Soyang Namgyal united the whole of the region, established his capital at Leh and built a palace at Tsemo along with a grand temple decorated with numerous Buddhist images. A brave warrior, he had conquered Shigar, Kharko and other areas of Baltistan in his youth and extended his domain to the outskirts of Lhasa in Tibet. He did not depose the ruling monarchs of those areas but allowed them to remain and rule under his authority. He devoted his time to public works and was responsible for the roads and bridges in both Baltistan and Ladakh before his death in 1555. The Namgyal dynasty of Ladakh exists even today – the Rani of Stok still occupies the Stok palace and has been elected to the Indian parliament.

Soyang Namgyal was succeeded by his brother Jamyang Namgyal, who immediately faced an invasion by the Muslim ruler of Skardu, Raja Ali Sher. Ali Sher's daughter, Khatoon, followed her father into battle and lost her heart to the Ladakhi king. Ali Sher too, was entranced by Namgyal's lovely daughter. There was a double wedding in Leh and the bleak capital overnight became a sparkling city for the splendid affair. The princess was crowned queen with the name Argiyal bestowed by a priest and Ali Sher went back to Skardu.

Their son Singe Namgyal assumed the throne in 1610 and defeated the king of Baltistan, who had attempted to invade Ladakh with the support of the Moghuls. Singe Namgyal was also interested in the construction of gompas and ordered the building of Hemis, Chemre, Themisgam and many chorten and mani walls.

Singe Namgyal divided the kingdom between his three sons. His descendant in Ladakh, Deldan Namgyal, ruled from 1645, had the golden Buddha statue erected in Shey and his generals sub-jugated the Baltis and made them pay tribute. Kashmiri troops, assisting the Baltis, were also beaten by the Ladakhis, but in the following years (around 1685) the Ladakhis were unable to repel invading Mongol forces. Ladakh once again came under Tibetan influence and in order to escape this domination the Ladakhis sought and received military support from their former enemies, the Kashmiris. The Governor of Kashmir sent troops to help the King of Leh regain his throne, but in return for this help the king had to pay a regular tribute to Delhi and a mosque had to be erected in Leh. Some sources maintain that the king actually had to convert to Islam but this is uncertain.

Delek Namgyal, who had ruled from 1655, was succeeded by Ngeume Namgyal in 1695. He maintained the good relationship with Kashmir, introduced the art of paper making into Ladakh, wrote many books on Buddhism and constructed a large fort in the Nubra valley. He died in 1750 but in the following years, until it was completely conquered by Kashmir, Ladakh was ruled by insignificant kings and fragmented into small, weak states.

After the establishment of Sikh rule over Jammu and Kashmir, Ladakh was invaded by Zorawar Singh, the general of Maharaja Gulab Singh. This event is known as the Dogra Invasion of 1834. At the head of 5000 troops Zorawar Singh was confronted at Mulbekh by the king Dorje Namgyal. Singh retreated to Suru for four months and then negotiated a peace. He retreated further to Lamayuru and then invaded the Zanskar valley. From there he marched over the Zanskar range, reached Spituk on the Indus and fired on the Leh Palace, destroying one wing. The shell holes and other damage remain to this day.

Dorje Namgyal then surrendered and his place was taken by various town governors appointed by the Maharaja of Jammu, who was descended from Ladakhi nobility (Chalons). Thus only the military was comprised of Kashmiris, the government was again in Ladakhi hands. The dethroned royal family received Stok, the palace where they still live today. The last king, Kunsang Namgyal, died in 1974 but is expected to be succeeded by his son when he reaches an appropriate age.

Since India's independence, and the resulting conflict between India and Pakistan over Kashmir, Ladakh, like Kashmir, has been divided between the two nations. Following the Chinese invasion of Tibet in 1959 there have been Indian and Chinese troops stationed on the eastern border and in 1962 there was another major conflict when the Chinese occupied part of Ladakh including the Changchenmo Valley. Since then Ladakh has been divided into three parts. Due to the strong military presence in Ladakh, India has considerably developed the region's infrastructure but the Chinese and Pakistanis have also been hard at work, building strategically important roads. There is now a road through the Chinese held part of Ladakh, close to the cease-fire line. Another road from Kashgar in north-west China goes over the Karakoram range into the Pakistani region to Hunza, Gilgit and the Indus Valley, west of Kargil.

PEOPLE & THEIR LIFE

The Ladakhis are Tibetan-Mongoloid in appearance – a healthy looking people, deep brown in colouring due to the strong summer sun. Many Ladakhis are nomads, herding their goats, noted for their fine pashmina wool, to high altitudes during the summer.

Their economy is mainly a subsistence one; woolen clothing, jewellery and religious objects are the main items they make. The Ladakhis have domesticated a range of animals including, of course, yaks and dzo. Horses, yaks, ponies and donkeys are used for transportation; the dzo for ploughing and horses for riding. Sheep and goats are kept for meat and wool while the short, stout and ferocious dogs keep invaders and wild bears at bay. Wild animals in the region include wolf, markhool, fox, hare, snow leopard, mountain mouse, marmot and bear.

Electricity is provided in the main towns by diesel generators. A large hydro-electric scheme at Stagna was destroyed by floods in 1978 and the rebuilding of the channels and weirs is very slow. Ladakhi houses were traditionally built on slabs made of stone and earth bricks with timber poles, then twigs and for the roof grass with mud on top. Now, however, Ladakhis have taken to building in fields and where the houses used to be three to four stories high, they are now only one or two.

In the Ladakhi family boys have a higher status than girls. A woman's work is regarded as being in the house where she holds supreme power. Polyandry still continues in some valleys in Ladakh.

A young and an old Ladakhi in Leh

Ceremonies

When a child is born the family usually holds a
festival for their relatives, neighbours and
friends after the first 15 days, at age one month
and after a year. All are invited to come to the
house and are given tsampa, butter and sugar,
along with tea to eat and drink all day.

When a marriage occurs festivities again
continue all day with musicians and dancing.
The first day is spent in feasting at the bride's
house, the second at the groom's place. When
the daughter of the family marries she goes to
live in the house of her husband's partner. Boys
are usually married or promised for marriage at
about 16, girls at about 12. To make a proposal
a relative of the boy goes to the house of the girl
and gives a ring together with presents of
butter, tea and chang. If the gifts are accepted
then the marriage follows some months later.

The boy offers a necklace and clothes to the
girl. The parents of the girl give the couple
clothes, animals and land if they are rich. These
gifts are known as a *raqtqaq* or dowry. When the
father of the family dies his place is taken by the
eldest brother. The other brothers must obey
the eldest brother. All inheritance of the family
goes to the eldest brother and then to the next
brother when he dies.

If the family consists of all girls, then the
father will bring the husband of the eldest
daughter into the house and all land stays in the
daughter's name and passes to her first son.
Both sets of parents must accept the proposal
of the boy for the girl. Usually the marriage is
negotiated by both sets of parents, who will
choose a suitable partner for their child on the
basis of manner, health and ability to earn
income and look after a house.

Ladakhi Dress

Men traditionally wear thick woollen robe
called *goucha*, fastened at the neck, under the
armpit and tied at the waist with a colourful
sash known as a *skerag*. The *skerag* is about two
metres long and 20 cm wide, wound round and
round and tucked in. In this sash men carry the
small essentials of Ladakhi life (flints, cap, tea
cup, etc).

The women wear a similar robe called a
kuntop but on their backs they add a colourful

Top: Women from the Temisgang region of Ladakh at the Hemis festival (BP)
Left: Kashmiri village woman, Wadvan Valley (GW)
Right: Bakharval girl (GW)

Top: Gujar man and woman (GW)
Left: Woodcutter at Phyang Gompa (BP)
Right: Bakharval shepherd with hennaed beard (GW)

shawl, the *bok* – in which a baby or parcels can easily be carried. it used to be worn for warmth and a protection on the back against heavy loads of sticks and rocks. Traditionally there was a brightly coloured design on the outside, with yak or goat skin on the inside to keep the wearer warm. This has now been changed by fashion to a simple ornament of brightly coloured material, although in winter many women still wear the goat skin for warmth.

The women wear their hair in two long pigtails, a style also followed by some men. They top the picturesque ensemble with a top hat or *perak* which somehow remains firmly balanced, perched on top of their heads. The traditional *perak* has three, five, seven or nine lines of turquoise, according to the rank of the wearer. Only the very richest and royalest of families could wear nine lines. When the woman dies the *perak* passes to the eldest child of her family. Shoes, known as *papu*, are made of woven yak hair or wool, often gaily decorated, with a sole of yak leather.

Although many men are abandoning their traditional dress for western clothing, the women still predominantly wear their colourful local dress.

GEOGRAPHY

The main settlements in Ladakh are strung along the Indus River Valley, which runs in an approximately north-west to south-east direction. In turn the Zanskar range parallels the Indus Valley to the south and separates Ladakh from the Zanskar Valley. To the north-east of Ladakh is the high Changtang plateau, reached by a number of passes, but this barren, sparsely populated area, with its high altitude salt lakes, is well into the restricted zone of Ladakh. Much of it is under Chinese control.

Only about 40 km from Leh, but again deep into the restricted zone where foreigners may not enter, is the lovely Nubra Valley, noted for its apple, apricot, walnut and mulberry trees. The river Shyok flows through this small and comparatively warm valley and yak, sheep and goats graze in small forests. The soda for Ladakhi tea comes from the Nubra Valley. The valley is only accessible for a couple of months each year since it is July before the snow melts back from the passes. Entry to the Nubra Valley is either over the dangerous, due to the avalanches, Khardung La pass at over 5300 metres or by the even higher (5500 metre) Digar La pass.

Ladakh is situated on a high altitude plateau between 3000 and 4000 metres above sea level. It is made up of two administrative districts, Leh and Kargil. Mountain ranges partition the region into six areas. Central Ladakh, around Phyang to Chemre, is relatively warm in the summer. The second area is Rong, on the eastern side of central Ladakh where the Indus valley narrows up to its headwaters above 4000 metres and where the climate is very cold.

The third area is Rupsho, in an open plain south-east of the Indus and around the Leh-Manali road. It lies between 4000

A young school girl in Pharka

and 5000 metres and is very cold and dry. The people are mainly sheep and goat herders. Tangse, the fourth area, is a small valley surrounded by mountains over 4500 meters near the monasteries of Tikse and Karu, over the Changla. The Nubra Valley is the fifth area while the Kargil-Zanskar region around the Nun and Kun range and the Suru River is the sixth.

There are three main routes into Leh. The Manali-Leh road and the Suru-Leh are not good for vehicles while the Srinagar-Leh road is closed from November to June each year. Special permission is needed to travel along the Manali-Leh road which is, in any case, sparsely populated. The Indus or Sindh is the main river through Ladakh but others include, in the Kargil area, the Drass, Suru, Wakkha, Shigar, Shingo and Phoo.

BUDDHISM

Although the Islamic influence extends out of the Kashmir Valley as far as Kargil in Ladakh, the predominant religion is overwhelmingly the Tibetan, Lamaist form of Buddhism. As the Kashmiris look towards Mecca, so do the Ladakhis look towards Lhasa and although it may be incorrect to refer to Ladakh as 'little Tibet' there is much evidence of Tibetan influence. This Lamaist influence extends to the use of Tibetan script for the holy books of *Kandshur* and the clear Tibetan architectural influence, particularly evident in the design of the Leh Palace which bears so many similarities to the larger Potala in Lhasa.

Lamaism is a form of Buddhism heavily influenced by the pre-Buddhist Bon religion of Tibet. This is especially noticeable on the stones and banners which carry pictures and carvings of Bon demons and gods. At the pinnacle of the Lamaist pantheon is the divine trinity of Avalokitesvara, Manjushri and Vajrapani, but there are an extraordinary number of other gods and demons. Their pictures totally cover the walls of many gompas

and to further complicate matters there can be unique incarnations only recognised in certain gompas!

Lamaism is the monastic side of the religion, the study of which requires long hours of meditation by the monks. This essential basis of Lamaist Buddhism contrasts with the visible rituals which most Ladakhis observe, such as pilgrimages to gompas, chortens, maniwalls, and holy tombs, or turning prayer wheels and chanting mantras. The observance of their religion is an everyday occurrence in the life of the people of Ladakh.

Lamaism probably came to Ladakh around the 10th century. It has been the religion of Tibet since 632 AD under the reign of King Srongbtsan-sgam-po, but had additions made to it under the influence of the magician Padmasambhava. Ladakhi monasteries belong to two main sects – the red-caps and the yellow-caps. The yellow-cap (or Gelugpa sect) are a reformed sect who follow the Dalai Lama as a reincarnation of the Bodhisattva Avalokitesvara. These sects are further divided with the Dukpa, Dekong, Saskin and Nyingma schools wearing red or maroon robes and caps and the Gyaldon and Ludok schools wearing yellow caps.

An important element in Ladakhi Buddhist society, as elsewhere, lamas are not solely confined to the priesthood, their main profession, but also work as teachers, physicians, medics and astrologers. Women too are admitted to the order and are known as tschomohs. They too have to get their head shaved. Both lamas and tschomohs work in the fields of the gompa. The head lama of any monastery is known as Khaushak, and next to him is the Loban.

Tibetan Buddhism places great importance on the doctrine of reincarnation. When a person dies their spirit may be born again in another body. Both in Ladakh and Tibet it becomes impossible to thoughtlessly kill a fly or squash an insect. In winter the people break the ice in the pools to save the fish before they freeze to death. They believe that the more life one saves the happier is the lot of the soul. Incarnations are created involuntarily through the forces of karma, or the law of cause and effect. Certain lamas are incarnations of Buddha and after years of study are entitled to be known as Rimpoche, or one who comes again and again to show the path to Buddhahood.

Monks are not allowed to have private possessions except their butter lamps and bowls and perhaps an icon or amulet box. Boys enter the monastery as young as three or four, as students, and don the red robe which they will wear for the rest of their lives. After 30 or 40 years of study and passing the final tests, they are then qualified for senior positions as lamas. Each must pass tests under the control of the Dalai Lama's own teachers.

The Dalai Lama always wears a yellow silk cap at receptions and ceremonies and all the objects in regular use by him are of the same colour. The use of yellow is a privilege he alone possesses. His robes, though, are always the red robe of a monk, once prescribed by Buddha, and differ in no way from that of monastic officials. The name Dalai Lama is not used in Tibet at all. This is a Mongolian expression meaning 'broad ocean'. Normally the Dalai Lama is referred to as Gyalpo Rimpoche, which means 'precious king'. He represents in his person the return to earth of Chenrezig, one of the thousand living Buddhas who have renounced nirvana in order to help mankind. Chenrezig is the patron god of Tibet and his reincarnations are always the Kings of Bo – as the Tibetans call their land.

In Leh it is possible to find families whose members are Muslims, Christians, and Buddhists since the Ladakhis are notably tolerant of other beliefs. As a rule, however, where there are different religious groups in the same area (as between Kargil and Shergol on the Srinagar-Leh road) the live quite separately from one another.

STATUES & SHRINES

To be able to make some sense of the many statues and shrines that you will see in the gompas of Ladakh, you will need to have some knowledge of the various deities and historical personages that you may see depicted. It is impossible to give anywhere near a full description here, as the various Buddhist sects have different representations of the same god, and within each sect there are regional variations. What follows is a very broad outline and should not be taken to be correct in any one situation.

Dhyani Buddha

There are five different representations of the Dhyani Buddha, each manifesting a different pose:

Vairocana This pose shows the Buddha preaching or turning the wheel of the doctrine of Dharma; in this pose both hands are held in a circular pattern in front of the chest and the Buddha is seated on the throne of a lion.

Aksobhaya In this pose, also known as the Miskyotpa posture, the Buddha is touching the earth with the fingers of the right hand and the palm facing inward as a gesture of calling the earth goddess to witness the Buddha's fitness for enlightenment. In this pose the Buddha is seated on the throne of an elephant.

Ratnasambhava (Rinjung) In this pose the Buddha's right hand is held low with the left open inwards and his is seated on throne of a peacock.

Amoghasiddhi (Tonyot Dugpa) The Buddha is in the gesture of fearlessness, which is interpreted as a sign of bestowing confidence or blessing, where the right hand is held upwards and the palm outwards, and the Buddha is seated on the throne of a garuda.

Amitabha (Otpakmet) The Buddha is seated in the Vajrasana pose holding the alms bowl of ambrosia. The earthly manifestation of Amitabha is the Panchen Lama, who is the spiritual guide of the Dalai Lama.

Amitayus (Tsepagmet)
Amitayus is the Buddha of long life and is widely worshipped in Ladakh and Tibet. He holds in his hand an urn of elixir and appears similar to the Amitabha.

Manjushri (Jampal Yangs)
Manjushri is a personification of the Buddha of wisdom. He carries a sword in his right hand, symbolising his power over the cords of ignorance. He book on a lotus signifies the power of learning.

Avalokitesvara
Also known as Chenrezig or Chanrazik, Avalokitesvara is the patron saint of Tibet. He is said to be incarnated in each successive Dalai Lama. This incarnation of the Buddha is the god of compassion and he taught to man the sacred mantra 'om mani padme hum'. There is another manifestation of Avalokitesvara known as Chughsig-Jal. He has 11 heads, the top one being that of Amitabha. He is the saviour of all living beings and is said to have burst his head at least 10 times when contemplating the suffering of men and animals. Among his 1000 hands there are eight principal hands – the central pair offers a blessing, the second right hand holds a rosary, the third holds a Shokra and the fourth is Veradamutra. The second left hand holds a bow and arrow and the fourth a drinking vessel.

Vajrapani (Chakra Dorje)
Vajrapani holds a Vajra in his right hand and his left makes the Korana Mudra. He wears tiger skin and has a snake coiled around his arms and feet. He is the god of energy and power and in his wrathful manifestation he represents the chief of the Tantric deities.

Buddha Maitriya (Chamba Gonbo)
This is a representation of the Buddha to come. He is usually depicted standing or sitting on the throne, never in a meditative pose. In his right hand he holds the wheel of the Dharma, on a plant, and in his left hand he holds a pot with a cactus plant.

As well as the various Buddhas and near Buddhas of Tibetan Buddhism there are the historical figures of Tibet and Ladakh, who have influenced the way Buddhism has developed, often dividing it into various sects.

Nagarjuna (Lhundub)
Nagarjuna was born the son of a Brahmin in south India. He became a great Mahayana Buddhist scholar of the Nalanda University.

Padmasambhava
Padmasambhava is the great master of the Tantra, established as the Nyingma school of Tibetan Buddhism. He is depicted in paintings and statues with his right hand holding a Vajra and the left hand holding a skull cap with ambrosia.

Rinchen Zangpo
Born in western Tibet, Rinchen Zangpo is celebrated as one of the great religious figures of Tibet. He showed such extraordinary skill at learning Buddhist texts that he was sent to Kashmir for higher studies. Following several years of study in Kashmir he travelled to the eastern regions of India where he studied under several famous Buddhists, saints and scholars.

On his return to Tibet he was recognised as the spiritual teacher of the land. He started work on the translation of Buddhist texts from Sanskrit into Tibetan. His work covered so many areas of Buddhist philosophy and thought that he is credited with being the father of the Buddhist religion in Tibet. He is depicted as seated on a lotus in the meditation pose and covered by a long yellow robe.

Throughout his life he is said to have been responsible for the construction of 108 monasteries and shrines, including those at Alchi, Sumdo and Mangyu.

Milarapa

Milarapa was born about 800 years ago in Lo in western Tibet. He was a disciple of Marpa, the first Mahamudra Guru of Tibet. He was a great scholar and is renowned as a poet.

Tsongkhapa

Tsongkhapa founded the Gelugpa or yellow-hat sect of Buddhism.

MONEY

Although there are banks with facilities for changing foreign currency in Ladakh note that India's perennial shortage of change can be particularly bad in Ladakh. Bring as many one and two rupee notes as possible with you. Free spending tourists have created the image that all foreigners have money to burn. This is not helped by the very high, by Indian standards, entry charges to all the Ladakhi gompas, but it must be admitted that the Ladakhis are certainly putting this new found monastic income to good use in restoring and renovating the gompas. Do not be too lavish with tips and donations. The inflation this brings about does not effect only tourists

Apart from in Leh, Kargil and Karu changing foreign currency will be virtually impossible. Banking hours are quite restricted. In Leh the summer hours are 10 am to 2 pm on weekdays and 10 am to 12 noon on Saturday. In winter the hours are shorter. In Kargil the Muslim holidays are also observed.

Begging

Begging has become an epidemic amongst Ladakhi children, although they do it more out of imitation and fun than in seriousness. Everywhere you go you will have children calling after you 'one pen', 'one bonbon' or 'one rupee'. Unfortunately this practice has been created by thoughtless and patronising tourists doling out pens, candy and rupees to the children. Ignore them or it will only become worse. It is said that enterprising professional beggars from Calcutta and Bombay are also beginning to make a summer appearance in Ladakh,

GENERAL INFORMATION
Post & Telegraph

There are telegraph and telephone offices in Leh and Kargil. Beside Leh and Kargil there are post offices at a number of the smaller towns such as Lamayuru, Khalsi and Sakti, but it is unlikely that they will be able to handle foreign mail. There is a radio link facility from Padum in Zanskar to Kargil.

There are J&K police stations in Drass, Kargil and Leh and office of the tourist police at the Leh Tourist Reception Centre.

Medical Facilities

There is a district hospital at Leh and Kargil and there are primary health centres at Drass, Sanku and Padum in Zanskar. There are a number of dispensaries on the Srinagar-Kargil-Leh-Upshi road. These are at Kharbu, Pashyum, Mulbekh, Khalsi, Chuchot, Tikse and Sakti. A dispensary is a small hospital with five beds and attended by trained medical staff. There are also dispensaries on the Kargil-Zanskar route at Tripson, Tampis and Pannikar.

General Advice

Take a sleeping bag with you, even in summer it can get very chilly at night and if you spend the night at a monastery or village you'll definitely need warm bedding. If you use public transport from Leh there are gompas which can only be visited if you stay overnight and return the next day – due to the bus timings. If you're planning to do much travelling around Ladakh a tent is also worth having. If you're trekking it's a necessity.

Be prepared for dramatic changes in temperatures and watch out for the sun's surprising intensity at this altitude. On a warm day the temperature can drop with striking speed when a cloud obscures the sun. You will find yourself putting on and taking off a sweater a dozen times a day. The burning power of the sun in Ladakh is phenomenal, if you want to avoid sunburn and a peeling nose you'll find a sun screen cream is essential. A hat also helps.

Remember the effects of altitude – people who fly straight to Leh from Delhi should take it very easy for a few days until they're acclimatised. Even from Srinagar at 1768 metres you're likely to feel breathless and light headed at Leh's 3554 metres. Take it easy, don't over-exert yourself at first. Bad headaches and nausea are common effects of lack of acclimatisation, they're particularly prevalent at night. Severe altitude sickness, which can be fatal, is extremely unlikely to afflict you unless you immediately start rushing up mountains. There's only one sure treatment for altitude sickness and that is to get down to a lower level. People with heart conditions should seek medical advice before visiting Ladakh – your heart has to work hard at this height. Remember that the effects of alcohol are compounded by the altitude.

Despite the officials' off-putting eagerness it's wise to register your name and passport number at the tourist office in Leh (if you arrive by air) or at the office in Drass (if coming overland). The Indian authorities do not like tourists selling cameras, watches and camping equipment in Ladakh. There are many traders only too ready to make you an offer, but take care in any negotiations.

Finally remember that much of Ladakh is a highly sensitive border area where India meets China and Pakistan. You are not allowed to go more than one mile north of the Srinagar-Kargil-Leh road. At Leh the road turns south through Upshi and eventually reaches Manali in Himachal Pradesh. You are not allowed east of a line

one mile west of this Leh-Manali road. People who ignore these regulations, so the story goes, may find themselves in an unpleasant jail for a week or three before the authorities get around to telling them how naughty they've been.

Ladakh in Winter

Winter is not the time of year to go to Leh, but we very much wanted to include at least a short visit and, of course, the rest of India is at its best at that time. Providing (as at other times of year) conditions are right Indian Airlines operate flights to Leh in the winter. Although one will probably not encounter other tourists on flights into Leh they are still likely to be fully booked so be as careful about booking – and reconfirming! – as for any other flights with Indian Airlines.

Whether the flights are more spectacular in the winter than at other times of the year I don't know, but certainly it's difficult to imagine finer flying weather than we experienced during our two flights in early January – beautiful blue skies and crystal-clear views of the white peaks of the Himalaya stretching as far as the eye could see in every direction. Although the route via Chandigarh is magnificent the Leh-Srinagar flight is even more awe-inspiring.

To the best of my knowledge, while we were there only one hotel was open in Leh – the Khangri. The family who run this small and simple hotel is very friendly and hospitable. Everyone did all they could to make us feel comfortable. Leh was particularly cold during our visit and even the Ladakhis were minding the cold. Our friends in Leh informed us that it had been -45° one night. At any rate soft drinks left on the window sill inside the room at the hotel were frozen solid in the morning. In addition to the stove which was set up and lit in the middle of our room late in the afternoon (a fascinating ritual), the hotel supplied us with hot water bottles and lots of blankets and heavy quilts.

If on a tight schedule, like we were, you tend to worry the whole time about whether or not the plane will arrive for the return flight. We heard many stories about winter visitors being stranded in Leh for 12 to 14 days. If you had an unlimited travel 'Discover India' ticket it might be interesting to fly in to Leh and straight out again, just for the superb views of the Himalaya and of Leh and its surrounding gompas from the air.

We experienced no problems finding taxis to take us to Tikse and Shey and enjoyed participating in an important religious festival at Spitok, otherwise attended by only the local inhabitants. If you decide to visit Leh in winter bring plenty of warm clothing and be prepared to still be bitterly cold much of the time. If you're lucky, as we were the day we arrived, the temperature will not be unreasonable during the day (it was -10° at noon) and there will be brilliant sunshine. All in all a winter visit is an exhilarating experience.

John Berridge

Photography

It is prohibited to take photographs of any military or strategic equipment or installations. This includes military camps, soldiers, military vehicles, bridges and even places or objects that in our eyes could be civilian installations such as the radio broadcasting station in Leh. This prohibition is strictly enforced and infringing it can result in the confiscation of cameras and films.

In the gompas you can generally photograph whatever you please, apart from very holy places, such as the Gonkhang room of Matho Gompa, where only monks are permitted to set foot. Nevertheless, you should exercise great restraint during prayers since flashes of light and the clicks of camera equipment are very disturbing.

THINGS TO BUY

You may dream of antique dance masks and tankas but you are not allowed to buy them! Antique dolls, swords, monastic antiquities such as Buddha figures, dance masks and tankas are all banned from being purchased, dealt in or taken out of Ladakh. Antiques are defined as being 100 or more years old. There has been a terrible drain of the accumulated treasures of the gompas due to the greedy actions of some over-wealthy and thoughtless tourists. The government has, belatedly, recognised the danger of Ladakh losing much of its cultural heritage and departing visitors have their baggage searched.

New tankas are now being produced, in fact there really aren't any old tankas around for sale – no matter what some fast talking salesman may tell you! The new tankas are generally painted in Darjeeling or Nepal.

There are many other items which you are free to purchase and export but first of all it is wise to identify whom you are dealing with. There are three groups of traders in Ladakh: Kashmiris come from Srinagar or Delhi just for the tourist season and they bring with them inflated prices and hard bargaining techniques. Tibetans come from Dharamsala and they operate many of the street stalls you will find near the tourist centre in Leh on behalf of Kashmiri traders. Finally there are the Ladakhis themselves, of whom there are very few. Naturally you have to be most careful when dealing with the Kashmiris.

There is a very small, but growing, local handicrafts industry, most of which is presently based on the Tibetan refugee camp at Choglamsar. The major craft here is Tibetan carpets. You may visit Choglamsar and buy them direct, or from the street stalls in Leh. They are cheap, compared to Kashmiri or Persian carpets, and also very durable although somewhat bulky to carry with you when you leave. It is possible, though naturally difficult, to find some old Tibetan carpets in Leh and in good condition.

You can also look for chang and tea-vessels, silver cups and butter churns or the mussel shells which serve as ornaments. For a few rupees you can buy a prayerflag or for a very large number of rupees you could invest in a new *perak* (they cost up to $10,000) – the headgear with hundreds of turquoise stones and silver pieces, worn at festivals and on special occasions. Or you may be satisfied with a tea kettle from the bazaar or search for silver-worked articles from China.

In practically all the gompas, during the tourist season, monks will have all sorts of items for sale – ranging from bells and

Butter lamp vendor

locks to small drums and musical instruments. There are many items which are easy to carry such as prayer wheels or dorjes. Since demand for 'authentic' items has outstripped supply you cannot be certain that anything is of any age. 'Antiques' in Ladakh are all likely to be 'instant antiques'. In any case authentic items should be left where they belong – in Ladakh.

Prices in Ladakh are generally quite high. Although there is much Tibetan and Ladakhi clothing, Tibetan jewellery and other Tibetan curios on sale, you should familiarise yourself with prices in Kashmir, Nepal, Dharamsala or other Tibetan centres before spending freely in Ladakh. You should bargain hard.

Tibetan Calendar
The Tibetan year is lunar, that is it has 13 months, and normally numbers 360 days. In

order to keep it in line with the moon's phases, one day is occasionally omitted and as it is the 'unlucky' days which are dropped, and these occur irregularly, the Tibetan year and months do not always correspond exactly with a normal lunar year or the Chinese months and years. Another complication is that, to keep the calendar in line with the solar cycle of the seasons, seven months are inserted each 19 years!

This makes comparisons between our calendar and their's rather difficult. Nevertheless, gompa festivals do fall at around the same dates each year – the important Hemis festival is usually in late June.

The year begins in February with the rise of the new moon. The months (Da-Wa) are named First, Second, etc, with the word Da-Wa (moon) prefixed. Thus the first month is Da-Wa-Tang-Po.

The week is divided into seven days (Za) named after the sun, moon and five planets. The days and their associated celestial bodies are:

Sunday	Nima (sun)
Monday	Da-Wa (moon)
Tuesday	Mig-Mar (Mars)
Wednesday	L'ag-Pa (Mercury)
Thursday	P'ur-Bu (Jupiter)
Friday	Pa-San (Venus)
Saturday	Pen-Ba (Saturn)

The different days of the week are associated with the elements – thus Sunday and Tuesday with fire, Monday and Wednesday with water, Thursday with air, Friday and Saturday with earth. Each hour and day of the week possesses a lucky or unlucky character, and the days of the month according to their order introduce other sets of unlucky combinations. Thus each hour of each day has some sort of astrological significance for the Ladakhis.

Every large monastery has a Tsi-Pa or astrologer lama, recruited from the cleverest of monks. Some monasteries also have an oracle lama. The astrologer lamas always have a constant stream of visitors asking for prescriptions as to what deities and demons require appeasing and the remedies necessary to neutralise these evils.

Like the Chinese calendar the Tibetan years are named after animals, in a cycle which repeats every twelve years. 1985 is the year of the ox – we'll then have the years of the tiger (or cat), rabbit, dragon, snake, horse, sheep, monkey, sparrow, dog, pig and rat before coming back to ox again. There is also a 60 year cycle of Jupiter which combines the 12 animals with the five elements: wood, fire, earth, iron and water. Each element is given a pair of animals, the first being considered male and the second female. 1984 was a water-mouse year!

FOOD

The staple food in Ladakh is *tsampa*, which is made by lightly roasting barley in a large metal pan, partly mixed with sand

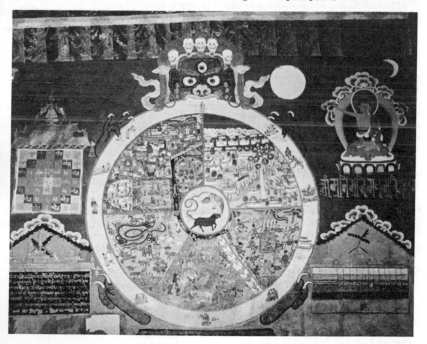

Tibetan calendar in Tiske Gompa

to prevent the barley catching alight. The barley is then sieved to remove the sand and the roasted grain is ground in a watermill. The resulting meal is sprinkled with *gurgur* (salt water) or mixed with a small amount of liquid to form cakes. Salted butter tea or *Chang* (a locally made beer) is often drunk with the tsampa. These dishes are called *cholak*.

If you eat in a local restaurant in Leh you will probably be offered the following dishes apart from *tsampa*:

Pava – peas and barley flour boiled in water for a long time until the peas are hard.
Cholak – a mixture of tea, butter, sugar and tsampa.
Khambish – bread made from wheat flour.
Thukpa – water and wheat flour made into noodles and dropped into boiling water and then served with a flavoured meat sauce.
Gugur chai – salt tea, made from green tea, salt, soda from the Nubra Valley, butter and milk.
Curd – made from yak milk.
Moe moe – steamed tsampa dough, usually with meat in the middle like dumplings.
Gyatug – a dish of long, vermicelli-like strips of tsampa over which minced meat and a flavoured sauce is poured.
Skir – a hotpot of meat, potatoes, grain and sometimes vegetables.
Kambir – small round breads, sometimes sweet.
Holkur – Ladakhi biscuit made of sugar, nuts and grain meal. Normally baked by the host himself to be served to the patrons.

There is much Tibetan influence and you will find many Chinese-Tibetan dishes like chow mein or *kothay* – meat or vegetables wrapped in thin dough and fried or steamed.

You may be surprised to see potatoes served in Ladakh. They were brought in by Moravian Christian missionaries from Germany in the last century. There are still about 200 Christians in Ladakh today. Food can get a little boring in Ladakh, the variety of vegetables and fruit grown locally is very limited – barley, potatoes, peas and onions are virtually the only locally grown produce on sale although fruit trees can also be grown in some areas. Mustard and a variety of herbs are also grown in Ladakh.

Much food and produce comes up from Kashmir, but only in the summer when the passes are open, of course. Prices are naturally inflated and in the last few weeks before the summer season commences with the opening of the road, when tourists are already starting to flood in by air, the supplies of food can be somewhat limited. It's worth bringing in a few menu brighteners like bars of chocolate or cans of apple juice. The usual Indian glucose biscuits are available everywhere and in Leh it is also possible to buy dehydrated soya-bean meal or biscuits, which provide a very useful and energy-giving carbo-hydrate supplement to your diet, especially at this altitude.

Although food production is limited in Ladakh what does grow there can be quite outlandish. The long daylight hours and the extra strength of the sun's ultra-violet rays at this altitude creates wonderous garden produce – cabbages with heads that have exceeded 14 kg, radishes or potatoes weighing up to two kg, turnips which reach five kg!

Ladakh is as insanitary as anywhere else in India so take care where you eat and beware of fresh fruit and vegetables. There is no piped water system in Leh so drink water at your own risk! Even boiling water isn't such a positive method of purifying it at this altitude since the boiling point is much lower. Remember to keep your fluid intake up as you can easily become dehydrated.

Tea & Butter Tea

The tea habit initially came to Ladakh, as to all of Tibet, from Imperial China, but due to the closing of the Tibetan border tea now comes from India. You may find Chinese/Tibetan tea smuggled over the border from Tibet on sale in the bazaar in Leh. It's more rare than expensive and the quality is not too high. The tea is often transported in pressed blocks which can frequently be seen as offerings in monasteries.

Traditional Ladakhi tea is made with butter and tastes more like a soup than our idea of tea. The tea is initially made very strong, brewed for a long time, then diluted to a drinkable strength. The tea is then put into a butter churn, a wooden vessel about 15 cm in diameter and 80 cm long, and bound with brass at the top,

Making butter tea

bottom and in the middle. A spoonful of salted butter is added and churned into the liquid. This broth is then reheated and drunk continually until it is all gone.

Every Ladakhi, no matter how poor, has his own tea vessel. In rich families the tea is served in three-part silver cups, the lower cup stands on a small pedestal and the cup itself is covered with a lid. The tea is generally drunk warm, not hot and during the colder part of the year the lower cup serves as a handwarmer. If you are invited for tea anywhere in Ladakh you will find that your cup is refilled as soon as you take a sip. Tea drinking continues until all the tea made is finished.

Tea is usually drunk during prayer ceremonies at gompas and you may be offered some, in that case you will be expected to have your own cup, an item every Ladakhi carries everywhere he or she goes. Cups are on sale at all the street stalls in Leh and at the general stores. In monasteries and for an average family's breakfast, the tea is accompanied by tsampa, which is either sprinkled into the warm brew, or kneaded into lumps and dipped into the tea.

Chang

Beware of the effects of the native beer – chang. High altitude and too much alcohol do not mix well! Nevertheless you should try some of this local alcoholic beverage. There is a chang 'pub' in Leh and the price is around Rs 1 per bottle. You should also try chang in a village at some stage, it usually tastes much better. Chang is a beer, home-brewed from barley and millet, partially seasoned by the addition of pepper and sugar. It is not filtered before serving so dregs and grains are found 'swimming' in the liquid. In short chang is a most unusual pleasure for the palate. In Ladakh you find, as in the other Himalayan states (except Tibet) with a population which belongs to the Tibetan group, no manufacture of spirit liquors.

LANGUAGE

Ladakh differs substantially from Tibetan although they belong to the same family of languages and Ladakhi is written in the Tibetan script. Dialects in nearby villages are very distinct and preserve their individuality to this day – a typical result of a society where few people travelled and there was little exchange of information.

In more widely separated towns, such as Leh and Kargil, the speech is so different that the inhabitants of one can hardly speak the dialect of the other.

There is one Ladakhi word you should learn even before you arrive since you will use it many, many times each day. That is *jullay* – the all purpose greeting that covers 'hello, goodbye, how are you', and simply 'greetings'. The Ladakhis are friendly, outgoing, spontaneous people and they call out *jullay* to everyone they meet – local or foreigner. In a region where passing travellers have traditionally been the most important source of news from the outside world everyone is eager to be friendly to visitors, friend or stranger.

Alphabet

The Ladakhis use a 35-letter alphabet known as ka-ga (ka and ga are the first two letters of the alphabet).

Pronunciation Guide

The vowels a, i and u can have two sounds. A can be as in *father* or in *am*. I can be as the i in *sin* or the ee in *seen*. U can be as the oo in *poor* or as the u in *pure*. Generally e is pronounced as in *them* and o as in *more*.

The usual form of the compound letters is:

ai as y	in m*y*
au as ou	in *ou*r
kh as koh	in *koh*lrabi
ng as ng	in si*ng*
ch as ch	in *ch*urch
ny as ny	in la*ny*ard
th as t	in *t*ub
ph as p	in *p*uppy
ts as ts	in ca*ts*eye
ds as ds	in win*ds*urfer
zh as z	in *z*ephyr
dj as dg	in e*dg*e

Numbers

1	*chig*
2	*nyis*
3	*sum*

4	*dji*
5	*nga*
6	*tok*
7	*dun*
8	*gyet*
9	*gu*
10	*chu*
11	*chu-chig*
12	*chu-nyis*
13	*chu-sum*
14	*chu-dji*
15	*chu-nga*
16	*chu tok*
17	*chu-dun*
18	*chu-gyet*
19	*chu-gu*
20	*nyis-chu*
30	*sum-chu*
40	*dji-chu*
50	*nga chu*
60	*tok chu*
70	*dun-chu*
80	*gyet-chu*
90	*gu-chu*
100	*gya*
1000	*stong*
100,000	*bum*

first	*dang-pa*
second	*nyis-pa*
third	*sum-pa*
fourth	*dji-pa*
tenth	*chu-pa*

Some useful Ladakhi phrase include:

hello, welcome, etc
 jullay
what is your name?
 khyoranggi ming la chi tzerchen?
how far is it to . . . . ?
 thi na cham shik thak ring yot. . . . ?
what time does the bus go?
 bus chuchot cham pey ka chat?
does this bus go to . . . . ?
 tje bus po cha nog ga . . . . ?
is this the road to . . . . ?
 tje lani bo tjenaggah . . . . ?
how much does this cost?
 tje bey rin cham in nak?

please
 katin chey
thank you
 thukjechey
good
 gella
can I buy some. . . . ?
 nya-chi tong rig no na diggah . . . . ?

Food Words

bread	*tagi*
potato	*alu*
tomato	*tamatar*
peas	*kanu*
white radish	*nungma*
red radish	*labuk*
corn, wheat	*zong*
barley	*nass*
barley flour	*tsampa*
cauliflower	*pulgubbi*
carrot	*shanma*
kohlrabi	*kuschulman*

Questions & Commands

where can I get water?
 nya chu kane thobin?
can I stay in your house?
 nya nerang ghi nang la thuk na diggah?
where can I find a room to sleep
 na nit lok sey nang ka ne thobin?
what is your name?
 nyan rang-ni ming-na-chaizer?
where do you live?
 nyanrang karwar zuksat?
where is the post office
 dakkhana-kaga yotkyak?
where is the medical shop?
 manai hati karwayot?
where is the hotel?
 hotel karwayot?
where is the tea shop?
 cha-hati karwayot?
where is the gompa?
 gompa karwayot?
where is the dak bungalow?
 dakbangla karwayot?
give me tea
 nya chha sal

give me food
  nya kharji sal
give me chang
  nya chang sal
give me meat
  nya sha sal
give me hot water
  nya chu-stante sal

wood	shing
matches	machi
candles	moom-bati
kerosene	sammar
stove	stobv
blanket	kambal
paper	shugo
please take tea	solja don

People

boy	nono
brother	acho
father	abba-laiy
girl	chocho
sister	achay-laiy
mother	ama-laiy

Other words you may come across include:

monastery	gompa
monk	lama
nun	tschomoh
flag	tartshco
flute	geihling
horn	thung
smoking sticks	spoz
prayer flags	tarchan

Om Mani Padme Hum

On thousands of prayer flags and mani stones in Ladakh you will see the phrase 'Om Mani Padme Hum' written, carved or painted. You'll hear the phrase murmured by the monks and believers in all monasteries. The generally accepted translation runs: 'Oh, thou jewel in the lotus'. It is usually addressed to Buddha or to Avalokitesvara, his Tibetan incarnation.

It is interesting to read the interpretation of this mantra by the clergyman Phuntsog, who went through training as a Buddhist lama before his conversion to Christianity: Om – the syllable which represents the basis of all being in Indian thought, in Buddhist thought it represents the trinity of speech, body and soul. Mani – the jewels which the god of the Tibetans holds in his right hand. They are arranged as a garland of roses and symbolise the way to holiness. Padme – the lotus flower which the god holds in his left hand. It is the symbol of purity. Hum – bless me. The whole phrase could thus be translated as 'Thou God with the jewel-rose-garland in one hand and the lotus flower in the other, bless my life, soul and spirit'!

GETTING THERE

Air Indian Airlines only started flying into Leh in 1979 – it's probably the highest airport in the world to be used regularly by jet airliners. More recently the original route from Srinagar to Leh has been supplemented by direct flights from Chandigarh to Leh. During the summer season there are four flights a week into Leh. Starting from Delhi one goes via Chandigarh, the other three via Srinagar with various stops between Delhi and Srinagar. One way fares are:

Srinagar-Leh	Rs 269
Chandigarh-Leh	Rs 387
Delhi-Leh (via Chandigarh)	Rs 606
Delhi-Leh (via Srinagar)	Rs 818

The short, less than half an hour, flight from Srinagar is extremely spectacular as it goes right across the Himalaya with superb views of Nun and Kun almost directly below you and K2 (Mt Godwin Austin), the second highest mountain in the world, away to the north in Pakistan.

Flying to Ladakh does have a few hassles. The weather in Leh is very changeable and unpredictable and the high winds that blow up virtually every afternoon means the flights can only be made in the mornings. Plus the approach is difficult, requiring clear visibility. Coming in you fly up the Indus Valley, the mountains rising above you on both sides, then turn left to the runway. Leaving Leh you have to bank right as soon as you're airborne because the Spitok monastery, perched on its hill, is not far to the left of the runway end. Approaches and departures can only be made in one direction because the runway runs steeply uphill away from the Indus.

The end result is that flights to Leh are frequently cancelled or aborted after crossing the mountains. To compound the difficulties, Indian Airline's tight scheduling and limited number of aircraft means that it is difficult to put on extra flights if necessary or even to replace cancelled or aborted flights. At the start of the season in particular the flights can be absurdly heavily booked – a full 737 load can be flown in but due to the altitude only a partial load can be taken out of Leh. Fortunately, at the beginning of the season the 'rush' is into Leh, not out.

If you arrive in Srinagar planning to fly to Leh, but without a reservation, or worse have a reservation but the flight is cancelled, you may have to do some hard work to get on a flight. Your houseboat/hotel owner or a local travel agent with some clout will know how to do it. On the other hand several travellers have written to report getting on the flight despite seemingly impossible positions on the wait list. Indian Airlines's booking system is not always super-efficient and the wait list can sometimes be quite meaningless.

At the start of the '80 tourist season a typical week of flying to Leh went like this: Monday flight – aborted. Tuesday – extra flight put on but again aborted. Wednesday, Thursday, Friday – no extra flights but the unlucky Monday-Tuesday passengers had to keep reporting back to the IA office to find out what was happening. Saturday – regular flight goes OK but there was no room for any of the Monday-Tuesday passengers. Sunday extra flight but again it's aborted! Monday – regular flight gets through OK but with only a dozen or so of the previous Monday-Tuesday's passengers. Tuesday – no extra flight. Wednesday – extra flight gets through and finally gets passengers, many of whom have been waiting in Srinagar for 10 days and have flown to Leh (unsuccessfully)

on three occasions, to their destination. Some passengers had crossed the Himalaya seven times before finally landing on the other side!

Still a few years back it was not unknown for unlucky Ladakhis to make a last minute trip down to Srinagar in October only to get stuck there when the snow came unusually early. In that case you just had to sit and wait for six months before you could get home. Today they can fly back although winter flights are, of course, even less predictable. The Indian Air Force flies to Leh from Chandigarh every day with a large transport aircraft – and their flight always gets in, bad weather or not.

Roads Buses depart from Srinagar for Leh every day during the season. Officially this is June to October but it's not unusual for the road to be closed until mid-June although on occasion it may be open by mid-May. Because of its strategic importance the army always tries to have it open by mid-June. The Zoji La pass is the last pass to be opened – although it is not the highest it is the one which gets the heaviest snowfall. The pass is usually closed around October/November each year when the heavy snowfalls begin. The Namika La and Fatu La are within Ladakh, where precipitation is very light.

Fares to Kargil and Leh from Srinagar are:

Leh – super de-luxe	Rs 153
Leh – A class	Rs 78
Leh – B class	Rs 58
Kargil – A class	Rs 39
Kargil – B class	Rs 29

The super de-luxe and A class buses operate Srinagar-Leh twice weekly, B class buses are daily. There is also a B class bus Srinagar-Kargil only on alternate days.

If you can afford it the super de-luxe buses are certainly the best as they will stop along the way to let you stretch your legs and take photographs. The seats have headrests and are much more comfortable. There is little comfort difference between A and B according to some travellers, enough to make it worth the extra according to others! A are four across seating with rudimentary headrests. B are five across seating. A class, however, provides reserved seats while on B class buses there will invariably be twice as many passengers at the end as they started with. Whatever class of bus you're on try to avoid seats at the back where you suffer much more bouncing around. The buses used on this demanding trip seem to be some of the oldest and least reliable J&K Transport can scare up.

The trip takes two days with an overnight halt at Kargil where there are plenty of hotels. You leave at 7.30 am each morning and arrive at around 5 pm each evening. The total distance may be only 434 km but it's a winding, often steep, road. At high altitudes the buses often crawl uphill at a snail's pace. There are often lengthy stops at road blocks as some stretches of the road are one-way and vehicles go across in convoy.

You can easily hire jeeps to make the trip but they will cost something around Rs 2000 — they'll easily accommodate six passengers if you tie your packs on the roof. If you take a jeep it's worth spreading the trip out by another day and making short forays off the main road to see some of the gompas along the way. If you watch around Srinagar it is sometimes possible to hitch or buy a ride on a private vehicle going to Leh.

Rides in trucks are also possible although trucks tend to go over the edge with much greater frequency than buses. After a tourist was killed in a truck accident last season the J&K government banned trucks from taking tourists. However, the ban is likely to soon be forgotten.

Before the Road Opens In the last few weeks before the Srinagar-Leh road opens it is possible to get to Ladakh by walking over the Zoji La pass. The pass marks the boundary to dry Ladakh and is the last pass to be cleared of snow. The chowkidhar at Sonamarg is the person to ask about the condition of the road. From Sonamarg the pass is reached by 26 km of winding road and is 800 metres higher.

To get to the pass you can either hire a jeep from Srinagar (say Rs 500) or overnight in Sonamarg and in the morning try to get the 7 am Beacon Patrol Truck up to the pass. It's wise to try and latch on to a party of locals to ensure you follow the correct path across the pass. There will usually be somebody crossing every day and it's often possible to hire ponies or porters. Porters from Sonamarg are likely to cost Rs 40 a day and you can double that since they also charge for walking back. Ponies are likely to be Rs 50 a day, with extra for the pony man and perhaps for feed for the ponies. There's usually transport across the pass since tourists start flying into Leh in increasing numbers shortly before the pass is open and food must follow. Supplies are driven up to the pass, carried across by yak and pony train, then loaded back on to trucks for the trip to Leh.

Towards the end of the melt the walk may be only a couple of kms, taking a few hours, but early birds may have to walk for more than a day — sheltering at an army hut on the way. In 1980, a month before the road opened, walking across entailed a 20 km trudge through the snow. In these early conditions the patrol may insist that you're adequately equipped and prepared before letting you cross.

You must take sunglasses and a good skin barrier cream. The deep snow and intense sunlight can easily lead to temporary snow-blindness or very bad sunburn. Late in the melt, or late on a hot day, you can get very wet from the slushy snow. Once over the pass you have to get a ride down to Drass. How easy this is depends on how many people are up at the pass working on the snow clearance. You'll quite possibly have to wait all day and if you're wet it will be an uncomfortable wait.

There's a Beacon Lodge or camp in Gumri, which marks the Ladakh end of the pass. This is usually operating from May, when bulldozers and snowploughs have driven in to begin their heavy work of clearing the road and reforming its surface. Matayin is the first village, about 10 km from the top of the pass at an altitude of 3179 metres, and there is a PWD Rest House there.

There's also a tourist hut in Drass, about 15 km further on. If you stay there, next day you should be able to get a ride down to Kargil. From Kargil there are buses on to Leh but only on two days each week during the winter. The pass is actually cleared of snow for some time before the road is open to traffic, but there are always road repairs to be done and debris, brought down with the snow, to be cleared. Jeeps can often cross the road before it is officially cleared for buses.

Srinagar to Leh

The road between the Kashmir Valley and Ladakh is surfaced almost all the way. It leaves Srinagar heading north-west and winds its way into the Sindh (Indus) Valley. The road goes through rice and maize fields and over partly submerged bridges – old wooden bridges over which the military have built pioneer bridges – crossing the Sindh River. It passes through the villages of Gandarbal, Kangan and Gund before reaching Sonamarg, the last sizeable settlement in the Kashmir Valley. The road was built after the 1962 Indo-Chinese conflict and this must be one of the most fascinating, terrifying and yet exhilarating roads and bus trips in the world.

Sonamarg is less a place to stay than a jumping-off point for trekking tours and riding trips in the mountains; in winter it is a paradise for skiers. Popular trekking tours include Sonamarg-Amarnath Cave, Sonamarg-Thajiwas Glacier, Sonamarg-Wangat. Beyond Sonamarg you reach the border to the Ladakh region. As you climb the Great Himalaya out of Sonamarg you leave behind one world and begin to enter a place that has for many become a sort of Shangri La. The world beyond the Himalaya has always been remote and inaccessible – soaring mountain ranges, snow-covered passes and impossible altitudes have always protected this region from invasion by conquerors or tourists.

SRINAGAR TO KARGIL
Zoji La (110 km from Srinagar)
The first pass, which the road approaches after many winding corners, is the Zoji La (3529 metres). After rainfall or during the spring snow-melt, one must beware of rock slides on this 1000 metre ascent. Due to these rock falls the road is very narrow in places and the Zoji La pass itself is not sealed and its condition depends on how

severe the past winter was. The road up to the pass is exhilarating but early in the season, when the Beacon Road Patrol crews are still working to shore up vast landslides, avalanches and ice slips that have eaten away huge chunks of the road, there are times when you will wonder if you were sane to make this trip.

The bus will crawl through vast walls of ice twice its height, cut by the snow plows and bulldozers, where melting snow rushes out from underneath a towering grey mountain of ice, which could at any moment slip and crush the bus. On other stretches, where the road has disappeared into the valley hundreds of metres below, there will be a narrow track, gouged out by bulldozers and compounded by the trucks and the picks of the labourers, that is barely wide enough to accommodate the wheels of the bus. If you have a window seat looking out into nothingness, reaching the Gates of India, that point in the roadway cut through a wall of rock just below the start of the pass itself, will be a great relief.

The pass is a low flat plain but beyond here the country seems bereft of any form of life. The mountains soar as bare rock and rubble while the river valleys are simply gravel and mud. Yet the clarity of the air and the nature of the countryside compels you to look closer and see the life which is everywhere. There are herbs growing on almost every slope, even the smallest trickle of snow melt will have an accompanying flash of green, and off in the distance you will see herds of goats that blend perfectly into the colour of the mountainside, tended by herders in black robes. Across the passes in the distance you will see laden black dzo plodding steadily onwards. It is as if the countryside, stripped of all its finery and lushness, becomes more visible not less. In a land where there are no trees, the merest twig becomes important. The road will lead you down from the Great Himalaya to a land of great peace and tranquility.

From the heights of the Zoji La pass, the road passes through the region where the Drass River has its source and along the river's valley. The first settlement after the pass is the town of Matayan on the Gumbar River, inhabited by Kashmiris, Dards and Baltis. The people speak Urdu, Dardi, Kashmiri and Balti. The further settlements are mostly on the mountain sides above the road, which passes through the villages of Prandrass and Murad Bagh before reaching Drass in a 15 square km valley.

Drass (147 km from Srinagar)

This is a small village with a TCP and a large military camp on the Drass River, en route to Kargil. The Public Works Department *Rest House* has a tourist officer and stands on the right hand side of the road from Srinagar. It can't be missed as it is directly opposite the *Rahi Tea Stall* where there is 'Hot Tea Available Anytime'. All the buses stop here and tourists are asked to register their names and passport numbers. Drass is famed for its freezing temperatures and heavy winter snowfalls. In this area the dialect spoken is named after the weather – *Hambabs* means snowfall. For trekking from Drass to Sanku (Suru Valley) see the Zanskar section.

From Drass to Kargil the road follows the river, at times running less than five to 10 km from the ceasefire line with Pakistan. At a left-hand curve outside of Drass four 7th century Buddhist bas-reliefs stand next to the road: the Maitriya Buddha, Avalokitesvera, an equestrian figure and a lotus. Beyond Tashgam the valley narrows and the mountain sides on both sides of the river are covered with rocks and pebbles. Shortly before the

Zoji La Pass

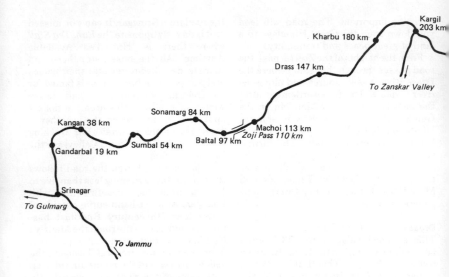

road from the Drass Valley turns off into the Suru Valley a reasonable bridge, passable by jeeps, crosses the Drass River towards the left. This bridge is barred to foreigners as it leads into a restricted military area.

From Drass the road runs to Kharbu (10 km), to Channigund (14 km) and then Kargil (10 km). The villages along the route are all hundreds of metres above the road, on small plateaux. Beyond Tashgam the landscape becomes more rocky, the mountains on both sides of the river reaching 5000 to 5500 metres. The road runs up and down steep passes, through narrow gorges with the river rushing alongside. The final couple of hours on the bus from Drass to Kargil are likely to seem never ending, although you can see tenuous log and rope bridges stretched across the Drass and Kanji Nallah River, and faint trails in the rocks leading upwards.

KARGIL (204 km from Srinagar)
Kargil, at 2650 metres, is the second

largest town in Ladakh and has a population of about 3000. It's situated in a lovely valley with apricot trees growing in the intensively cultivated fields. By the time you get to Kargil you will have been struck by the artificially irrigated fields. Since irrigation is so important in this region, the distribution of water requires great care. Every village is divided into groups, called Gowar, of from five to 10 families, to ensure an equitable arrangement. Willows and poplars grow beside the irrigation ditches which lead to the terraced fields and line the road for much of its length in this region. They furnish building materials for the construction of houses in this nearly treeless land.

The Kargil region actually gets more rainfall than in the rest of Ladakh and the area grows plentiful wheat, barley, vegetables and, of course, the apricots for which it is famous. Peas have been recently introduced and are flourishing.

The town was once an important trading post due to its strategic location at the intersection of trade routes from

Srinagar — Leh
Kilometres from Srinagar

Shergol 237 km
Mulbekh 244 km
Namika Pass 259 km
Bodh Kharbu 274 km
Khalsi 337 km
Lamayuru 310 km
Nurla 348 km
Rizong 363 km
Saspul 372 km
Alchi 370 km
Lekir 382 km
Bargo 392 km
Nimmu 398 km
Spitok 421 km
Leh 434 km
To Manali

Russia to India and from China to the west. Over the last 30 years political changes have considerably reduced its importance. Today it is just a village at the junction of the Drass and Suru Rivers, 20 km from the Indus; a stopping point with hotels, camping facilities and a service station on the road to Leh. The buses to and from Leh stop for the night here and leave for Leh between 4.30 and 5 am.

With the construction of the Zanskar road to Padum, Kargil's importance is likely to increase once again. While in 1974 you could hardly buy anything in the bazaar, it is now possible to purchase everything you would need for a trek, even kerosene stoves. If you are contemplating trekking in Zanskar or Ladakh it is worth pointing out that until Padum travellers must live off their stored supplies for virtually the entire distance and in Padum the choice will be very limited. Anything forgotten in Srinagar should, therefore, be bought here. Due to the strong religious beliefs, great difficulties accompany the purchase of alcohol!

The dialect spoken here is called Purik and shows its relationship with the dialect spoken in Skardu, Pakistan. In contrast to the rest of Ladakh, the children here are taught in Arabic. A momentous occasion in Kargil is the archery contest in May.

Trespone and Sankhoo are two 'Imambaras' found in Kargil. These Turkish-style buildings have Persian and Arabic-speaking Muslim mystics, known as Aghas, in residence. Kargil also has a mosque, the Jami Masjid. Kargil's Muslims are noted for their extreme orthodoxy women are conspicuously absent from the streets and all forms of entertainment are frowned on. Like the Iranians the people follow the Shi'ite sect.

Information
The Kargil tourist office is up the hill behind the Government High School, off the main street. It is open from 10 am to 4 pm, but closed on Sundays. The tourist officer here is less than helpful, but he does have some interesting maps on his

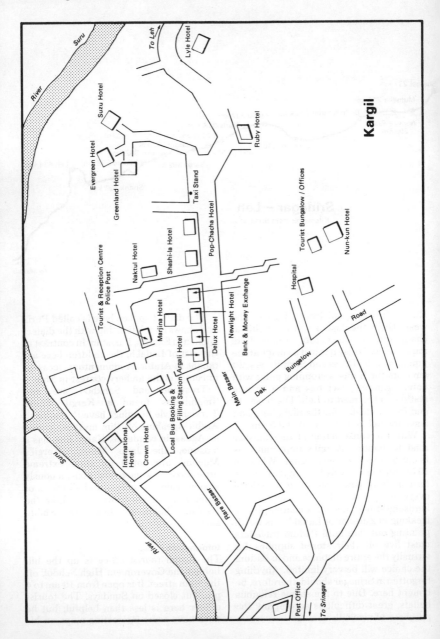

Kargil

wall of the Zanskar region, and a fascinating file on the fate of injured or missing foreign tourists in the region. Beware of the Himalayan black bear, avalanches and bus accidents.

Mohammed Rahi, who owns and operates the Yak Tail Hotel & Restaurant in the main street and the Hotel Marjina, just off the main street, is a good local information source. He is knowledgeable about trekking trails of the area and can offer advice about the condition of the road to Zanskar.

Kargil has two banks; there are no banking facilities in Sonamarg and the only other places in Ladakh are at Leh and Karu.

The main bazaar has many Kashmiri products including embroidery, turquoises, tobacco, raw sugar and exotic spices. You will also find cloth woven from the finest wool from the long-fleeced mountain goats, brass bowls, flower vases, wine cups and tall jugs (used for coffee, tea or other liquors), leather shoes embroidered with silk or gold, silver chains, rings, bracelets and charms, paintings, pashmina shawls, brightly coloured rugs and other more Chinese-looking items. Nearby Tsaluskot is the granary of the region, attracting people from Zanskar and Leh, who come to buy grain. The houses have stone foundations and a superstructure of unbaked, heavy clay bricks.

Trekking Equipment The tourist office in Kargil has some trekking equipment for hire under the same conditions as the Leh office. The equipment includes a number of tents, foam mattresses, sleeping bags, alpine jackets, rucksacks, climbing equipment and so on. Kargil is the starting point for most of the treks and journeys into the Zanskar valley, although it is also possible to enter it from other points along the side of the Leh-Zanskar range.

People of the Kargil Region
Kashmiris once came to the Kargil region to graze their cattle, and were followed by the tribes from Gilgit, Chitral and Mongols from Baltistan who settled there permanently. Later the Mongols were driven out by an Aryan tribe, the Purkpas, who now live around Drass, and the Dokpas, who are Aryan Buddhists, who live in the villages of Durchik and Gurkun, north of Kargil.

The Dokpas, who are Buddhists, are a community of about 700 people, descended from migrants from Gilgit, found mostly in the Indus Valley villages of Durchik and Gurkun. They are known for the striking Aryan beauty of their women, and for their fair skin. They are fond of ornaments – even men wear earrings, necklaces, bracelets and strings of imitation pearls. Both sexes decorate their caps with a variety of blood-red flowers, which puts them apart from all the other races in Ladakh. The Indus Valley here is rich in fruit, particularly grapes, and the Dokpas delight in drink and dance – milk however is taboo. This curious mixture of Buddhist and Hindu religion means their respect for the cow is so intense that even cow dung is never used as a manure or fuel. The people grow their hair long and rarely bathe.

The route to their region, over the range from Kargil to the Indus Valley, and thence down to Leh, is forbidden to tourists because of the border dispute with Pakistan. The remote locality of the lower Indus villages and the custom of marrying mostly among themselves has preserved their distinctive identity. The government of a village is a seven-man council, elected by all the men. In July these villages celebrate a harvest festival which lasts for several days. Gurkun, the main village of the region, is 80 km from Kargil.

Places to Stay
Kargil is a bit of a wild-west town and consists basically of two streets running at right angles to each other; so it's no problem finding anything. If you arrive just after the Zoji La pass is opened you may find accommodation in short supply and prices appropriately higher. Normally throughout the season you should be able to find a double room for around Rs 20, or up to Rs 250 with full board.

The main street hotels are mainly of a pretty poor standard and seem to be getting worse each year. In Kargil's cheap hotels bed bugs seem to be standard equipment. You need to walk down some of the short and dark alleyways to find something reasonable. Most of the hotels cluster around the bus station where the buses arrive around 6 pm and depart around 6 am. This can be important if you are a heavy sleeper!

The better hotels include the *Marjina*, with singles from Rs 80. It has an almost Swiss-alpine look, with its three storeys stacked into a small courtyard behind the first row of shops on the main street. The *Hotel d'Zojila*, which is run by the J&K Tourist Corporation, is inconveniently situated almost three km from town and has doubles from around Rs 90. At the top of the Kargil price scale is the *Highlands Hotel* with 80 beds and doubles at Rs 300.

Altogether Kargil has one A class hotel, two B class, three C class and nine or more D class. Singles/doubles in D class hotels are supposed to be Rs 40/60 but the hotels in that category are generally much cheaper, and deservedly so! The *Yak Tail* charges Rs 5 for a bed or Rs 20 for a double. The *Argalia Hotel* is probably better (cleaner!) value although it is uncomfortably close to Kargil's diesel electricity generator. Fortunately the power goes off at 11 pm. Like all Ladakh towns, Kargil only has electricity from 8 pm.

The *Suru View*, behind the bus stand, has doubles from Rs 50 but it's not all that good. The 'incredible' *Crown Hotel*, down the main street towards the river, has singles at Rs 10, doubles at Rs 15 to 20 and has been recommended. So has the *Hotel Greenlands*, behind the bus stand on the way to the Suru View, where clean doubles with bathroom and blankets are Rs 40.

Kargil has two *Tourist Bungalows*, one with six double rooms, one with 10 double rooms and one deluxe rooms. The ordinary rooms cost Rs 25, deluxe rooms Rs 45. Deluxe rooms have running water. Catering facilities are available at extra cost. The rooms at the new *State Tourist Bungalow*, near the river, are clean, simple and adequate – good value. There is a sign to follow from the main street. Kargil also has a circuit house and a good *PWD Rest House* in a nice location and with good big rooms at Rs 25 for doubles.

Places to Stay around Kargil

Drass has a *Tourist Bungalow* with six double rooms. Tourist bungalows are being built at Mulbekh and Pannikar. Costs are as in Kargil. There are *PWD Rest Houses* at Sanku and Rangdum on the route to Zanskar and at Bodhu Kharbu. Reservations must be made with the Executive Officer in Kargil. Tourist Bungalow reservations can be made with the Tourist Officer in Kargil.

Places to Eat

Food in Kargil tends to be rather expensive and mediocre but the *Light Restaurant* on the main road has good food and is run by friendly folk. They have an interesting variety of teas and home made curd, and they open early enough in the morning to breakfast before the bus departs.

Getting Around

There are local buses around Kargil as well as the summer services between Srinagar and Leh which overnight in Kargil. From Kargil there is a daily bus to Mulbekh (Rs 4.85), to Sanku twice daily (Rs 5.40), to Pannikar on alternate days (Rs 9.55), to Drass on alternate days (Rs 7.20) and to Srinagar on alternate days (Rs 39 A class or Rs 29 B class). The fare to Leh is Rs 35.

Provided the Zanskar valley road is open there is a bi-weekly truck service to Padum with a night halt at Rangdum. Buses on this road are terrifying, they often have to back up to get around sharp corners. The fare to Padum is Rs 35.

Other fares in the area include Khangral Rs 7.45, Chiktan Rs 8.60, Bodh Kharbu Rs 8.40, Menjee Rs 1.50, Trespone Rs 2.65, Silmoon Rs 7.85.

AROUND KARGIL

Mount Kala Pahad (4575 metres) near to Kargil, was under Pakistani control until the 1971 India-Pakistan conflict. In that war the borders of India were pushed further to the west but one still cannot travel directly to the Indus valley and along the Indus to Leh. One must still take the hard way over the Namika La and Fatu La passes and reach the Indus valley by Khalsi. A road is being built around the Namika La pass – 'which touches the sky'. It runs through the forbidden zone, west of the present road.

In this region are the interesting villages of Garkon, Dards, Dardchik and Dha Hanoo, whose population (altogether about 700 people) is light skinned and speaks a language which sounds like Russian, although it also contains elements of Persian and Sanskrit, the languages of Aryan invaders. The remote locality and the custom of marrying only amongst themselves has preserved their distinctive identity right up to the present day. The government of the village is the responsibility of a seven-man village council, chosen by all men in the village. In July these villages celebrate a harvest festival which lasts for several days. Garkon is 80 km from Kargil.

Muta & Polyandry

The custom of 'muta', limited-duration marriages, is still practised in Kargil. The marriage contract signed at the wedding ceremony only applies for a limited time – in some cases only for one day. Another Tibetan marriage custom, which often strikes westerners as remarkable, is polyandry, the simultaneous marriage of more than one man to the same woman. Today polyandry is only practised in outlying villages like Saliskote and Trespone (in the Zanskar region). In this situation a woman marries her husband's younger brothers, except for any who may be monks. Together with the great number of unmarried monks and nuns, this practice functions as a social form of birth control – from Cunningham's visit to Ladakh in the mid-19th century, up to the latest

Monk at Mulbekh

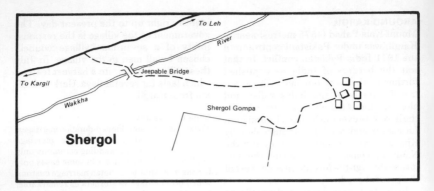

Government of India census, the population of Ladakh has hardly altered.

Zanskar

The recently completed road through the Suru Valley, along which is the Rangdum Gompa, turns south from Kargil and crosses over the Pensi La pass to Padum. The extremely heavy winter of 1983 destroyed much of the road on the passes leading up past Nun and Kun to Rangdum and the road was only open for vehicles as far as Pannikar. At the best of times the road is very rough and negotiable only with difficulty. If the road is open all the way the fare on a truck from Kargil is around Rs 39 or a jeep can be hired for around Rs 2300.

Information on trekking in Zanskar will be found in the Zanskar section. Even in the winter months it is still sometimes possible to reach Srinagar from Kargil by going via Kishtwar, following the Suru River and going over the Bhoktal Pass at a height of 4380 metres.

KARGIL TO LEH
Kargil-Shergol

The road starts to climb shortly after Kargil and leaves the Suru Valley over a small pass in the Wakkha Valley. Here you cross the religious border and see the first smiling Ladakhis with their typical Tibetan-headgear. As the river valley broadens, more and more irrigated barley and wheat fields appear. In early summer there will always be women plowing and planting, in mid-summer women weeding and tending the irrigation canals, and in late summer women harvesting the crops.

Shergol (237 km from Srinagar)

The small village of Shergol is 33 km from Kargil and is the first true Ladakhi village. The village, on the right hand side of the Wakkha River, is hard to see from the road as it lies in a ravine behind a mountain, on the opposite side of the river from the road.

The only visible evidence of the village is the small gompa perched half-way up the eastern slope of this mountain – appropriate to its size the gompa has only two monks who are tended by a single nun. Some of the rooms, such as the kitchen, are hewn from the rock and resemble holes more than rooms. The gompa has some beautiful wall paintings which are well worth seeing. At the foot of the mountain, near the 35-house village (210 inhabitants), there is a less important gompa.

Mulbekh (244 from Srinagar)

A further seven km brings you to this

Wakkha Valley village. The palace of Raja Chalon of Mulbekh is on the left hand side of the road. Above the village on the slopes is a double monastery. It's a difficult ascent, particularly if you are not yet acclimatised to the altitude of Ladakh. Two paths lead to the gompa and the right hand path (monastery mountain to the left) is the easier.

Here, as with all gompas in Ladakh, one should make enquiries beforehand in the village as to whether the monks are present. Often the gompas may be deserted for days at a time as the monks may be out in the fields or in other villages tending to their normal work, leaving the monastery closed up. Only in the mornings and evenings can one be sure of encountering lamas who are not engaged in prayer. We were able to put two lamas of Mulbekh Gompa into action by showing them pictures of the Dalai Lama. These pictures of a holy person are, naturally, also holy and are handled accordingly – carefully touched, pressed on the forehead and reverently returned. With amazing speed the lamas then ascended the mountain and opened the gompas (the Serdung and Gandentse Gompas) for us.

Choose the direct path up to the gompas even though it seems steep for it gives a better view of the Wakkha Valley. A festive highpoint is the harvest thanksgiving festival (Shuba) which is celebrated at the same time in practically all larger Wakkha Valley villages. Mulbekh Shuba is a great attraction during the harvest time when the oracle of Mulbekh makes an appearance. In contrast to the oracle of Shey this one is incarnated in a young farmer.

One should always remove one's shoes when visiting a gompa. If you do not like going barefoot – the floors are often coated with rancid butterfat – take along socks or stockings for these visits. Obviously one should also have a reverent attitude; don't make loud noises or touch holy figures. Remember that mani walls or chortens should always be walked around clockwise with the structure on your right.

Chamba Statue

A km beyond Mulbekh, beside the road on the right hand side, is a seven metre figure

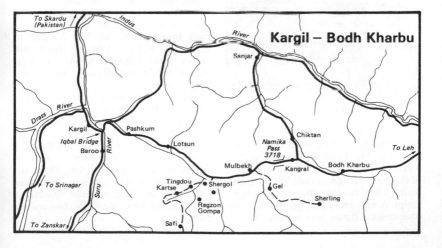

Chamba Statue at Mulbekh

Gel

If you wish to make more than a short pause at Mulbekh and to experience a little of the local way of life then visit the village of Gel. The small village, picturesquely situated on a steep slope above the Wakkha River, still lives (like many Ladakhi villages) in a bygone era. Although it is only a few km from the surfaced road Indian soldiers rarely come here and during a visit there time seems to stand still. When we visited Gel not only did the children cry when they first saw us, but adults held the animals fast in their quarters, barricaded the doors and observed us suspiciously from the roofs of their houses. The ice was rapidly broken, however, when we wanted to buy an expensive *giri* (hand-spindle with distaff). With the construction of the new jeep-road to the Namika La, the modern world is now encroaching upon Gel.

Mulbekh-Lamayuru via the Namika La & Fatu La

From Mulbekh the road climbs through a sandhill landscape to the 3718 metre high Namika La. The descent from the Namika La, with its twisting and turning razorback road, is quite an adventure. The first village beyond the pass is Kangral; a small collection of houses where it may be possible to obtain fuel. Here also a dirt road branches to the left, leading to Stakchey, Samra, Chiktan (with old palace ruins), Sihakar, Sanjar and along the Indus to eventually meet the Kargil-Khalsi road.

The principal town in the valley of the Kanji Nallah is Bodh Kharbu, a large military camp which stretches out on both the right and left sides of the road. In the *PWD Rest House*, on the left hand side of the road, the two travellers' rooms can sometimes be used by tourists. There are many government projects underway during the beautiful summer months so your chances of finding a room free are not good.

The road follows the river for a short

of the Maitriya, or future Buddha, cut into the rock. The figure is thought to date from the Kushan period, around the time of the birth of Christ. Inscriptions found on the side of the rock are in the Kharoshti script. A new small temple, which partly obscures the figure, was built in 1975.

time and then winds its way up to the 4094 metre high Fatu La pass, which is always cool and often windy. This is the highest pass on the Srinagar-Leh road. Although you think you are traversing the most logical point on the pass, you will see yak trains much higher up on the right hand slope, crossing in apparent isolation with their easy and slow gait. If your eyes are good you will be able to see their Ladakhi herders walking along perhaps several hundred metres away. From the top of the pass you get a good view down the river valley towards Kashmir, while ahead you are looking towards the Indus River valley, over several mountain ranges and towards Tibet.

The stretch of road from the pass to Khalsi is one of the most fascinating along the whole route. About 15 km from the top of the pass the old Tibetan monastery of Yungdrung at Lamayuru stands below the road on a crumbling mountain. There is a village on the mountain side.

Lamayuru (310 km from Srinagar, admission Rs 5)

According to an old legend there was, in the valley of Lamayuru, in the time of the Sakyamuni Buddha, a crystal clear lake where the nagas lived. Arahat Madhyantaka prophesied that in later times a monastery would be built there and through a supernatural force he emptied the lake. In the 10th century Naropa, one of the 80 wise men, visited the Valley of Lamayuru and spent many years meditating in a hut.

The first Lamayuru monastery was built under Rinchen Zangbo at the end of the 10th century, under orders from the king of Ladakh, who altogether had 108 gompas built in west Tibet. It was built on the broken mountain in the valley and consisted of five buildings, of which only the central building stands today. One can still see some remains of the four corner buildings to the west. The gompa has an impressive 11-headed, 1000-eyed image

Lamayuru Gompa

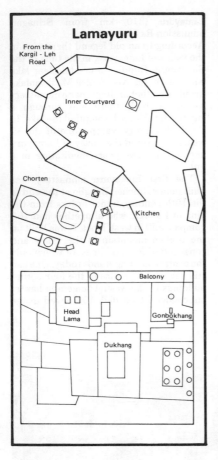

Lamayuru

From the Kargil - Leh Road

Inner Courtyard

Chorten

Kitchen

Balcony

Head Lama

Gonbokhang

Dukhang

Although the monastery has some fields they are insufficient to feed all the monks. Therefore, like practically all other Ladakhi monasteries, they are dependent upon the donations of believers. In order to channel these donations small daughter gompas were erected in outlying villages, their superior lama being the head lama at Lamayuru. Similarly the Sankar Gompa in Leh is an 'under-gompa' of the Spitok Gompa. Several times each year the monks from all the under-gompas come to Lamayuru for general prayers. These colourful occasions, when mask dancing goes on for three days, fall in the second month of the Tibetan calendar (February-March) and in the fifth month (July). During the first festival, which attracts many people from the districts of Sham and Stod, the ritual of hurling a votive offering is observed.

The Drogpo Valley and Lamayuru Gompa first come into sight 14 km beyond the Fatu La pass. The road leads into the village of Lamayuru and on into the valley a short distance beyond this viewpoint. If you do not have a four-wheel drive vehicle and wish to go to the monastery you must continue a few km further along the main road towards Leh. A steep route then leads to the right into the valley, again for four-wheel drive only. It ends at a low, small gateway into a small inner courtyard. Before this gate there is nowhere for a vehicle to turn around. If you wish to see more than just the gompa you should descend to the valley where the village (population about 500) follows its medieval lifestyle at the foot of the monastery mountain.

You should also take a short walk into the fields to see the mani walls, being sure to pass the wall on the left side – ie with the wall on your right. Here at Lamayuru it is interesting that the mani walls, piled up by devout pilgrims, stone by stone, often dragged there from many km away, and

of Chenrezig. In its heyday up to 400 monks lived in the monastery but today there are only 20 to 30 who belong to the yellow-hat sect. Many lamas from Lamayuru now go out to other parts of Ladakh as teachers.

In the 16th century the monastery was declared a holy site in which even criminals could seek sanctuary. For that reason even today it is known to Ladakhis as Tharpa Ling, 'Place of Freedom'.

Right: Lamayuru Gompa

with the mantra 'om mani padme hum' carved on them, have more than a religious significance. These stone walls protect the fields in the valley bottom from the avalanches which can be loosened by snow and rain. Similar mani-guard-walls can be seen past past Khalsi and at Hemis. Leh has the longest mani walls but it is no longer possible to walk the full pilgrim path of several km because it leads into military areas.

Wanla Gompa

Slightly south-east of Lamayuru this gompa is reached by a climb of several km up to the top of a pass. The old monastery was built about a thousand years ago during the time of Rinchen Zangbo. Its main image is of the 11-headed Mahakaruna or Avalokitesvera, which stands more than two storeys high. The wall paintings are of the Buddhas, Bodhisattvas, mandalas and other religious icons. There is also a sacred image of Atisha. Wanla is a point of pilgrimage for people from the districts of Sham, Stod and other parts of western Ladakh and Zanskar. It is on the trekking route from Lamayuru to Padum.

Khalsi (Khalatse, 337 km from Srinagar)

Beyond Lamayuru, the military road winds round many sharp curves, the so-called Langro Curves, on a slope in a side valley of the Indus, then crosses over a barren rocky slope to the river banks. Beware the speedbreakers before the last curve! Near the ruins of old fortifications, with the remains of a hanging bridge, the road crosses a stable iron bridge on the right bank of the Indus. After some sharp bends it passes through a military camp close to where the Khalsi-Gurgurod road branches off to the left. This road will eventually lead directly to Kargil, avoiding the Fatu La and Namika La passes, Khalsi today is a rest stop for buses and has many restaurants on the main road offering reasonably priced food – usually dahl and rice. It's a charming village with abundant dried apricots.

Rizong (363 km from Srinagar)

The Rizong Gompa, and its associated nunnery Julichen (Chulichen), are two of the more interesting places in Ladakh and well worth a visit. Both are of the Gelugpa or yellow-hat sect of the Shas Rimpoche in Dharamsala. Rizong is an active teaching gompa and while 20 to 30 lamas live there, including some young novices, more often than not many of them will be out in villages or other gompas. The monastery was founded in 1829 and stands at 3450 metres. There is always the resident 'manager' Lobsang Tsundus, who is happy to show you around and offer butter tea although he speaks no language other than Ladakhi.

The gompa is built on a sheer rock face and sprawls over seven levels. The approach, up a twisting, narrow gorge of dry, crumbling shale, is spectacular. *An English Buddhist in a Tibetan Monastery*, mentioned in the introductory section on books, describes a stay in the Rizong Gompa. The walk to the gompa takes about 1½ hours from the turn-off. The road was washed away in several places by the heavy snow of 1983 and may not yet be repaired. The last half hour of the walk is steep. Women are not allowed in the gompa after 4 pm, but this rule is flexible – if you arrive at 3.30 pm you will probably be allowed to stay for about an hour.

Follow the road for about about 45 minutes to its end at a low, stone wall, which marks the boundary of the birch woods, apricot groves and barley fields maintained by the nuns at Julichen. The path rises steeply to the left, then flattens out and after about 10 minutes you come to the nunnery. You can camp in the woods at the end of the road and it would be a good idea to set up camp and leave your packs here before tackling the more strenuous part of the walk. There is plenty of wood and fresh water for cooking. You can also leave your packs at Julichen before heading up to Rizong.

Inside the nunnery to the left is a large courtyard where you will find nuns busy

Top: Lamayuru Gompa (GW)
Left: Traversing the Great Himalayan range at Zoji La before the road is open to traffic (BP)
Right: Tanka in Lamayuru Gompa (TW)

Top: In the back streets of Leh (TW)
Left: Monk in Spitok Gompa (TW)
Right: Wall painting in Shergol Gompa (TW)

spinning wool, weaving and drying barley. Some of the nuns object to being photographed. Women may stay at the nunnery but not at the gompa; the opposite situation applies to men. If you do stay you will be expected to survive on tsampa and butter tea unless you bring and prepare your own food.

From Julichen the track winds through barley fields and apricot trees to a fork marked by a chorten, mani walls and blue prayer banner. Take the track to the left, away from the fields and up the dry gully. The track winds steeply upwards past new mani walls and inscriptions – and graffiti – on the slate and mudstone.

As you reach the first chorten the gompa comes into view, at once commanding and surrounded by the sheer, bare hillsides. Just past the gateway chorten is a sign telling visitors that smoking, drinking intoxicating liquor and the eating of meat are forbidden beyond this point. Behind and to the right of the tree on which this sign hangs are two very low-roofed huts, one surrounded by a wall. These huts house pools fed by the spring which is the sole source of water for Rizong. Legend has it that the founder of the monastery caused the spring to appear.

The path now winds steeply up the hillside to the entrance to the gompa, which is a small door on the left side of the third level, not visible from anywhere but the short level path leading to it. The gompa is well maintained and has several large prayer halls, an impressive array of thankas, a large library of well cared for books – most stored behind glass, and a small printing shop for preparing several of the texts from the hand carved wooden blocks, and a fine array of statues.

The most striking aspect of the gompa, however, is the variety, colour and number of the wall paintings. Three stand out: the Tsarchu or 10 lives of the Buddha, which

Left: Mandala in Rizong Gompa

runs around three walls of the chamber with the statues of the Chamba and Cho, the colourful Checkchik to the left of the of the entrance to the Chikhang, and a very old painting of Chinese style and origin of a Chinese scholar in the chapel next to the quarters of the head lama. These latter two are kept covered.

You can also see the stone drum with which the Rizong monks beat out their prayers. The drum is made of a hollowed out tree stump which has been covered with a stone slab. It is hit with a small stone hammer.

Alchi (370 km from Srinagar)

Although there are a great many temples, caves and stupas built in Ladakh by Rinchen Zangbo, Alchi Choskor is the largest and most famous of them all with a widely renowned collection of paintings and painted wooden statues. Some of the artwork here reminded one traveller of Eastern European folk art. A road leads off the highway to a bridge over the Indus at a point 33 km beyond Khalsi and two km before Saspul. The old bridge, which could only be crossed in a small jeep, has been replaced by a new bridge which buses are able to use. Travellers can now travel directly to Alchi along the new graded road.

In the village of Alchi there are many chortens, some of which possess gatelike openings and others have the bases of small towers at their four corners. Alchi is unusual in that it is on lowland, not perched on a hill top like other Ladakhi gompas. Built in the 11th century it is noted for its massive statues of Buddha and its lavish wood carvings and artwork – almost baroque in style. The main structures include the principal one of the Rinchen Lhakhang, the Lotsa Lhakhang

School for Monks in Lekir Gompa

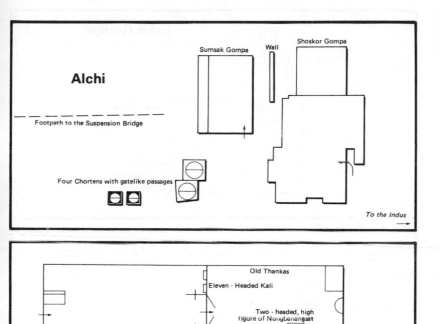

Alchi

Sumsak Gompa

Wall

Shoskor Gompa

Footpath to the Suspension Bridge

Four Chortens with gatelike passages

To the Indus

Old Thankas

Eleven - Headed Kali

Two - headed, high figure of Nungbanangaat

Chorim Bodche

Big Chamba Statue

Shoskor Gompa – Alchi

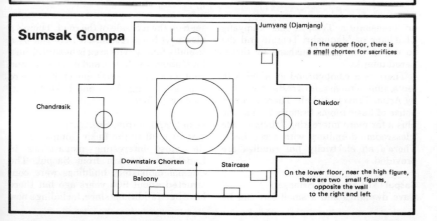

Sumsak Gompa

Jumyang (Djamjang)

In the upper floor, there is a small chorten for sacrifices

Chandrasik

Chakdor

Downstairs Chorten

Staircase

Balcony

On the lower floor, near the high figure, there are two small figures, opposite the wall to the right and left

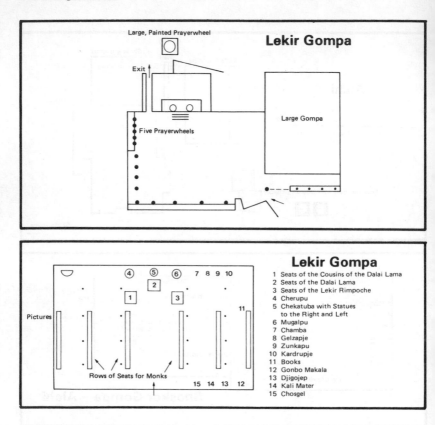

Lekir Gompa

1 Seats of the Cousins of the Dalai Lama
2 Seats of the Dalai Lama
3 Seats of the Lekir Rimpoche
4 Cherupu
5 Chekatuba with Statues
  to the Right and Left
6 Mugalpu
7 Chamba
8 Gelzapje
9 Zunkapu
10 Kardrupje
11 Books
12 Gonbo Makala
13 Djigojep
14 Kali Mater
15 Chosgel

or Translator's Temple, the Jamyang Lhakhang or Manjushri Temple and the so called Sumtsag Lhakhang or three-tiered temple.

There is a campground at Alchi with tents, simple rooms and a restaurant – run by Artou Travels of Leh. There is a row house of basic rooms from Rs 20 a single plus a far more interesting Tibetan-style 'classroom' dormitory with three beds. There's no electricity but candles are provided.

Saspul (372 km from Srinagar)
Cave dwellings and a small fort can be

seen on the left side of the road. There's a nice new hotel-restaurant here run by a friendly family. The area is beautiful, on a bluff above the Indus, and it makes a good spot for a day or two stopover. From here you can Rizong, Alchi and Lekir by bus, jeep or on foot.

Lekir (382 km from Srinagar)
The turn off to the Lekir Gompa, one of the most interesting monasteries in Ladakh, is 9.5 km from Saspul. The original monastery buildings were constructed about 900 years ago but there have been additions since, including a new

Gonkhang which was built in 1983. The gompa looks very much like the Potala in Lhasa. The steep road to the gompa has many hairpin bends but is now a good, all weather road although the bridge over the Lekir River is not very stable. Both the approach to Lekir and the view from its roof are quite outstanding. There are approximately 150 yellow-cap lamas

belonging to the large gompa and the head lama is Tensing Chergal. At Lekir the monks ring out their prayers by hitting a wooden beam which they use as a bell.

The gompa school has 30 pupils who learn three other languages beside Ladakhi. They are Tibetan for religious purposes, Hindi and English. The pupils, who are prepared as recruits for the

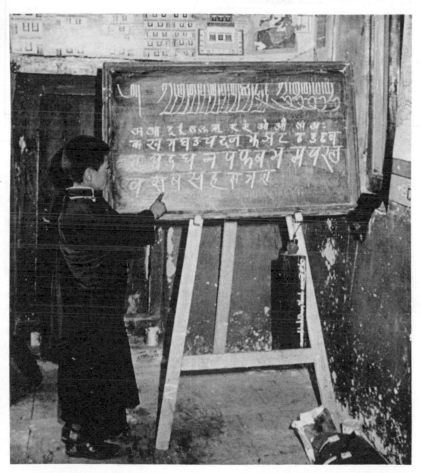

Monk school in Lekir

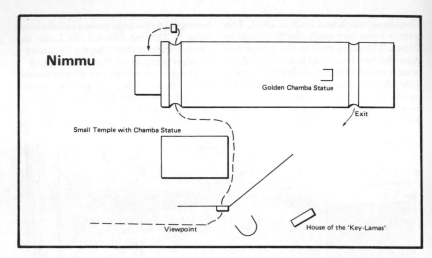

monastery, live part of the time with their parents and part of the time in the monastery. The Indian government also has two elementary schools in Lekir village. There are three grades of lamas – Chunjung, then Gyetsul and the highest grade – Gyelong.

Basgo (392 km from Srinagar)

Above the road at this small town is the heavily devastated Basgo Fort. Basgo Gompa is worth a visit on account of its Buddha figures but, unfortunately, its wall paintings have been badly water damaged. The first gompa has a two-storey high golden Chamba statue in a 'European' sitting pose. The temple has the second

largest Buddha statue in Ladakh and this too is in a 'European' sitting posture. Smaller Chamba statues stand in front of the figure of the white-clothed Chamonada. One of the three monks who live below the gompa in a small house will have the gompa key.

Nimmu (398 km from Srinagar)

On the right hand side of the road in the green fields there are four 'gate' chortens. Just 2.5 km beyond Nimmu the road leads to the place where the Zanskar River flows into the Indus through the Nimmu Gateway (Nimmu Gyasgo), a large cleft rock. From here it is only 35 km to Leh.

Leh & Ladakh

LEH

The capital of Ladakh, Leh is about 10 km north-east of the Indus at the exit of a fertile side valley. From the town down to the Indus, the landscape is almost completely barren. Leh (3505 metres) has a population of 20,000 and a large military camp stands between the town and the airfield, which is also down towards the Indus. There are a number of interesting places to visit in and around this fascinating town but it is equally interesting just to wander the winding back streets of the old town. At one time Leh was a major stopping point on the Asian 'silk route' and a commercial capital in its own right. Today it's important mainly for its military base but also, more recently, as a tourist centre.

Information

The Leh Tourist Office has some climbing and trekking gear for hire at reasonable rates. The quantities are limited but they include waterproof tents (Rs 7 a day), foam mattresses (Rs 2), down jackets (Rs 2), sleeping bags (Rs 3), backpacks (Rs 3) and a variety of climbing gear including ice axes, pittons, rope and so on. The sleeping bags tend to be grubby; get them early enough to be able to wash and dry them before you depart.

Artou Travels have a bookshop in Leh. Try Syed Ali Shah's Postcard Shop for postcards. There is a medical clinic upstairs at the corner of Main Bazaar Rd and Lal Chowk Rd. It opens around 5 or 6 pm. There's also a pathology department at the hospital. Dr Narbu, at the hospital and clinic, has been recommended.

Leh Palace

The old palace of the kings of Ladakh (open 6 to 9 am and from 5 pm) overlooks the town from the south-west slope of the Tsemo hill. It has eight storeys and was built by King Singe Namgyal in the 16th century, at much the same time as the famed Potala of Lhasa – which it resembles. The damage to the palace, one side is gaping open, stems from the Kashmiri invasions of the last century. Like the Shey Palace the Leh Palace still belongs to the Ladakhi royal family, who now live in their palace in Stok.

Few of the palace wall paintings are worth looking at since they have been scratched and smeared over the years. The small Khar Gompa within the palace is also of little interest. In fact the main reason to make the short, steep climb up to the palace is for the superb views from the roof, over which the coloured prayer flags wave in the wind, the lines of which begin on the blue-white-red-green-yellow Tarchock mast. Beware of the many holes in the floors while you're wandering around the palace. In good weather the Zanskar range, snow covered until early summer, appears close enough to touch although it rises from the other side of the Indus.

If you can, get a monk, if one can be found, to unlock the preserved but now unused central prayer room; a dusty, spooky place with huge faces looming out of the dark and two walls lined with religious texts on rice-paper, allegedly 600 years old.

Leh Town

The old town of Leh, with its houses for the aristocrats and servants of the royal household, is clustered at the bottom of the hill under the palace. The new city spreads away from the hill on land which once belonged to the royal family. Due to steady growth in recent years, Leh is becoming increasingly westernised. At one time Leh had a city wall with three gates, one of which still stands close to the market – to the right and uphill towards

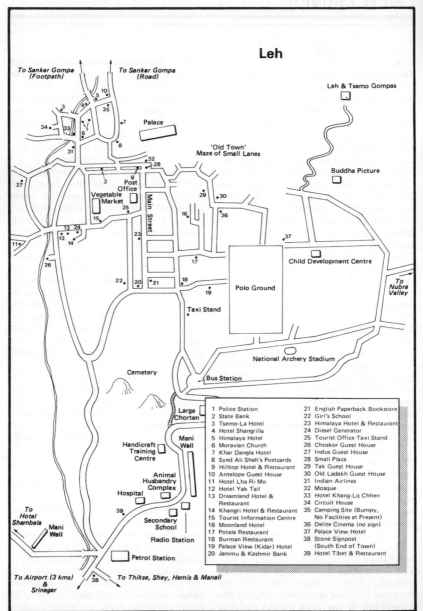

Leh

To Sankar Gompa
(Footpath)

To Sankar Gompa
(Road)

Leh & Tsemo Gompas

Palace

'Old Town'
Maze of Small Lanes

Buddha Picture

Post
Office

Vegetable
Market

Main Street

Child Development Centre

Polo Ground

To Nubra Valley

Taxi Stand

National Archery Stadium

Cemetery

Bus Station

Large
Chorten

Mani
Wall

Handicraft
Training
Centre

Animal
Husbandry
Complex

Hospital

To
Hotel
Shambala

Mani
Wall

Secondary
School

Radio Station

Petrol Station

To Airport (3 kms)
& Srinagar

To Thikse, Shey, Hemis & Manali

1 Police Station	21 English Paperback Bookstore
2 State Bank	22 Girl's School
3 Tsemo-La Hotel	23 Himalaya Hotel & Restaurant
4 Hotel Shangrilla	24 Diesel Generator
5 Himalaya Hotel	25 Tourist Office Taxi Stand
6 Moravian Church	26 Choskor Guest House
7 Khar Dangla Hotel	27 Indus Guest House
8 Syed Ali Shah's Postcards	28 Small Plaza
9 Hilltop Hotel & Restaurant	29 Tak Guest House
10 Antelope Guest House	30 Old Ladakh Guest House
11 Hotel Lha Ri Mo	31 Indian Airlines
12 Hotel Yak Tail	32 Mosque
13 Dreamland Hotel &	33 Hotel Khang-Lq Chhen
Restaurant	34 Circuit House
14 Khangri Hotel & Restaurant	35 Camping Site (Bumpy,
15 Tourist Information Centre	No Facilities at Present)
16 Moonland Hotel	36 Delite Cinema (no sign)
17 Potala Restaurant	37 Palace View Hotel
18 Burman Restaurant	38 Stone Signpost
19 Palace View (Kidar) Hotel	(South End of Town)
20 Jammu & Kashmir Bank	39 Hotel Tibet & Restaurant

the palace. The gate is called Kingsgate because only the king and his family were allowed to use it. The chorten above the city is the remains of a royal leisure site.

Leh Gompa

The Leh Gompa stands high above the palace and also overlooks the ruins of the older palace of the king of Tagpebums. The Red Gompa (Tsemo Gompa) was built in 1430 by King Gvags-Pa-Bum-Ide and has a fine three-storey high seated Buddha figure flanked by Avalokitesvara on the right and Manjushri on the left. The walls have recently been brightly painted and the gompa is open from 7 to 9 am. In all there are three gompas at the top of the hill, the topmost one is in a very ruined condition but offers extremely fine views over Leh and the surrounding countryside. To the right of the palace you can see a Buddha painted on the rocks, a remnant of an earlier monastery.

Other Leh Gompas

There are a number of lesser gompas in the old town of Leh – such as the Guru Lakhang to the left of the palace, beneath the large chorten. The Chamba Lakhang, south of the palace, and the Chenrezig Lakhang, to the south-east, are similarly neglected since they contain little of interest compared to other more splendid gompas around Leh.

In the centre of Leh the new monastery or Gompa Soma or Jokhang was built by the Buddhist Association of Ladakh in 1957. It contains an image of the Buddha Sakyamuni that was brought from Tibet. Meetings of the Buddhist Association are held in this monastery.

Mani Walls

Near the Leh radio station there are two long mani walls. The one in the centre of the open plain is known as Rongo Tajng and was built as a memorial to Queen Skalzang Dolma by her son Dalden Namgyal about 1635. It is about half a km long and contains many hundreds of thousands of mani inscriptions carved in stone in Tibetan. At its end there is the Stupa of Enlightenment and the Stupa of Victory.

The second long mani wall, further down the hill from this one, is said to have been built by Tsetan Namgyal in 1785 as a memorial to his father King Tsewang Namgyal, and is about 350 metres long.

Leh Fort

The Leh fort, built by Zorawar Singh, contains three temples but cannot be visited because it is within the military camp area.

Wedding Ceremonies

A visitor to Ladakh rarely has a chance to see a Buddhist wedding performance according to the old customs and ceremonies. Today too much foreign influence is likely to have crept in, European clothing is slowly replacing the traditional dress. In 1975 we were fortunate enough to be guests at a wedding performed according to the old rites.

The celebration began at 10 pm in the house of the bride. The all-male party celebrated with chang which, according to custom, one must take in three consecutive draughts. As a special sign the host improved the chang by adding butter. A celebration meal was served at 2 am, but again only men partook. The bride remained in her mother's kitchen, symbolically indicating where her place was! Clothed in a wedding gown with a silver-embroidered cape, decorated with old family jewellery, the bride is overwhelmed with lucky white ribbons (katahs) and given gifts of money by her relatives and friends. While the men sing and the mother laments, the bride then goes to the family of the bridegroom, where she is met, in front of the house, by lamas.

Now the celebration proper begins. In a long ceremony, in which the bride must first of all refuse the food which is offered to her, the bride is led from her father or a friend of the family, to her husband, with whom she then symbolically partakes of a meal. She is then shown the house, with particular emphasis on the (her) kitchen. By sunrise the ceremony is concluded, but not the celebration which is a social occasion for the families with musicians, food and much, much chang.

Funeral Ceremonies

Near to the palaces at Stok, Shey and Leh you may notice a large number of chortens, the old 'pleasure gardens' of the kings of Ladakh. If you go into the side valley, to the north-east of Leh, on whose eastern slopes the road to the Nubra Valley begins, you may find (particularly with the help of a local) a large stone where a curious funeral practice was once conducted. The bodies of the dead were hacked to pieces and ground up with stones then left to be devoured by vultures. This practice was also followed in Tibet and is still followed in the Mustang region of Nepal.

Today the site of dismemberment is used for cremations. After a ceremony in the house of the dead person the corpse is tied up in a covered sedan chair. Accompanied by lamas the procession makes its way into the side valley near Leh. A few hundred metres north-west of the chortens the procession halts and the chair is placed in a walled oven. This is really only a vertical tube with a firehole underneath. The fire is started with many prayers and during the long ceremony oil is frequently thrown into the oven until the cremation is complete. The ashes are scattered into a holy river or, in the case of a person of high standing, placed in a chorten.

Places to Stay

There are an amazing number of hotels and guest houses in Leh and it is also relatively easy to arrange accommodation in private homes. Indeed many of the smaller guest houses are simply private homes which rent the odd room out. Prices are extremely variable, dropping right down in the off-season when there are very few visitors in Leh and shooting up in the high-season. Many places close down completely over the winter. Prices quoted below are for the high-season; cheaper places may halve (or more) their rates during the off-season although the more expensive hotels are less likely to be so variable. Leh's hundred-plus hotels and guest houses are categorised by the tourist office with official room prices ranging from around Rs 10 to nearly Rs 500. There's also a hotel tax of 5% on rooms at under Rs 100, 8% for rooms from Rs 100 to 200, 12% on rooms above Rs 200.

Places to Stay – bottom end

In the rock bottom category you can find doubles under Rs 30 (less in the off-season) and dormitory beds at Rs 5. Some places in this bracket also provide bed bugs at no extra cost so take care! Popular cheapies include the *Palace View Kidar Hotel*, close to the polo ground. It also has a collection of braying donkeys for your night time entertainment but it's 'run by a lovely woman who usually meets the bus dressed in her traditional costume. You eat meals in her elaborate kitchen, lovely breakfasts; nice atmosphere'. There's a second, unrelated, Palace View Hotel on the other side of the polo ground.

The *New Antelope Guest House* has dorm beds for Rs 5. The *Moonland Guest House* is in the upper-cheap bracket, the *Old Ladakh Guest House* (quite close by) is similarly priced – both in the old part of town. The *Rainbow Guest House* has doubles from Rs 15 or 20 and is run by a pleasant family who prepare good food. It's far enough away from the generator to be quiet. The *Himalayan Hotel* is friendly, with a garden and doubles at Rs 35.

In the middle price category there is the *Khangri Hotel*, just down the road from the tourist office and uncomfortably close to the diesel generator. As in Kargil the power goes off around 11 pm. Rooms cost from Rs 100. The side-by-side Glacier View and Karakoram have been renovated, upgraded and amalgamated to create the *Tsemo-La Hotel*. It's fairly close to the centre and has a pleasant garden, an attraction shared by many of Leh's hotels. The *Hotel Yak Tail* is also in this price category and is next to the Dreamland Hotel, on the road leading to the Lha-Ri-Mo. There are a number of good guest houses out in the fields beyond the Lha-Ri-Mo, off the road to Skara village.

Right: Looking over Leh with the Leh Palace in the background

With rooms from around Rs 50 (none of them with attached baths), a pleasant garden and one of the best restaurant in town, the *Dreamland* is a very popular hotel choice and also very close to the centre. In a quiet area of the town, directly beneath the ruins of Leh Palace, the *Hotel Kardungla* has rooms from around Rs 120 although they're often available cheaper. The upstairs doubles have attached bathrooms, thick carpets and blankets and hot water is available in the evenings. The new and clean *Kahyul Hotel* costs Rs 40/60 for singles/doubles in season; rooms have attached bathrooms. It's very quiet, well away from the generator, but the owners are Kashmiris so you have to be certain you know what you're getting for your money – exactly how many buckets of water.

Places to Stay – top end

As Leh's status as an international attraction grows the number of 'upper notch' hotels is rapidly increasing. Most of Leh's more expensive hotels are fairly new, almost without exception they quote all-inclusive prices. There is not a great choice of restaurants in Leh. Upper bracket hotels include the *Shambala Hotel*, rather a long way out of town, off towards the edge of the valley.

Two recently completed hotels closer to the centre are the *Kang-Lha-Chhen* (tel 39) and the *Hotel Lha-Ri-Mo*, both with rooms from Rs 350 and both within easy walking distance of the centre of Leh. The fourth more expensive hotel is the *Hotel Indus*, out of town on the Hemis road. There are many, many other hotels all around the town – some in the winding, narrow streets of the old town; others out in the rice paddies to the other side of town. Leh also has several 'official' places which you are less likely to get in to: there's a *Dak Bungalow*, in which the tourist office is located, and the *Leh Motel* out towards the airport.

Places to Stay around Leh

There are places to stay in a number of the villages and gompas around Leh. The tourist department has *Tourist Bungalows* in Sakti, Saspul and Khalsi as well as in Leh. Each has a minimum of six double rooms and costs Rs 25 for an ordinary double, Rs 45 for a deluxe room and an extra Rs 4 for bedding.

Many villages are now taking advantage of the number of tourists and have established small co-operative hotels:

Alchi A guest house with eight beds.

Chipkyangchen At this village, between Kargil and Leh near Lamayuru, the hotel is near the road, not in the town and consists of a guest house with six beds.

Hemis A hotel-restaurant with 10 beds and food served on order. There are numerous camping sites near the monastery.

Khalsi A hotel-restaurant with 10 beds and a *PWD Rest House* with 10 beds.

Lamayuru Three hotel-come-restaurants with a total of 22 beds. There is also an excellent camping site.

Nemo A forest rest house with six beds but no food is available.

Nurla A guest house-restaurant with six beds and a good camping site.

Phyang A hotel-restaurant.

Sakti A *Tourist Bungalow* with eight beds.

Saspul Two hotel-restaurants with 12 beds, a *Tourist Bungalow* with eight beds and a good camping site.

Shey A tea stall near the foot of the Shey palace where accommodation can be obtained.

Stok A hotel-restaurant with 30 beds in Yurt tents. There is also an expensive A class hotel here.

Tikse There's the popular *Shalzang Chamba* hotel-restaurant with 16 beds and doubles at Rs 15. There's also a forest rest house with four beds but no food is available.

Places to Eat

Leh's restaurant possibilities have definitely improved in recent years, a result of the growing tourist trade. The better restaurants now offer a variety of Chinese, Indian and Tibetan meals with chow mein, mo mo and various other noodle and rice dishes high on the list of favourites.

For a long time, far and away the best place to eat was the *Dreamland Restaurant*, right by the Dreamland Hotel and close to the centre. It's still a very popular place to meet and eat but other restaurants now give it stiff competition. The Dreamland is clean, friendly and very reasonably priced – most dishes are around Rs 10. Tibetan kothay, various chow meins and other noodle dishes top the bill and make a pleasant change from rice, rice and more rice if you've been in India long. They also do nice jasmine tea and breakfast here, of Ladakhi bread and apricot jam, is terrific.

Just across the road and up the stairs is the newer *Om Restaurant*, which is trying to be all things to all people. The service can be a little slow and the food is a little more expensive than elsewhere but it's very good – a spot for a real night out. Just up the road from the vegetable market or down the road from the State Bank of India, the *Tibetan Restaurant* maintains its reputation for excellent, cheap and nourishing food. The staff also get the prize for being the most entertaining, especially as you walk through the kitchen on your way in and out. The Tibetan still has no windows and you sit virtually in the street, which can be a disadvantage when the beggars arrive.

Almost next door to Dreamland is the *Khangri Restaurant* which is nice (but not quite so nice) and fairly cheap (but not quite so cheap). Good for a change of pace. The unlikely named *Chopsticks* sells wonderful pies and cakes and late night snacks. It's on the road which leads down to the library at the end of the street with all the Tibetan clothing stalls. The *Hotel Pamposh* tea stall on Lal Chowk is good for tea, coffee, curd and fresh bread. The *Nepali Cafe* is also good.

After these places the standards drop rapidly. There are many little places around the town centre and a string of Indian restaurants at the bottom end of the main street selling good Indian sweets and remarkably insanitary looking food. OK for a cup of tea but take care with anything else.

Or you can buy fresh vegetables from the pavement market at the top of the main street. There's a more official vegetable market too. Early in the morning you can get delicious hot, freshly baked bread from the cluster of little bakery stalls in the back streets by the mosque. They're clustered on the road that leads up to Ali Shah's Postcard Shop or the Hotel Kardungla. It's cooked Middle East style in hole-in-the-ground ovens and is great for breakfast with honey – bring the latter with you from Srinagar. Most hotels and guest houses will provide a basic Tibetan breakfast of bread, jam and tea, and in some cases eggs, if you ask. Some hotels will also provide evening meals.

Schools

Besides the monastery schools the Indian government has 380 educational establishments including over 200 primary schools in Ladakh. In 1971 literacy in Ladakh was still only 14%. There are over 200 Ladakhi students at universities in Srinagar, Jammu and elsewhere in India. They receive a monthly stipend of Rs 75 from the Indian government. We always found it interesting to visit the primary schools. We took some film in the village school at Parka, I photographed a schoolgirl standing with the typical wooden panel on which they write with a wooden stylus and thinned clay-liquid. The pupils draw a line for writing in a noteworthy manner – a string with chalk rubbed in is pressed onto the board and then plucked like a musical string. The result is a very sharp line. The Tibetan alphabet is learned by the pupils singing together.

Getting There

See the introductory Ladakh section for information on getting to Ladakh by air or land. Getting bus tickets for the return trip to Srinagar can be rather confusing. They're reluctant to sell tickets to Srinagar until they know the buses have turned up from Srinagar. If you want to travel by truck the truck park is next to the bus stand, prices are generally Rs 40 or 50 but the tourist office does not approve of visitors using trucks and may make it difficult for you. The trucks driven by Sikhs are probably best.

Official rates for hiring jeeps or taxis from Leh to Kargil or Srinagar are:

	Kargil	Srinagar
taxi	Rs 700	Rs 1575
jeep	Rs 805	Rs 1811
Jonga*	Rs 840	Rs 1890

*six seater

If the road from Kargil to Padum is open a jeep from Leh to Zanskar will cost Rs 3500 one-way or Rs 5100 return.

Getting Around

Buses One of the easiest ways to get around the Indus Valley is to use the local bus service. The buses are extremely crowded, run down and look as though they will never get to where you want to go, but they always do. It is one of the better ways of getting close to the local people. You will share the bus with Ladakhis, Zanskaris, Dards, goats, chickens, monks, bales of hay and piles of wood. The local custom is that everyone, including women and children, stand up to give their seats to a monk.

However unreliable they may look, the buses are cheap and they usually run on time. The main problem is that there are not enough of them and there may be only one service a day to the more remote parts where you want to go. Another local custom is that you need to get to the bus stop in Leh almost an hour before the bus goes if you want to get a seat. This has its advantages and disadvantages. If you are likely to be on a very crowded bus, and you are jammed into a seat by an aisle full of people, you may not be able to get out when you want to, or even to get fresh air. On the other hand the roofs on the buses are very low and it is impossible for an average sized westerner to stand up in them. In this case your journey can be quite uncomfortable.

If you are not sure if you are on the right bus just ask. Ladakhis are very friendly and helpful people and they will soon tell you what you want to know, as best they can. In season the J&K Tourist Office may offer bus tours of the area. The main services from Leh are:

route	dist.	buses daily	fare
Choglamsar	8 km	4	Rs 1.20
Chushot	25 km	3	Rs 3.30
Hemis	45 km	1	Rs 6.00
Khalsi	98 km	1	Rs 12.95
Matho	27 km	2	Rs 3.75
Phyang	22 km	3	Rs 3.10
Sabu	9 km	2	Rs 1.35
Sakti	51 km	1	Rs 6.95
Saspul	62 km	1	Rs 7.90
Shey	16 km	2	Rs 2.10
Spitok	8 km	2	Rs 1.20
Stok	17 km	2	Rs 2.85
Tikse	20 km	3	Rs 3.00

For trips further afield there are daily buses to Kargil costing Rs 39 (A class) or Rs 34 (B class). For Lamayuru (124 km) take a Kargil bus (Rs 16.10). For Lekir (54 km) a Khalsi or Kargil bus will get you there (Rs 7.10). For Karu (40 km, Rs 4.85),

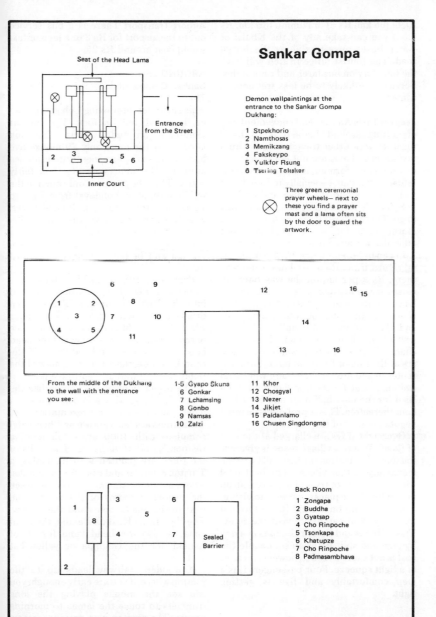

Sankar Gompa

Seat of the Head Lama

Entrance from the Street

Inner Court

Demon wallpaintings at the entrance to the Sankar Gompa Dukhang:

1 Stpekhorio
2 Namthosas
3 Memikzang
4 Fakskeypo
5 Yulkfor Rsung
6 Tsering Tsltaker

Three green ceremonial prayer wheels— next to these you find a prayer mast and a lama often sits by the door to guard the artwork.

From the middle of the Dukhang to the wall with the entrance you see:

1–5 Gyapo Skuna
6 Gonkar
7 Lchamsing
8 Gonbo
9 Namsas
10 Zalzi
11 Khor
12 Chosgyal
13 Nezer
14 Jikjet
15 Paldanlamo
16 Chusen Singdongma

Sealed Barrier

Back Room

1 Zongapa
2 Buddha
3 Gyatsap
4 Cho Rinpoche
5 Tsonkapa
6 Khatupze
7 Cho Rinpoche
8 Padmasambhava

Alchi (65 km, Rs 8) or Nimmu (36 km, Rs 4.50) you can take any of the Khalsi or Kargil buses operating along the Kargil road. The tourist office in Leh will have the full story on bus fares and timetables. Services are likely to be less frequent in winter.

Jeeps & Taxis An easy and convenient way of getting around Ladakh is to band together with other travellers and hire a taxi or jeep. Taxis are not cheap and the drivers have formed a union and now refuse to bargain, especially in Leh, but if you cannot stand the crush and endless delays of the buses, they are the only way to go. There are set fares for some longer journeys and for certain local trips, but other destinations must be by negotiation.

In general taxis charge Rs 3 per km or, on return trips, Rs 3 per km on the way there, Rs 2 per km on the way back. In most cases a loading of 30% is added for longer routes and sightseeing tours. The charge for the long tours to monasteries and places of interest usually includes a wait of one hour for which there is no charge. Beyond one hour wait the charges are at the rate of Rs 10 an hour. For local routes in and around Leh there will be no waiting charge for the first half hour, then Rs 5 for the next half hour and Rs 10 an hour thereafter. This is probably the most negotiable part of the taxi trip.

Overnight stays are charged at the rate of Rs 80. Where a village name is given as the route destination the fare will be to the monastery of that village. The best deal will probably be to try and negotiate an all in cost for all the places you wish to visit in one day. Count on around Rs 300 to 350 for a day. You can easily visit the Shey, Tikse, Hemis and Spitok Gompas in a day by jeep and split between six people the cost is not excessive. Six, however, is a bit of a tight squeeze. Four passengers fills a jeep comfortably and five is getting tight.

Airport Transport There is a bus service out to the airport for Rs 2 or a jeep or taxi would cost around Rs 25.

AROUND LEH

Sankar Gompa (3 km, entrance fee Rs 10)

This small but interesting Leh gompa can easily be visited on foot. The Sankar Gompa is an under-gompa of Spitok Gompa. At the most only 20 monks live here and few are permanently in residence although the monastery itself is fairly active. Thus the gompa is only open to the public (except on holidays) from 7 am to 10 am and from 5 to 7 pm. It is, however, well lit, so an evening visit is worthwhile. At these times the monks will welcome you and may offer you yak butter tea, tsampa and boiled and spiced mustard plant.

From the yard you climb the steps to the front room or Dukhang. Double doors lead into the Dukhang proper. Three green drums immediately attract the eye, under which, to the right of the door, is the place of the Gyeskos. From the seat of the head lama, who is also the head lama of the Spitok Gompa, there is a good view of the richly painted wall and entrance door.

The upper floor of the gompa has the Dukar Lakhang with a Dukar figure – a most impressive representation of Avalokitesvara (also known as Chenrezig) complete with 1000 arms (all holding weapons), and 1000 heads. The walls of the room are painted with mandalas, a Tibetan calendar and rules for the monks. Above a wooden stairway you can also see the residence rooms of the head lama, next to the guest rooms and the library. The Venerable Kushok Bakula, the head lama, is also the head lama for all of Ladakh for the Gelugpa or yellow-hat sect.

A wooden stairway leads up to the rooftop where, if you are early enough, you will see the monks playing the long trumpets to rouse the lamas to morning prayer. The rooftop also provides a view

Top: Crossing the Himalaya from Srinagar to Leh, with Kun and Nun below (TW)
Left: Window shopping in Leh (TW)
Right: Main street of Leh (TW)

Top: Leh, with the palace in the background and the Leh Gompa above it (TW)
Left: Tikse Gompa (TW)
Right: A visit to the tailor in Leh (TW)

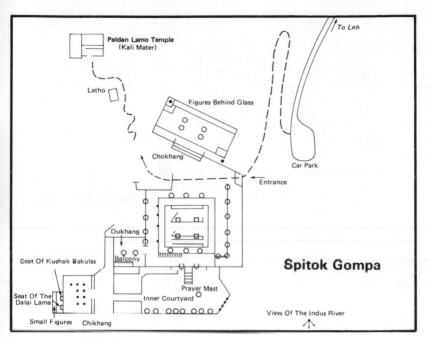

Paldan Lamo Temple
(Kali Mater)

Latho

Figures Behind Glass

Chokhang

Car Park

Entrance

To Leh

Dukhang

Seat Of Kushok Bakula

Balcony

Seat Of The Dalai Lama

Small Figures   Chikhang

Inner Courtyard

Prayer Mast

Spitok Gompa

View Of The Indus River

Wallpaintings in the high prayer room of Spitok Gompa:

1 Maharkala
2 Jame Daka
3 Mahakala
4 Jamaransa
5 Setapa
6 Kali Devi
7 Chamching
8 Wamchass

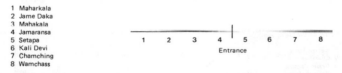

1   2   3   4   5   6   7   8

Entrance

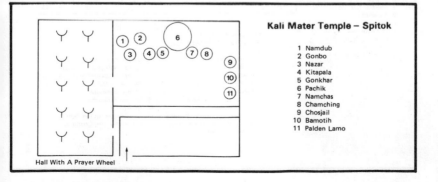

Kali Mater Temple – Spitok

1 Namdub
2 Gonbo
3 Nazar
4 Kitapala
5 Gonkhar
6 Pachik
7 Namchas
8 Chamching
9 Chosjail
10 Bamotih
11 Palden Lamo

Hall With A Prayer Wheel

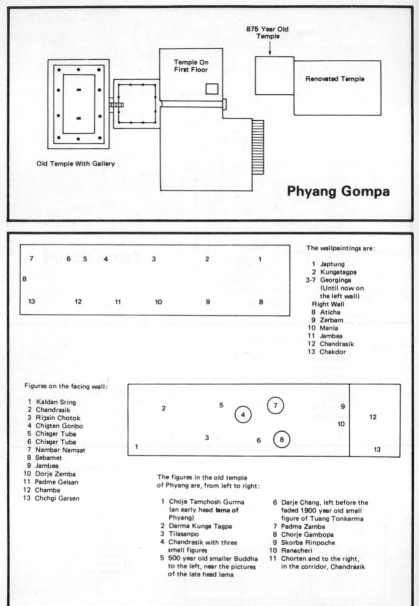

875 Year Old Temple

Temple On First Floor

Renovated Temple

Old Temple With Gallery

Phyang Gompa

The wallpaintings are:

1 Japtung
2 Kungatagpa
3-7 Georginga
(Until now on the left wall)
Right Wall
8 Aticha
9 Zerbam
10 Manla
11 Jambea
12 Chandrasik
13 Chakdor

Figures on the facing wall:

1 Kaldan Sring
2 Chandrasik
3 Rigsin Chotok
4 Chigten Gonbo
5 Chisger Tuba
6 Chisger Tuba
7 Nambar Namsat
8 Sebamet
9 Jambea
10 Dorje Zemba
11 Padme Gelsan
12 Chamba
13 Chchgi Garsen

The figures in the old temple of Phyang are, from left to right:

1 Choje Tamchosh Gurma (an early head lama of Phyang)
2 Darma Kunga Tagpa
3 Tilasanpo
4 Chandrasik with three small figures
5 500 year old smaller Buddha to the left, near the pictures of the late head lama
6 Darje Chang, left before the faded 1900 year old small figure of Tuang Tonkerma
7 Padma Zamba
8 Chorje Gambopa
9 Skorba Rinpoche
10 Ranacheri
11 Chorten and to the right, in the corridor, Chandrasik

out across the endless valley and the town of Leh.

There is a concrete path all the way from Leh to the front door of the gompa. You find the path by going past Ali Shah's Postcard Shop, turning left at the Antelope Guest House and right at the first path which runs alongside the stream.

Spitok Gompa (10 km from Leh, entrance fee Rs 13)

There are 125 yellow-cap monks at this monastery which stands on a small mountain above the Indus. You pass it on the way into Leh on the right hand side of the road and it's also very close to the end of the Leh airport runway. You can walk to the monastery from Leh in two hours but take care not to wander into the military zone.

There is the grave of a very high reincarnation at the gompa and the Spitok head lama is also the head lama of the Sankar Gompa in Leh. He also represents Ladakh as a member of the Indian Parliament. Gurphug in Stok and Pashi Gephel in Sabu are also under-monasteries of Spitok. The gompa has three chapels of which the highest, the Paldan Lamo Temple (Kali Mater), is the most impressive. The temple (Gonkhang) is approximately a thousand years old.

From the highest point on the Spitok hill you have a good view over the Indus Valley, the village of Spitok at the foot of the hill, of Pharka lying opposite, of the mountains, usually snow-covered even in summer, which divide the Indus Valley from Zanskar and last, but not least, of Leh. Don't take photographs looking back towards Leh because the airport, between the monastery and Leh, is classified as a military area. From Paldan Lamo Temple, on the peak of the mountain, a small path leads past a red Latho to the monastery proper. The built-in Dukhang is well worth seeing.

The area around the wall paintings, with its tankas, prayer-flags, bookshelves and books, is well illuminated. Near the Dukhang there are several other chapels of which the new Chokhang is above some stairs. Here funeral ceremonies can be witnessed. Many of the small, old prayer rooms, the head lama's room, and the rooms of the monk are, unfortunately, no longer shown to foreigners. They contain some wonderful wall paintings, tankas, silver chortens, Buddha figures, statues of other deities and hundreds of books but some thoughtless tourist took objects as souvenirs.

From the level of the Dukhang 19 steps lead up to the inner courtyard with a flagpole around which, on the 28th and 29th days of the 11th month of the Tibetan calendar (mid-winter), the Spitok Gostor is celebrated with mask dances. At this festival the 'Jelbagh' dance masks, like those hanging on the walls of the monastery, are no longer used but rather true-to-life representations. The monastery has a statue of Kali whose face is only shown once a year.

Phyang (or Fiang) (24 km from Leh towards Srinagar, entrance fee Rs 10)

An access road leads to the monastery to the right of the main road. Phyang village is in the river valley, a few hundred metres walk away. Again you must take care when photographing – the barren mountainside opposite Phyang is a military zone! Phyang Lake, to the north of the gompa, is in a restricted area and off limits.

The Phyang Gompa has 50 lamas and seven 'novices' of the red-cap sect and possesses five chapels. The monastery is interesting for its museum containing some old Chinese, Tibetan, Mongolian and possibly Serasan weapons and armour. The museum room itself is said to be nearly 900 years old. The monastery has had several renovations recently, including the addition of a large house for the head lama and a new entrance hall with a large prayer wheel. The 650 year old Dukhang Temple was renovated in the late '70s.

Signpost for the Beacon Highway

Phyang's large and colourful festival rivals that of Hemis in the crowds it attracts. However, it had always been held in winter, until recently, when the lamas decided to move it to summer to take advantage of the tourist season! New rest houses have been built by the lamas to accommodate the anticipated crowds.

If you go down into the village of Phyang from the monastery or the main road you may be able to see a wonderful kitchen in a Phyang farmhouse. The summer kitchen in the upper storey is so lavishly equipped with dishes inherited over the generations that you feel like you are in a living museum. The sturdily built farmhouses generally have three storeys. The stables and storerooms are found on the ground floor. Above these is the so-called 'winter kitchen', which also serves as the living and sleeping room for the entire family during the winter. These close living arrangements, plus 'floor heating' from the stables beneath, conserves precious fuel (usually wood or dried cattle dung). A small animal may also be kept in this collective living room over the winter.

In the summer the family moves up to the top storey, which is often just a summer kitchen set on the roof. They sleep under the stars in summer. In Leh you may also see houses on whose roofs groundsheets are spread out, under which the house owners live, as if they are camping in tents. The summer night temperatures are low enough to make westerners reach for their sleeping bags, but they don't bother the Ladakhis at all. They're a hardy race! At a festival in Bodh Kharbu we saw a cook who, in the absence of a drinking vessel, took a draught of boiling butter tea in his cupped hands and drank from that as if it had been no more than a handful of cold water. Rich farmhouses will have special drinking vessels for butter tea or chang.

Beacon Highway

The Beacon Highway leads from Leh into the Nubra Valley over a pass at 5606 metres – making it probably the highest road in the world. 'You can have dialogue with God' according to the road builder's sign! Only in September and October is the road open, at other times ice covers the road on the northern side of the Nubra Valley. For foreigners the road is closed year round since the Nubra Valley is in the restricted area and can only be visited with special permission. The Nubra Valley may, however, soon be opened to visitors.

Tibetan Refugee Camp (9 km from Leh)

Near Choglamsar, on the left side of the Leh-Shey road and close to the Indus, is the Sonam Ling refugee camp. More than 2000 refugees have lived here, under the most primitive conditions, since the early '60s. They have managed to grow some vegetables on this rocky ground but live mainly on the donations of international aid organisations, having had to come to terms with the change from the mountain heights to the banks of the Indus. They also earn some money from handicrafts, particularly the manufacture of Tibetan carpets. The Tibetans are known as fair dealers and have only slowly infiltrated the Kashmiri dominated artifacts business in Ladakh.

View from Phyang Gompa

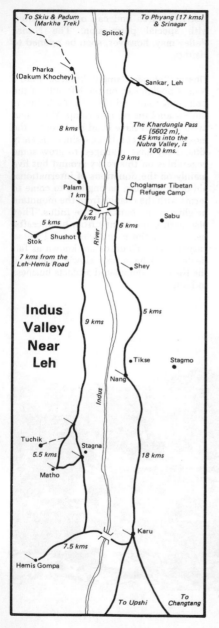

To Skiu & Padum
(Markha Trek)

To Phyang (17 kms)
& Srinagar

Spitok

Pharka
(Dakum Khochey)

Sankar, Leh

8 kms

The Khardungla Pass
(5602 m),
45 kms into the
Nubra Valley, is
100 kms.

9 kms

Choglamsar Tibetan
Refugee Camp

Palam
1 km

2
kms

Sabu

5 kms

6 kms

Stok   Shushot
            River

7 kms from the
Leh-Hemis Road

Shey

**Indus
Valley
Near
Leh**

9 kms

5 kms

Tikse   Stagmo

Nang

Tuchik   Stagna

Indus

5.5 kms

18 kms

Matho

Karu

7.5 kms

Hemis Gompa

To Upshi

To
Changtang

Choglamsar is the main training place for Buddhist monks in Ladakh. Since the Chinese invasion of Tibet the School of Buddhist Philosophy school, on the right-hand side of the road from Leh to Hemis, has become an important centre for the study of Tibetan literature and history and of Buddhist philosophy in its pure form. Many westerners, interested in Buddhist learning and meditation, have also studied here. Choglamsar has an extensive syllabus and its library is worth seeing, even for the casual visitor.

In 1977 the old bridge at Sonam Ling was replaced with a new one able to take heavy vehicles. There are mani stones in the village of Palam (across the road and turn right) which has a mixed Buddhist and Muslim population. The Hemis-Stagna-Palam road is very rough and there are some river crossings to be made, but there is a regular bus connection.

Shey (15 km from Leh towards Hemis, entrance fee Rs 5)

The old 'summer palace' of the kings of Ladakh built about 550 years ago by Lhachen Palgyigon, the first king of Ladakh. It stands next to the remains of a larger construction on the east side of a hill which runs south-east towards the Indus. From the palace you can see over the fertile Indus plain north-east to the Tikse Gompa and over the Indus to the Zanskar mountain range. Hundreds of chortens of the most diverse forms and sizes stand on the barren plains to the north, separated from the fertile riverbank land by the Hemis road.

The old Shey palace has the largest golden Buddha statue in Ladakh in its gompa. The statue is worked out of gold and gilded copper sheets, stands 12 metres high and has blue hair. It was erected by King Dalden Namgyal in the middle of the 17th century. Sacrificial offerings (grain, jewels), holy signs and mantras are contained inside the figure. The most important moment in the construction of such a figure is when the

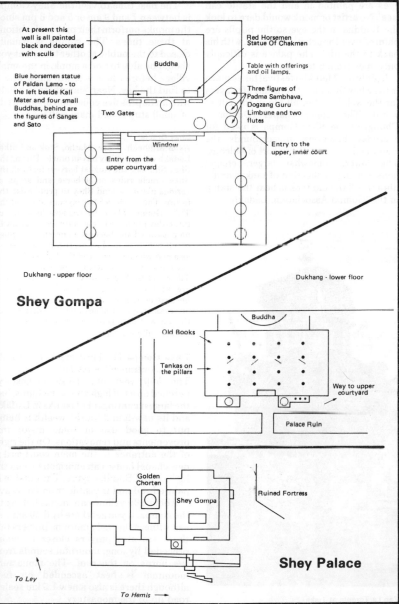

At present this wall is all painted black and decorated with sculls

Buddha

Red Horsemen Statue Of Chakmen

Table with offerings and oil lamps.

Blue horsemen statue of Paldan Lamo - to the left beside Kali Mater and four small Buddhas, behind are the figures of Sanges and Sato

Three figures of Padma Sambhava, Dogzang Guru Limbune and two flutes

Two Gates

Window

Entry from the upper courtyard

Entry to the upper, inner court

Dukhang - upper floor

Dukhang - lower floor

Shey Gompa

Buddha

Old Books

Tankas on the pillars

Way to upper courtyard

Palace Ruin

Golden Chorten

Shey Gompa

Ruined Fortress

Shey Palace

To Ley

To Hemis ➜

eyes are painted in and the statue can 'see'. No artist or monk would dare to look the Buddha in the eye so the pupils are painted over the artist's shoulder, with his back to the idol. The palace is officially only open from 6 to 9 am.

In July the Metukba festival takes place in the Shey Gompa with one day of prayers for the well being of all life in the entire world. The upper chapel (Dukhang-Chung) of the Shey Gompa is used for everyday functions, it surrounds the Buddha figure's head as a sort of balcony. The lower, somewhat larger, chapel houses a large collection of tankas and a library. All the old tankas bear the stamp of the 'Gompa Association, Ladakh'.

Zan La Temple at Tiske

The best time to visit the Shey Gompa is between 7 and 9 am or 5 and 6 pm since the monks perform their prayer-devotions at these times. The gompa is usually closed to the public at other times but you should be able to find a monk, in the small village before Shey, who will know where to find the key. Near Shey there is a field with an impressive collection of hundreds of small stupas and mani walls.

Shey Oracle
As in Mulbekh, Tikse, Matho, Stok and other Ladakh villages, Shey has an oracle. During the Shey Shublas, the August harvest festival, the Shey oracle rides on a horse and stops at various places around Shey to prophesise the future. The oracle, a Shey layman, starts at the Tuba Gompa where he engages in a two or three-day prayer, while in a trance, in order to be possessed and become an oracle. The Shey oracle is held in the highest regard and viewed as a god who has achieved the highest level of existence. Other oracles, especially those in Tikse and Stok, are not so well regarded, but are at the same time feared and revered because of their spiritual state. It is said that if one asks a question of an oracle, but disbelieves the answer and goes to another oracle, no answer will be given.

Tikse Gompa (17 km from Leh towards Hemis, entrance fee Rs 10)
The 500 year old Tikse monastery, perched on a hill high above the Indus, has the largest contingent of monks in Ladakh and its new-found tourist wealth is being put to good use in some major improvements and renovations. On the right of the entrance to the main courtyard a new chapel houses an enormous 15 metre high seated Buddha figure. The outside is painted red and is visible from far away.

About 100 yellow-cap monks belong to the gompa. If you get there by 6.30 am you can witness the daily morning prayers but there are also prayers closer to noon, preceded by long, mournful sounds from the horns on the roof. The monastery mountain is best ascended on foot although there is also a new 1.5 km sealed road up to the monastery.

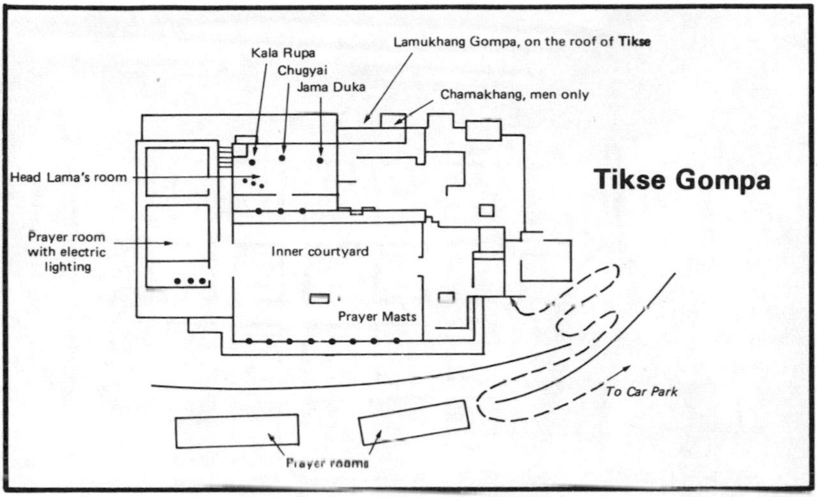

Tikse Gompa

Labels on the diagram:
- Kala Rupa
- Chugyai
- Jama Duka
- Lamukhang Gompa, on the roof of Tikse
- Chamakhang, men only
- Head Lama's room
- Prayer room with electric lighting
- Inner courtyard
- Prayer Masts
- To Car Park
- Prayer rooms

Wallpaintings in the high prayer room of Tikse Gompa:

Left	Right
1 Gonbo Ping	1 Chamsing
2 Gonbo Chakjipac	2 Lamo
3 Gonbo Chhak Tukpa	3 Chosgialckhor
4 Gonkar	
5 Sangdu	

5 4 3 2 1 | 1 2 3

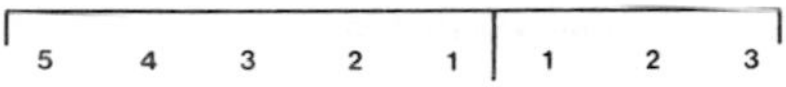

Figures:

Flag pole (Gyaltsan) in the middle, to the right of Chosgial, left of Tsepakmet.

In the prayer room there are two seats, one for the Dalai Lama who visited Tikse in 1973 and 1976, and one for the head lama of Tikse.

Behind the prayer room:

1 Sharipu
2 Buddha
3 Mongalpu
4 Shikdan and Chamsing
5 Chandajik

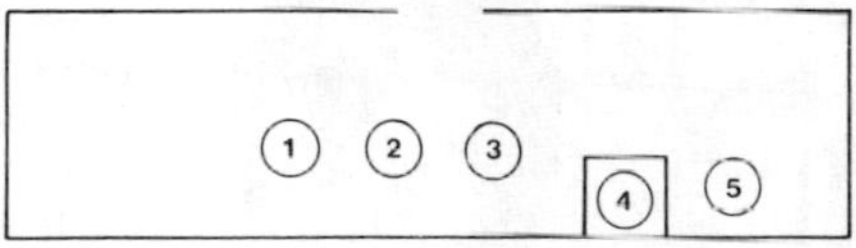

(1) (2) (3) (4) (5)

The small temple of Zan-La is beside the car parking area on this road. In the gompa courtyard there are some interesting Tibetan calendars on the walls. In the chapel there is a picture, near the central Chamba statue, of Tsung-Khapas, the founder of the Tugend (Gelugpa) sect. Some steps run up to a roof balcony from which there is access to the rooms of the head lama. Above everything is the roof top Lamukhang chapel, to which the Chamakhang also belongs, where only men may go. If you remain very quiet you may see mice nibbling at the offerings of grain and drinking the water. Whereas a few years ago travellers could buy, for a few rupees at the most, a printed prayer flag, today the monks wait in the

Below: Pages from a book   Above: Library at Tiske Gompa

monastery yard with portable stands from which they sell monastic souvenirs!

Below the monastery there are further chapels which are not very attractive. The 'houses' of the monks stretch out towards the foot of the hill. Tikse has an important festival with mask dances, the Tikse Gostor, on the 18th and 19th day of the 12th month of the Tibetan calendar.

There's a popular small hotel at Tikse and from here it's a picturesque walk through the fields and villages, instead of along the road, between Shey and Tikse. In October, when they're busy threshing the barley, the villagers will be singing in the fields. They have different traditional songs for each task.

Monks

When asked what criteria are used to choose lamas, or which sons in a family will become monks, a monk of Tikse told us that he came from a family with four sons. His eldest brother is a farmer, the second eldest is a teacher and his youngest brother a monk like himself. In principle all could become monks but the father must give his consent. This he will certainly not give to all his sons because some must stay on to run the farm and look after the rest of the family.

Tikse Oracle

The Tikse oracle is the most important oracle in Ladakh. An old man in the village is supposed to have supernatural powers. In a trance this layman, for he is not a lama, is possessed by a spirit and speaks Tibetan, a language which he cannot normally understand. He is said to be able to perform miraculous cures on beasts and men. With the help of a small tube he can 'suck' diseases from the bodies of the ill. He also gives advice for healing and can predict the future. In 1975 a new oracle appeared, the young wife of a Leh carpenter. Even in her youth there were special indications of her status as an oracle.

Printing

Tikse Gompas possesses a rich and beautiful library with many hand-written or painted books. Recent editions are produced by block printing, as in old Tibet. This procedure is also used today for the printing of the holy books Kandshur, Tibetan gka-hgyur, 'the translated word' of Buddha and Tandshur, 'the translated teachings' of the Lamaist religious teachers Bu-Ston (1290-1364 AD). The latter consists of a 225 volume commentary on the Kandshur!

Wooden printing plates are made up for each page and pressed by hand. The many hundred volumes indicate how much space the printing plates must take up in the monastery. Older and more highly regarded editions are often printed not black on white but painted with gold ink on black lacquered paper. These are decorated with Buddha figures. The individual pages are not bound up but kept as collections of loose sheets, wrapped in cloth between two wooden boards, tied up with a strap and stored on the shelves.

Tikse Gompa has the most beautiful library. In Hemis Gompa there are some rarities such as bilingual books in Tibetan and Sanskrit. You may meet one of the porters who has to lug the heavy books from the gompa to a village for a festival – the monks themselves follow on much later.

Hemis Gompa (45 km from Leh, entrance fee Rs 10)

Porter carrying books

The Hemis Gompa is famous far beyond the borders of Ladakh for its Hemis Festival (Hemis Setchu or Mela of the Hemis Gompa). This takes place every year with mask dances on the 9th to 11th day of the fifth Tibetan month. This date usually falls in the second half of June, although it sometimes goes into the beginning of July. Hemis also has a gigantic tanka, one of the largest in the world, which is only displayed to the public every 12 years at the Hemis Festival. It was unveiled at the 1980 festival so it will not be shown again until 1992.

The festival draws pilgrims, dressed in their finest costumes, from all over Ladakh and, since 1975, tourists from all over the world. Apart from being one of the largest in Ladakh it is one of the few major religious festival in Ladakh which is held in the summer, when the passes are open. Other monasteries are considering switching their festivals to the summer months, however.

Hemis Gompa is the largest and one of the most important in Ladakh quite apart from its annual festival. It was founded about 350 years ago by Stagtshang Rinchen, who was invited to Ladakh by King Singe Namgyal. You can gain an

Hemis Gompa

impression of the extent of the monastery area on the climb to the so called eyrie, a hermitage (Gotsang or Kotsang Gompa) reached by a one hour, three-km climb to 3900 metres, 1000 metres higher than Hemis. The 13th century monastery predates the Hemis Gompa and was built by Syalwa Gotsang-Pa, who meditated in a cave nearby. A small shrine has been built around the cave, where you can see his foot and hand print in the rock.

There are about a dozen monks living there; the small gompa serves as a retreat for many of the lamas from Hemis and it also services many of the monasteries in Ladakh by printing religious texts using carved wooden blocks, yak oil and lamp black, and rice paper imported from Burma. The climb is quite strenuous because of the altitude; you should not undertake it lightly. While the Ladakhis, who are used to the scarcity of oxygen, will virtually sprint up the mountainside you will need to take quite a few rest breaks.

The thousand square metre courtyard of the Hemis Gompa is entered from the north-east. The two prayer flags, in front of the first steps up to the Dukhang, form the middle point during the festival. A few places are reserved for guests but it is sometimes possible to buy 'admission tickets' to the gallery from business-minded monks! The day before the two-day festival is devoted to demonstrations. On the first day of the festival the part which foreigners can watch begins at 10 am with ceremonies in the courtyard. After prayers in the Dukhang the Rimpoche climbs the steps up to the courtyard, accompanied by musician monks, crosses it and takes his place underneath the gallery.

Shortly afterwards the dances begin, which have as their theme the struggle against evil and infidels and the inevitable victory of good and of Buddhism. The Padmasambhava dance, which shows the conquest of the Ruta demons, is part of this dance. Other figures which the dancers represent are Yama – the God of

Spectators at the Hemis festival

that the front room stands behind, its roof supported with four poles. The side walls of this front room are covered with partially damaged frescoes of the watchers of the heavenly directions. In the Dukhang, the general assembly room, the throne of the Rimpoche dominates the sitting places of the monks.

In the Lakhang there is a large gilded statue of the Buddha Sakyamuni with blue hair, surrounded by several silver chortens which, as in Spitok Gompa, are decorated with semi-precious stones. There are also beautiful frescoes in the Lakhang Nyingpa which is otherwise practically empty. The hands of the artists who prepared the gompa's giant tanka are revered as holy relics, but Hemis also has many lesser, but still interesting, tankas. Hemis also has an excellent library, particularly well preserved wall paintings and good Buddha figures.

In the second and third storeys, near the other chapels like the Zankhang, there is the Kharrabgysal, the rooms of the Rimpoche or head lama. The Rimpoche, spiritual overlord of Hemis, is a reincarnation of the monastery's founder, Stagtshang Raspa, who built Hemis in the first half of the 17th century, under King Singe Namgyal who also established the monasteries of Chemre, Hanle and Themisgang. The last overlord of the gompa was a reincarnation who, as a five-year old child, was undergoing training in Tibet when the Chinese invaded. Since then the Chakzot (manager), a brother of the late king of Ladakh, has conducted the business of the gompa. Because of the Chinese takeover of Tibet the monastery has had no communication with its Rimpoche since the '60s. During the 1975 festival Drugpa Rimpoche, a 12-year old youth, became the new Rimpoche as a new incarnation.

He is at the same time the overlord of the Drugpa Kargyupa, one of the six divisions of the red-cap sect who, before the Chinese invasion of Tibet, possessed influence practically only in Bhutan and

Death, the black-hatted sorcerer Guru Trakpo – the vanquisher of all demons, and various other forms of Padmasambhava. The sequence of the dances changes with time – often to present a different finale for the benefit of distinguished guests! The dancing continues to late afternoon, with a brief stop at mid-day. Locals and foreigners find time to patronise the many small stands outside the monastery walls where tea, soup, tsampa, sweets and other refreshments are sold. If you wish to take photographs take account of the position of the sun when selecting your vantage point. In the crowded conditions during the dancing it is virtually impossible to leave your place.

If you visit the gompa outside the festival time you will be impressed by the stillness of the valley. You will also have the opportunity to see the various chapels. Near the Dukhang is the Lakhang, which is the first one after a small set of steps from the yard. The doors are placed inwards so

Ladakh. In Ladakh the Stagna and Chemre monasteries belong to this order, while Spitok belongs to the yellow-cap (Gelugpa order). Drugpa Rimpoche currently lives in Darjeeling, where he is completing his training.

Most of the 500 monks who were once based at Hemis have now moved to other monasteries throughout Ladakh and the monastery is maintained almost entirely for tourism. The monastery is growing rich from the proceeds of its festival – for tourists it costs Rs 20 for each day of the festival. The monks are now building a new shrine with a two-storey tall statue of the Sakyamuni Buddha.

Getting There Hemis is easily reached by car or jeep as a day trip from Leh, but more time consuming to visit by public transport. By car you follow the Upshi road past Shey and Tikse, this is the Manali road which follows the Indus. Past the TCP checkpoint at Karu (where foreigners have to show their passports) you turn to the right to cross the Indus over a new bridge and follow the winding road up towards the gompa. Unlike many other gompas Hemis is not visible from afar – it only comes into view when you're right beside it.

During the summer there is one bus a day to Hemis which leaves Leh around 11.30 am and arrives at the monastery around 12.30 pm, departing on the return trip about 1 pm. These departure and arrival times appear to be very variable. This means you have to stay overnight if you wish to see the monastery. There is plenty of good camping space in the woods nearby, which is usually full of campers during the festival time. The wood is extremely beautiful and well maintained and cared for by the monks. There is a small stream which feeds the trees, the grass of the wood and, in the small stone house near the centre of the wood, drives a water wheel which grinds the grain for the monks' tsampa.

There is also a rest house and

Dancer at the Hemis festival

restaurant, with four bedrooms. You can buy cheap meals and plenty of tea here. You cannot, however, buy any other supplies and if you are camping overnight you must bring most of your needs with you from Leh. The 'parachute restaurant', near the bus stand, has cheaper food and good accommodation. The monastery itself has a diesel generator, housed in the stone structure that looks like a garage. Don't camp near it.

If you feel, after an afternoon's exploration and night's camping, that you want to get back to Leh, you can walk down to the Upshi road before 7 am and catch the bus up from Sakti at Karu. During the festival there are several buses from Leh to Hemis and back each day but you will be missing something if you do not camp with the many hundreds of people who flock to the gompa for the festival.

Tagthog Gompa (entrance fee Rs 10)
Also known as Bragthog, this is the only

monastery of the Nyingma school of Buddhism in Ladakh. Tagthog means the place with the rock ceiling and it is built around a cave which, as legend has it, was used by the Padmasambhava (Guru Rimpoche) in the 8th century. He is believed to have stayed in the cave for meditation and thereby blessed it with his presence.

There are three main shrines, the cave hall is the oldest and from time to time sacred water drops from the cave ceiling. Within this temple, the statues of Padmasambhava include one in the wrathful Tantra form. The Lakhang (main assemble hall) was built a hundred year ago. The tantra deity is the Buddha Heruka and the wall paintings show 100 deities in their peaceful and wrathful forms.

The new Lakhang was completed in 1966 and was conceived and planned by the Stakling Rimpoche, who was abbot of Dorje Tag in Tibet for several years before coming to Tagthog. The statues in this temple are of Padmasambhava in different forms. The frescoes have images of renowned spiritual personalities of the various schools of Buddhism.

There is a bus from Leh to Tagthog and back in summer. The bus leaves Leh about 4 pm and arrives at Tagthog about 7 pm. The bus stays overnight in the village of Sakti and leaves Tagthog the next day around 7 am, passing through Sakti 10 to 15 minutes later. It is possible to catch this bus at Karu, if you walk down from Hemis, around 7.30 to 8 am. However, it is the first bus down the valley to Leh for the day and will be very full. Cost from Leh to Tagthog is Rs 7.

Festivals

Most of the great religious festivals of Ladakh fall in the winter. The major exception is the Hemis festival, the biggest of them all. Other summer gompa festivals include the Phyang monastery's festival in mid-July. The monasteries at Thagtog and Chemre usually hold theirs in November, before the real depths of winter. More festivals, which used to be associated with certain religious, cultural or agricultural meanings, are now being adjusted to coincide with the June to September tourist season. Festival dates tend to vary by several weeks from year to year due to the 13 month Buddhist calendar's variation from our western calendar

In addition to the monastery festivals practically all the villages have harvest thanksgiving festivals and archery events during the summer. There are also private parties in which dance plays an important role. In these slow, sustained dances the dancers appear to be between dream and trance. Many of the dances, which have a musical accompaniment of drums and flutes, show interesting elements from the daily life of farmers. Hand movements, for example, are unmistakeably taken from the actions involved in sowing seeds. In general men and women dance totally separately. If they are together on the same 'dance floor' they will still do their own, unrelated, dances. We experienced a special feature during a celebration at Bodh Kharbu – a dance master selected from the crowd some women and young girls to dance. After initial

Dancer at the Hemis festival

reluctance they seemed to quite enjoy it.

Ladakhi archery contests, which are followed by more dancing, are only a pale reflection of similar festivals in other Himalayan states. Whereas in Bhutan specially designed and fashioned bows would be used for such a contest, in Ladakh the bows are much cruder. Nevertheless these contests have their own charm and they do give you the opportunity to see the making of chang, butter-tea and tsampa. No matter what else happens at a festival these three ingredients must be included. Festival musicians are generally paid in local produce. After a good meal they receive, with their cup of butter-tea, a cup of tsampa meal, sometimes also sugar and a piece of butter. The whole lot is wrapped up in a piece of cloth and knotted for transport.

Anyone wishing to tape record festival music should keep their microphone concealed. Otherwise all that will result is a wild medley of noises since the Ladakhis are fascinated by these strange technological instruments. They will point it out to the audience and comment loudly! A cassette recorder with an inbuilt microphone can be kept out of sight, even inside a carrying bag.

In Leh itself, especially during the summer, there are often cultural nights with dancing, singing and other entertainment put on by the people from the Tibetan refugee camp at Choglamsar. The tourist office in Leh is now also organising festivals with archery contests, polo games and wedding and dance feasts. The Dalai Lama's birthday on 6 July is a festival in Leh, mostly for Tibetans. Leh also has a picture theatre in the town and another at the army base; they usually show Indian movies.

Chemre Gompa

If you turn to the left at the Karu TCP you will, after five km, reach Chemre Gompa on a ridge above the village of Chemre. Like Hemis it was founded by Stagtshang Raspa but in contrast to Hemis the mask dances are held at the turn of the year in the Tibetan calendar – in mid-winter. The Dukhang and the three further chapels above it are not really worth visiting.

The small, but noteworthy, Trak Tok Gompa is 10 km further on. The old Trak Tok Rimpoche, who came from Tibet, is highly revered by the Ladakhis. The old cave-chapel, which is reminiscent of Dakum Khochey, is especially interesting. Although they both lie in a restricted zone tourists may visit the Chemre and Trak Tok Gompas.

Leh-Manali Road

At the Upshi TCP (a km before Upshi) the road deviates to the right, crosses a pioneer bridge across the Indus, and turns into a side valley. Up to the Upshi TCP no special documentation is required, but from here on special permission is needed from the District Commissioner in Leh since the 'restricted zone' extends eastward from one mile *west* of the Leh-Manali road. The Leh-Manali road is 475 km long and is only recommended for fully equipped four-wheel drives since no refuelling or repair facilities are available.

The road is normally open only in September and October, the highest pass is the Tanglang La (5429 metres), 65 km beyond Upshi. There is no public transport along this stretch although in summer there is a bus service between Keylong and Manali, a distance of about 117 km crossing the Rohtang Pass. Two km before Miru a line of mani-pennants spans the whole valley.

Hemis to Leh on the other side of the Indus

The Hemis-Stagna-Choglamsar road on the left bank of the Indus is sealed for a short distance but was badly damaged in 1978 due to unusually severe weather.

Matho Gompa

Matho lies five km from Stagna in a southern side valley. The monastery is above the village with many grain mills, on a long ridge surrounded by a small forest. The gompa was founded in the 16th century by Tungpa Dorje but was almost destroyed during the war between the Muslim invaders and the Ladakhis in the late 16th century. It was saved a few years later by the arrival of another lama, Chokyi Lodo, who renovated the monastery

Top: Monks at Tikse Gompa (TW)
Bottom: Wall-painting at Tikse Gompa (TW)

Top: Monks chant pujar inside Hemis Gompa before the start of the festival (BP)
Left: Guru Padmasambhava makes his final appearance at the Hemis festival (BP)
Right: A Ladakhi woman offers yak butter oil to the monks at the Hemis festival (BP)

Elderly pilgrim at a gompa

and restored its activities. Today it has 60 monks and 30 novices from the larger monasteries. It belongs to the Sakyapa sect.

Near the chapels, which were renovated for the visit of Sakya Trinzin Rimpoche, overlord of the sect, is a small room which is very interesting. This room, called Gonkhang, is filled 50 cm high with grain. According to an old custom every family from Matho brings a small bowl of grain from the first harvest for this room. This is not accompanied by any special ceremony. There is a lama who is particularly responsible for the Gonkhang room; he is changed every three years. The room has a special significance during the two-day Nagrang Festival (at the Tibetan New Year, in February) and a one-day festival on the 8th day of the second Tibetan month (usually March) called the Nispetsergyat.

During these two festivals two special monks (called Rongzam) go into a trance in this room and then, adorned with old weapons, run over the mountain ridges in the area and over the roofs of the monastery. During the Nagrang Festival the lamas are evil-minded on the first day (they hit spectators) but very peaceable on the second day! At the Nispetsergyat these two Rongzam ride the stretch which they went over on foot at the beginning of the Tibetan year. Both of these festivals are accompanied by mask dances. For

these two monks there stand two Lathos, red chortens of a special style from which prayer flags flutter. They are situated high in the mountains, about five or six km from the monastery, close to a glacier.

The monks, also known as Luyar, are just like other monks at other times of the year, but if someone in the village doesn't believe in or has lost faith in the powers of Buddhism, these two monks batter themselves on the arms, feet and tongue with their old weapons. The wounds do not bleed and their injuries heal so quickly that they are able to dance a short time later. They do this in order to show that they possess divine powers. This ritual is still practised today on the 14th and 15th days of the first month of the Tibetan calendar. Like the monks of the Gonkhang room they are replaced every three years, the choice is made, following a prayer, from four or five candidates. All 60 monks write the name of their candidates on a small piece of paper. The head lama draws two of these pieces of paper out and those are the monks for the next three years.

In front of the door to the Gonkhang room there is a prayer mill made out of oil cans – a sign of the times, but still adorned with the mantra 'om mani padme hum' in addition to other prayers. They are written on a paper roll, not on little scraps of paper. The Gonkhang room, in which meditation takes place, is ascribed its own spiritual power. Thus one cannot in any circumstances take photographs here because pictures of the room would take away a part of the power.

Matho is famous, at least amongst Ladakhis, because of its oracle. The Lhaba of Matho is, in contrast to the oracle of Tikse, a priest and lives in the monastery. On special days (in winter on the 8th day of the second month of the Tibetan calendar) the oracle runs all over the mountains near Matho; he is blindfolded and 'sees' only with a painting on breast and back. The oracle speaks to the village dwellers by a small spring at the foot of the monastery mountain.

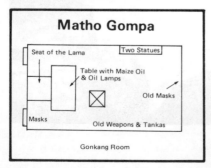

Matho Gompa

Seat of the Lama

Two Statues

Table with Maize Oil & Oil Lamps

Old Masks

Masks

Old Weapons & Tankas

Gonkang Room

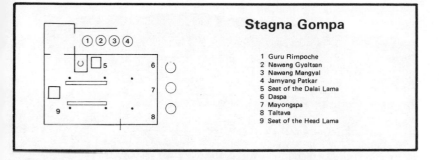

Stagna Gompa

1 Guru Rimpoche
2 Nawang Gyaltsan
3 Nawang Mangyal
4 Jamyang Patkar
5 Seat of the Dalai Lama
6 Daspa
7 Mayongspa
8 Taltava
9 Seat of the Head Lama

Stagna Gompa

This gompa lies on a sugarloaf mountain on the west bank of the Indus River. The hill is said to be shaped like a tiger jumping up to the sky and since the monastery is built on the tiger's nose it took the name stagna or 'tiger's nose'. It cannot be reached directly from the Leh-Hemis road because there is no bridge, one must use the Choglamsar or Karu bridge.

The most important image in the monastery is one of Avalokitesvara which is said to have come from Assam. In the chapel there are three new paintings – a large picture of Choshikzal, the red figure of Standin and the blue figure of Dorje Chang. In the wooden cupboard there is a large standing figure of Dorje Phakma besides eight Sashan Gyat. Under this major chapel there is another chapel which may only be entered by lamas. Stagna has 25 red-cap monks and the head lama can offer his visitors a European sofa with two easy chairs – of which he is more than a little proud.

Under monasteries of Stagna are those of Mut, Karu and Stakrimo in Ladakh and of Bardun and Sani in Zanskar.

Stok Palace (entrance fee Rs 20)

Eight km towards the Indus from Stagna, then four km over a rubble slope at the outlet of a side valley, will bring you to the palace of Stok. Coming from Leh you cross the Indus at Choglamsar then travel a km towards the Indus and turn to the right. The palace is about 200 years old and is the only Ladakhi royal palace which is still inhabited. The last king, Raja Kunsang Namgyal, died in 1974 and, as is customary for personalities of high standing, a chorten was erected in the village where he was cremated.

One of his brothers is now the 'manager' of the Hemis gompa but only his widow, the Rani of Stok, and his youngest son live in the palace. The widow, who was formerly revered as the Gyalmo, Rani Parvati Davi Deskit Wangmo, the 18th Queen of Ladakh, was born in 1936. She has four children – the eldest son will become the next King of Ladakh when he is 20 to 25 years old. The exact date will be set by lamas and people of high standing. Gyalpo means king, Gyalmo is queen, Gyallu is prince, Gyalmo Chhunun is princess. The King of Ladakh formerly had a cabinet of five ministers and the influence of Ladakh's kings once reached from Demchok (on the present day Chinese-Tibetan border) to Mulbekh and in the north over the Nubra Valley. Today the political power rests with the Indian governor, the District Commissioner.

The palace of Stok has 80 rooms, only 12 of which are now used. There are 25 servants working for the Rani, but because the palace is so difficult to heat the Rani moves south to Manali for the winter months. Three rooms, which make up the museum, are open to the public and

Royal Palace at Stok

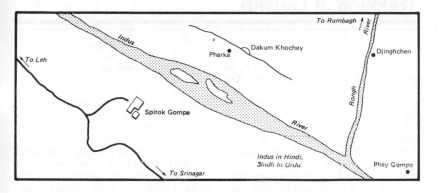

it is also possible to visit the small gompa, with the lama's permission. A guide with reasonable English unlocks the museum which contains the royal family's jewellery, noted for its turquoise and red coral, and also a superb collection of 35 400-year old tankas, coloured using paints made of crushed semi-precious stones. Some visitors feel that unless you have a distinct interest in the Ladakhi Royal Family visiting the palace is barely worth the Rs 20 entrance fee, but others find it very interesting.

Apart from the palace Stok's only other attraction is the July archery contest. As in Matho you can see the small water mills in which the roasted grain is ground into meal. There are two lay oracles in Stok and they give their 'performance' at the Lchagrang Festival on the 9th and 10th days of the third month of the Tibetan calendar. There is a variety of accommodation available at Stok and you can also camp there. There is a small tent restaurant also.

Pharka

The village of Pharka is on the opposite side of the Indus from, and in sight of, the Spitok Gompa. You can only reach Pharka by the Choglamsar route, the last kms must be made on foot but up to that point the road is jeepable. At the village of Pharka there is a cave in the sandstone bank of the Indus. The cave gompa, Dakum Khochey, was built by Lotsava Rinchen Sanghpo and is older than Spitok Gompa. In front of the gompa cave there is a building housing a small primary school. The teacher enjoys painting 'modern' tankas in his spare time.

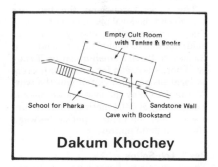

Dakum Khochey

Trekking in Ladakh

Ladakh offers many possibilities for trekking and mountain climbing. The Suru Valley (reached from Kargil) and Zanskar are especially good for trekking. Zanskar can only be reached along the Suru Valley from Kargil; it is possible to trek from Nimmu directly into the Zanskar Valley only with the greatest difficulty. The Zanskar Valley can be reached in about a week of walking from Kargil, less if the road from Kargil is open. Treks into Zanskar or within Zanskar are covered in the Zanskar section. There are also numerous mountain climbing possibilities in Ladakh.

MARKHA VALLEY TREK

The Markha Valley is a popular trekking route, adjacent to the Indus Valley and south-east of Leh. This is an eight or more day roundtrip trek from Leh. Part of this excellent trek follows the same route as the trek from Leh to the Markha Valley and on to Zangla and Padum in Zanskar. See the Zanskar section for more details on the route on into Zanskar. The trek can be made in either direction.

The views throughout the trek are superb and the local people very friendly. They can generally offer you accommodation and food but don't depend on it. Be sure to leave a small donation if they do. There's no need for guides or porters as local people always tell you the way. Within the valley the best known peak is Kang Yissay at 6401 metres, but there are many other un-named peaks between 5000 and 6000 metres.

Day 1: Leh-Spitok

There are several buses a day or you can take a taxi. It's possible to stay in a villager's house in Spitok or camp by the Indus.

Day 2: Spitok-Rumbagh

This is a long day's walk. You start by bearing north-west along the Indus from Spitok until you reach a good suspension bridge which leads over to the southern bank. You then walk eastwards to the flanks of the foothills directly ahead of you. Sketchy paths traverse these flanks parallel to the Indus. Follow these across a large dry ravine until you hit a very well defined path and river running south-west.

This is the path to Rumbagh. The path follows the river valley all the way through via Jingchan (Zinchan) before turning south to Rumbagh. It's possible to overnight with villagers at Jingchan or Rumbagh, which is in a side valley to the left of the main valley. The day's walk is strenuous, a steady ascent throughout.

Day 3: Rumbagh-Skiu

Another long day starts with returning down from Rumbagh to the main valley. You continue south for a short time before turning west (right) up the first side valley. This path leads up to the village of Yuruche then to the Ganda La at 5000 metres. The long ascent to the path takes up most of the day. After the pass the walk is straightforward, you head south-west down the obvious path, following the river valley to Shingo then Skiu. Accommodation is possible with the villagers at either place.

Day 4: Skiu-Markha Village

The true Markha Valley is joined at Skiu. The easy day's walk follows the Markha Valley upstream to Markha. There are many paths in the main valley and no steep gradients. The Markha River has to be crossed twice but bridges may soon be completed. There is abundant wood and water and the people are very friendly. Accommodation is possible in old buildings below the village or you can camp by the river. Markha village is the starting point for the trek to Zangla in Zanskar.

Day 5: Markha Village-Longmaru La

This is another long day's walk but by this time you should be well acclimatised. Start by following the Markha River upstream past the villages of Umlung and Hankar. It's very important to turn north-east (left) away from the Markha Valley soon after Hankar, where an obvious path leads up a narrow side valley and over a wooden bridge from where a good path follows the side river up towards Nimaling and the Longmaru La. Nimaling is reputedly very small and very old – if you can find it! You can camp by the river below the Longmaru La, but it's very cold although the views of the Himalaya are superb.

Day 6: Longmaru La-Chokdo

The ascent northwards to the pass at 5200 metres takes about two hours through the snow. It's easier than the Ganda La. The views from the top are good, but the pass is followed by a tedious descent northwards towards Larsa. The rocks here are very loose. Continuing north down the river valley the path is very ill defined but as you follow the main stream down and say 'Hemis?' to anyone you meet you won't go wrong! At the end of the day you reach Larsa and Chokdo is only half an hour further on. There are friendly people and accommodation is possible at either place.

Day 7: Chokdo-Hemis Gompa

A leisurely last day starts with an easy morning clambering down river to Martseland and the Indus Valley. The path is still poor, just follow the river valley. From Martseland to Hemis bear north-west above and parallel to the Indus Valley for three km or so. There's accommodation and food available at Hemis and transport back to Leh.

KONGLACHA PEAK

The Konglacha Peak (6700 metres) lies south-east of Leh and it is reached via Rumbagh, the first day's walk on the Markha Valley trek. From Leh you go to Stok where you can hire porters and donkeys. From Stok you go past the Kurphuk Gompa and on to the 4800 metre Namlung Pass then descend to the village of Rumbagh at 3270 metres. From there it's another day's walk to the base camp of Konglacha Peak, it takes a further two days to climb the peak.

STOK BASE CAMP

This trek starts out like the Konglacha trek. You can hire donkeys at Stok for about Rs 17.50 to 20 per day, inclusive of the donkeyman, so long as you hire two. They're not really necessary, you can make this trek without them, but it does ensure you have a good guide.

The first day's walk out of Stok follows a river valley for about five hours, keeping to the left of the valley and ascending about 1000 metres. You pass some summer dwellings and the eroded landscape is very beautiful. There's a good camping place at the end of the day. The second day continues up the valley, easier walking than the first day. In four hours' walk you ascend about 600 metres to the Stok base camp at about 5200 metres. The sun at this altitude is very strong and at night the fast flowing mountain stream nearby may freeze over.

You can spend another day or two around the base camp, perhaps ascending to nearly 6000 metres (20,000 ft). There is some animal life to be seen including the Ladakhi desert-rat. From the base camp you can descend all the way back to Stok in one day, perhaps even back to Leh if you arrive early enough to catch the bus.

KOCHTET PEAK

The Kochtet Peak (7015 metres) is in the restricted zone. From Leh to Changla is 79 km along a jeepable road. You leave Leh on the Indus road to Hemis Gompa. At

Karu you turn left into the restricted zone. The ascent takes four days. Note that north of the Srinagar-Leh road and east of the Leh-Manali road is a restricted area so all treks must be confined to the other side of these roads. You should be well-equipped with mountaineering rations.

LEH-MANALI

Before setting out on this 14 day trek you must obtain a permit from the District Commissioner in Leh. Otherwise your trek will come to an end at the control post before Upshi. You follow the Indus Valley as far as Upshi where you turn into a side valley over the Miru, Gya and the Tanglang La pass to Rukchen. Then it is over the Marang La pass, past Sutak, over the Lachalang La (5070 metres) and the Baralacha La pass (5100 metres) and through Darcha to Keylong. Finally you cross the Rohtang Pass to Manali. Kargil-Manali is covered in the Zanskar section.

OTHER TREKS

Other treks in Ladakh include the eight to nine day trek over Shang from Leh to Sihumar. The Alchi to Chiling and Sumdah trek takes four days.

MOUNTAIN CLIMBING

Ladakh was practically shut off from the outside world between the end of WW II and 1974 so the mountaineer will find many 5000 to 7000 metre peaks which have not yet been climbed. Some have not even been named. Since the Ladakh valleys are at altitudes of 3500 to 4000 metres the mountain ascents are only 1000 to 3000 metres and sloping sides and deep ravines make them comparatively easy to climb. The remainder of the 1980s is likely to see a large influx of western mountaineering enthusiasts. Japanese teams have already started conquering some of these virgin peaks.

One of Zanskar's many terrifying suspension bridges

All foreign climbing expeditions to India require permission in writing from the government of India through the Indian Mountaineering Foundation. Violation of this regulation may entail arrest and prosecution. Intending climbers should contact the foundation for applications forms and other details. The address is Secretary, Indian Mountaineering Foundation, Benito Juarez Rd, New Delhi.

Karakoram

The range of mountains north of Ladakh, and thus north of the Himalaya, has 10 peaks over 7000 metres including, at 8611 metres, the world's second highest peak, Mt Godwin Austen, also known as K2. It stands in the Pakistani held part of Kashmir. Because the mountains in the Karakoram rise from a base altitude averaging close to 3000 metres they do not look as impressive as the Himalaya. This region is outside the permitted zone.

Around Leh

Across the Indus to the south of Leh, beyond the village of Stok, there is a range of mountains that is popular with climbers. The base camp for climbing in this region is about two day's trek from Stok, along the trail towards the Ganda La, one of the entrances over the range to the Markha Valley.

Most of the peaks in this area are unnamed but Stok Kangri at 6150 metres, Gulap Kangri at 5900 metres, Mashiro Kangri at 7537 metres and Kantaka at 5275 metres are among some of the named peaks.

Around Kargil

The Suru and Zanskar Valleys provide some of the more spectacular and difficult climbing in Ladakh. The Nun-Kun Massif is one of the most frequent climbing areas of the region and is booked out for months ahead, sometimes years, by climbing expeditions. The approach to the twin

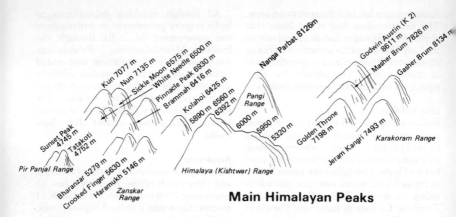

Main Himalayan Peaks

peaks is from the Kargil-Padum road, about 70 km south of Kargil. The main approach is either from Tangole or Gulmadong. Some expeditions have also approached from Parkutse along the Kangri Glacier. To reach the base camp for Kun it is necessary to cross the Suru River, and at present there is no bridge.

The Nun-Kun Massif, which lies on the Great Himalayan range, is the highest peak in Ladakh at 7077 metres (Kun) and 7135 metres (Nun). Other named peaks within the Suru and Zanskar areas are Pinnacle at 6930 metres, White Needle at 6500 metres, Z1 at 6400 metres and D41 at 5600 metres. In this region, along the Great Himalaya to the south of the valley and the Zanskar range to the north, there are many peaks between 5500 and 6500 metres which are unnamed. Zealous climbers could even claim some of these

higher peaks for their own although all claims must be registered with the Indian Mountaineering Foundation.

Zanskar Range
This range is north of the Suru River along the Kargil-Padum road. The most frequented area is around the village of Trakkur, just over the 4400 metre Pensi La pass from Padum and near the foot of the Turung Drung Glacier. Named peaks of the region are Z2 at 6175 metres, Z3 at 6270 metres and Z8 at 6050 metres.

Pir Panjal
This mountain range is south of the Himalaya. The Vale of Kashmir is between the Pir Panjals and the Himalayas. The Lahaul Valley, north of Manali and south of Ladakh, is similarly sandwiched between the two ranges.

Zanskar

Zanskar, the region between Kargil and Lamayuru in the north and Kishtwar and Manali in the south is, at the moment, an ideal trekking area. The new road from Kargil, over the Pensi La to Padum has brought some of the trappings of civilisation to the Zanskar capital but one severe winter proved how tenuous a connection that road is. You won't find hotels in Zanskar but nor will you find military installations and soldiers, a common part of the scene in Ladakh. The most you'll come across is a mounted patrol or pony caravan of the J&K Police. As for foreign visitors they are still few and far between in this far 'off the beaten track' Himalayan valley. The valley is about 300 km long and is unusual in that access is only by high passes from the sides. A unique feature of the Zanskar area is the twin peak of Nun and Kun.

The whole of the Ladakh region is extremely arid but the Zanskar Valley gets more snow than other areas, with snow falling for seven months of the year. The people spread gravel on the snow to melt it. In the depths of winter all the rivers freeze over. Even the Zanskar River freezes on the surface and the Zanskaris walk along it to reach the Indus near Nimmu – an otherwise inaccessible route. The Indus Valley in Ladakh is warmer than the Zanskar Valley.

TREKKING IN ZANSKAR

On all the trekking reports that follow note that the day by day sequence of events can vary enormously from trekker to trekker and season to season. If you start earlier or later, walk faster or slower, where you get to each day is bound to vary. River levels in Zanskar are even more likely to cause variations in the itinerary. Many treks in Zanskar, and the Padum-Markha Valley trek in particular, involve many river crossings. If, due to heavy snow from the previous winter, the river levels are high then crossings will take longer and distance covered will be shorter. Additionally the rivers tend to be higher later in the day, as the snow melts faster. Thus if the rivers are high you are likely to be stopped by a high water level earlier in the day than in a year when in general the river levels are lower. So take the trek reports that follow as a general guide, don't think that your trek will duplicate day to day itineraries.

Trekking in Zanskar is not easy. The trails are often rough, the river often deep, the passes always high. This is not a place for beginners. Nevertheless, certain precautions will make a Zanskar trek an easier proposition:

Survival Anyone intending to trek in Zanskar should be completely outfitted in Srinagar or, at the latest, Kargil. Very little will be found in Padum and in the small villages along the trail it is not always easy to buy even tsampa meal. If you have porters or pony-leaders you should ensure that they feed themselves. Most important you must take sufficient kerosene (and ensure the containers do not leak!) since there is very little fuel for burning.

Food Westerners should take along tinned meat (unless they're vegetarians!) and other food suitable for strenuous walking at altitudes from 3000 to 5000 metres. A larger group could take along a sheep as live meat. If you wish to (or have to) survive Zanskari style you should bring tsampa (roasted grain) with tea, water and chang. A kind of noodle known as pakthuk can be prepared for a change and tsampa can also be baked as a flat bread called takir or, in Tibetan, pakleb. Chuli pak is a real Zanskari appetiser – it consists of apricots (chuli) cooked in butter which is then eaten with flat bread for breakfast.

Packing Clothing and equipment should be packed in a rucksack or kitbag, the latter are easier to transport on pony back. Waterproof individual items by putting them in dustbags sealed with rubber loops.

Shoes Light running shoes with rubber soles are recommended for trekking; they dry quickly after crossing streams. The rocky trails, however, are very hard on running shoes which may not stand the abuse. Some trekkers feel that trekking boots are better. In no circumstances try to cross streams or rivers barefoot.

Other Equipment A sturdy walking stick is important, especially for crossing streams, snowfields or ice. Take a sun hat but ensure it stays firmly in place or it will soon be blown away. A chap stick is important if you want to avoid burnt, dry lips. Sunglasses are very important in the high mountains – good quality and 85% filter factor. Have some safety pins on hand, not packed somewhere far away or where they could be lost in a fall. Your parka and sleeping bag should both be good quality since the nights can get very cold. Make sure your tent is waterproof, some monsoon rains creep over the mountain barrier and bring heavy downpours.

Ponies for Trekking Ponies are indispensable for riding and haulage in the Kashmir Valley, particularly on the Pahalgam-Amarnath trek although many westerners manage without them on that route. They're also useful in Ladakh, particularly on treks into Zanskar, although in many places you find donkeys rather than ponies.

Locally supplied saddles tend to be very uncomfortable – in Pahalgam they are often made of iron: hard, inflexible, awkward and with just a little leather on top. In the Suru Valley the saddles are all made of wood. In either case riding rapidly becomes impossible. Not only are the saddles a nightmare, the bridle and stirrups are equally bad. In fact stirrups are often completely lacking on Suru Valley and Zanskar ponies and the bridle may be simply a loose rope tied around the animal's neck. A tall westerner, with his legs reaching almost to the ground, looks like Don Quixote!

The reason for this poor equipment is quite simple – apart from water crossings ponies are primarily used only as beasts of burden and rarely ridden. If you wish to use your own saddle it is not necessary to bring it with you since saddles are sold in the neighbourhood of the Shah Hamdan Mosque in Srinagar. They can easily be resold after you complete your pony trek.

In choosing a pony, if you should be so fortunate as to have a choice, considering the limited number available, pay close attention to the rear and withers. Otherwise you will have an uncomfortable time on horseback. Forget whatever you know about horses when viewing these animals – they fly in the face of our preconceptions and are unbelievably nimble and surefooted. If you decide to entrust yourself to such a 'disguised deer' do not try to steer them, they find their own way with remarkable certainty. If you do want to direct the pony with the reins (they do not seem to understand hints on the shanks) then give a gentle indication and allow one or two seconds reaction time. They're not machines with instantaneous reactions! Over-strenuous tugging at the reins leads to defensive resistance.

Allow the ponies sufficiently long rest stops and opportunities to relax. The animals don't always find enough food at overnight halting places (at least in Zanskar) so they are allowed to wander in search of food at night. Don't blame the horse-drivers if it takes some time to round them up in the morning. The mid-day stop should, if possible, be at a place where ponies can graze. Unload them at this time and remove the saddles, you will see the ponies roll on their backs to reduce the flatulence caused by the tight belly

Top: A trekking group on Kanital Glacier (GW)
Left: Campsite at Wadvan Valley (GW)
Right: Kashmiri horsemen (GW)

Top: Fatu La, highest point on the Leh-Srinagar road (BP)
Left: Lingshot Gompa, Zanskar (GW)
Right: Rafting on the lower Zanskar River (GW)

band. The pause should not be too short or, further down the trail, the docile beasts may suddenly decide to throw off their load or rider and settle down to some serious grazing.

Bear in mind that the smell of westerners is still unusual to Zanskari horses. A local horse-leader can be very reassuring for the ponies – if you ride alone it is important to tether your pony during stops. Otherwise it will gallop off home at the first opportunity.

The lightly tinkling bells found around the neck of Zanskari horses drown out the noise of falling stones and reassure the horses. Despite such precautions against panic horses do sometimes fall, as happened on our trek from Zangla to Nerag (see Padum-Lamayuru Trek) when our horse was drowned. This is naturally seen as a bad omen for the trip and porters and horse-drivers may desert you after such an accident. Financial compensation for the dead animal will help; it is often the horse-drivers' sole possession. You must reckon on Rs 1000 to 2000. In general Zanskari horses and porters are more reliable than those from Kashmir. For horses from the Suru Valley the rope suspension bridges at Padum constitute an insurmountable obstacle on a trek to Zanskar and you will have to switch to Zanskari horses from Thonde or Zangla. They are able to get across these frightening bridges. Many porters from the Kashmir Valleys are unwilling to go beyond Padum since they are unused to the high altitude passes.

At Rangdum porters (who will carry 15 kg) cost about Rs 30 a day, ponies are Rs 45 plus Rs 5 for the pony man and they will carry about 50 kg. At Sanku and Pannikar porters and ponies are slightly cheaper. Kargil will probably be cheaper again although the price there is variable.

RELIGIOUS FESTIVALS IN ZANSKAR

Mune Gompa Anchog takes place on the 15th day of the 11th month but it is only prayers.

Karsha Gompa Gostor on the 25th-29th days of the 11th month of the Tibetan calendar – usually from mid-December to the first week in January. Features cham dance with masks.

Thonde (Stongde) Gompa Gostor from the 29th day of the 11th month of the Tibetan calendar, it follows the end of the Karsha Gostor.

Tagrimo Gompa A one-day prayer festival takes place on the 29th day of the 11th month, at the same time as the Karsha Gostor.

Phuctal Gompa Gostor is on the 29th and 30th day of the 12th Tibetan month and features prayers but no mask dances.

Bardan Gompa Gertsa on the 15th day of the fourth month (usually the first week in June), features cham dance with masks. This is the major Zanskar festival that takes place in the summer, the Hemis festival in Ladakh takes place at the same time.

Zongkhul Gompa Zongkhul Huchot takes place on the 16th and 17th days of the fourth month but there are no mask dances.

Sani Gompa Nungnes does not have a fixed date but usually takes place in July.

Sani Gompa Sani Nasjal takes place between the 15th and 20th days of the sixth Tibetan month, usually the first week in August. The festival takes place during the blooming of the 'Guru Neropa Flower'.

Padum The Padum Hurim or Skurim is on the 28th and 29th days of the 10th month of the Tibetan calendar and features cham dances with masks.

Zangla The Zangla Hurim is on the 28th

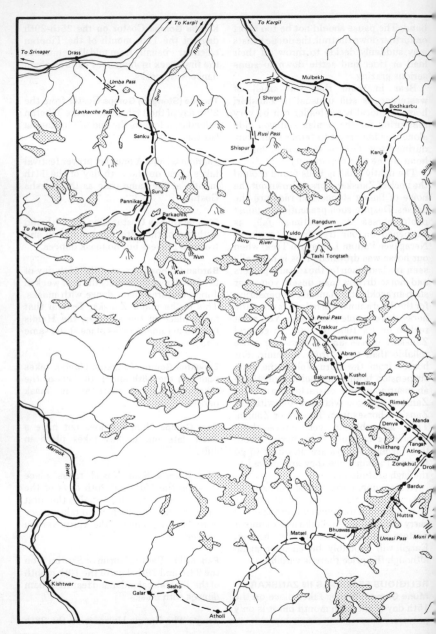

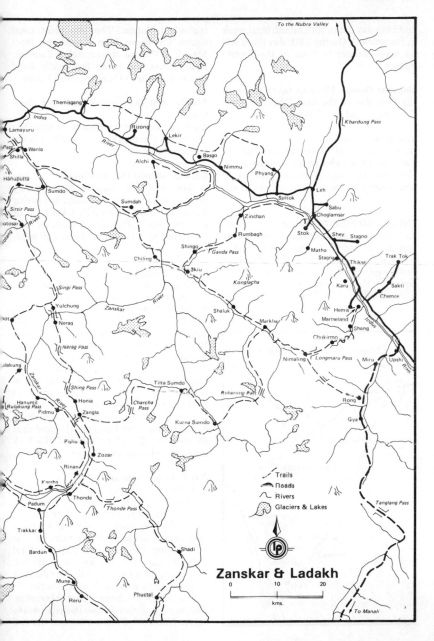

To the Nubra Valley

Khardung Pass

Themisgang
Indus
Lamayuru
Rizong
Lekir
Pass
Shilla
Wanla
Basgo
Nimmu
River
Alchi
Phyang
Hanuputta
Leh
Sumdo
Spituk
Sabu
Sirsir Pass
Sumdah
Choglamsar
otosar
River
Zinchan
Stok
Shey
Stagno
Rumbagh
Matho
Trak Tok
Shingo
Ganda Pass
Stagna
Chiling
Thikse
Skiu
Konglacha
Karu
Sakti
Singi Pass
Chemre
Yulchung
Zanskar
River
Shaluk
Hemis
Neraq
Marklha
Martseland
Nerag Pass
Shang
Chikirmo
Nimaling
Longmaru Pass
Miru
Upshi
ulakung
River
Tilta Sumdo
Kulun
Hanumil
Honia
Charcha
Rulakung Pass
Pidmu
Zangla
Pass
Rong
Kurna Sumdo
Gya
Pishu
Zozar
Rinan
Karsha
Padum
Thonde
Tanglang Pass
Trakkar
Thonde Pass
Bardun
Shadi

Trails
Roads
Rivers
Glaciers & Lakes

Mune
Phuctal

Zanskar & Ladakh

0   10   20

kms.

Reru

To Manali

and 29th day of the 10th month (first week in December). On the 29th day there will be mask dances in front of the Zangla Palace.

Lingshot Gompa Monlam takes place on the 15th day of the first Tibetan month (February) and consists of prayers.

Visiting Gompas
At present most of the monasteries in Zanskar do not charge any entrance fee. However, the monks prefer tourists to arrive early in the morning or late in the evening.

TREKS TO/FROM ZANSKAR
Zanskar is often pronounced as Zanhar and still appears on many maps as Zaskar – one of those Victorian-era errors which cartographers have perpetuated right down to the present. There are many routes leading in to Zanskar, despite the

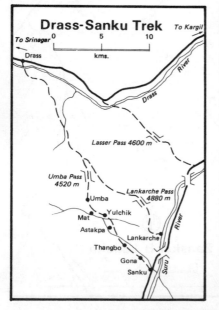

region's isolation. The two most used routes are those from Kargil and from Manali to Padum, the capital of Zanskar. Apart from the most frequently used routes there are others less well known.

PAHALGAM (Kashmir)-PANNIKAR (Suru Valley)
An eight-day trek continuing on from the Amarnath Cave trek and described in the Kashmir section.

DRASS-SANKU (Suru Valley)
A three day trek from the Drass Valley directly into the Suru Valley, bypassing Kargil. It is suitable for a Zanskar trek, for a Drass-Sanku-Pannikar-Pahalgam trek or simply as a Drass-Sanku-Kargil mini-trek.

KARGIL-PADUM
Although the Kargil-Padum road was completed in the early '80s the severe winter of '83 knocked much of it out. Even at the best of times it's a rough road suitable only for the hardiest of vehicles. When the road is repaired, including the bridges over the tributaries of the Stod in Zanskar, the Kargil-Padum road will be passable from early June to late October. If the road between Namsuru and Parkachik is open and a vehicle is available then it is possible to go from Kargil to the Pensi La in one day and thus shorten the first four days of the trek detailed below to one.

Day 1: Kargil-Namsuru
The first day consists of preparation in Kargil, then a bus or jeep trip to Namsuru. Beyond Kargil you do not follow the Leh road, which crosses the Suru at Chanchi over a metal bridge, but turn right into the Suru Valley. The route goes past the Hotel d'Zojila and for 15 km is surfaced, continuing over Grantung to the village of Rispong (20 km) which has a mosque.

The route continues past Martodas, Skininurai and Sanskritwe (Sanskarwe) to Sanku (Sankoo). Sanku was once the end

of the bus route, 42 km out, and has a school and Dak Bungalow. The road switches to the right-hand side of the river four km past Sanku and continues for 7.5 km before changing back to the left-hand side towards Namsuru. From Sanku to Namsuru you pass through the villages of Kur, Phokra, Partik and Yoljok.

Day 2: Namsuru-Pannikar-Parkutse
Horses and porters can be hired in Namsuru or Pannikar but it is a good idea to book horses in advance as they may all be out on the trail. The road continues along the river valley, but the trekking route cuts off the wide river bend. The Suru River is crossed over a large wooden bridge near to Namsuru, the route climbs over the town of Pannikar in zig-zag curves to a ridge, from which the Nun and Kun massif can be seen to the south-east.

Most of the horses hired in the Namsuru-Pannikar region for trekking in

Zanskar will be hired from Kashmiris because this is where the last major settlement of Indo-Aryans and Muslims is to be found. Note that on the road to Pannikar roads marked 'impassable' may only be partially blocked by landslides and can be carefully crossed. Beyond the ridge of Pannikar the trekking route winds down to a good camping spot with fresh grass at Parkutse. Here you meet the road again; from here to the Rangdum Gompa it runs along the northern river bank.

Day 3: Parkutse-Parkachik-Yuldo-Rangdum Gompa
Parkachik is the approach base for the Nun Glacier and the last Muslim village en route to Padum. Between the village of Parkachik and the next camping place at Gulmatang there is some absolutely breathtaking scenery in this practically uninhabited valley. On the other side of the river the Ganri Glacier extends directly from the Nun and Kun saddle to

the river below, it's coloured green from the high copper content in the subsoil (Zan means copper, skar means valley). The Kargil region is rich in other minerals too; chromite, sulphur, limestone, borax, soda and gold have been extracted from some of the rivers.

Closer to Gulmatang, opposite the Shafat Glacier, there is a fantastic view to the right of the Nun and Kun massif. The Nun peak is approached from the village of Tangole, the Kun peak from Shafat. Past Gulmatang the road continues through Zulichok, then past the ruins of the village of Shakar on the left; depopulated some years ago by smallpox.

Yuldo is the first town with a Zanskari population, situated six km before the Rangdum Gompa. Travellers are likely to get a friendly welcome in the small (just 10 or so houses) village. If you do not wish to continue by car to Padum or Karsha you can leave your vehicle here and take native Zanskar ponies. Prices range from Rs 25 a day and up.

The journey from here to the gompa can be shortened by cutting across the many corners along the road, especially where it runs on the northern slope of the wide, gravel plain. You have to cross a network of rivers which meander through this plain and here, as elsewhere on this trek, the river crossings are easier earlier in the day. Melting snow raises the rivers later in the day. From Yuldo the Rangdum Gompa, where 40 Gelugpa (yellow-cap) monks reside, is already visible in the distance, perched on a steep, sugarloaf mountain.

According to an inscription the monastery was built about 250 years ago by Gelek Yashy Takpa during the reign of King Tsewang Namgyal of Ladakh. As in other monasteries travellers are expected to make a donation when visiting the gompa. The small mani walls, here and further along towards Padum, are more ornate than in Ladakh. Buddha reliefs are arranged on the stones and some of the stones are carved not only with the usual 'om mani padme hum' mantra but also

with pictures of chortens and mandalas. There is a field suitable for camping about 1.5 km from the gompa towards the Pensi La pass. Gnats from the nearby swamp can be a nuisance but in compensation edelweiss grow in profusion.

Day 4: Rangdum Gompa-Pensi La

By vehicle you could have got to the Pensi La in one day, as noted in the introduction to this trek. It's about 25 km from the gompa to the 4401 metre Pensi La pass into Zanskar. The road runs along the north-eastern slopes, giving beautiful views of the mountains to the west. If you have come the whole way on foot and become reasonably acclimatised to the altitude, the climb to the Pensi La will be relatively easy. On your way to the pass you come across stone heaps with prayer flags; travellers add their mani stones or small flags with a picture of a horse's head and the usual mantra.

There are 20-odd ponds at the top of the pass where you should have no difficulty in finding a good camping place. The pass is an alpine high plain with firm, soft grass, rosemary and other alpine flowers and many red-brown marmots who pop up out of their holes to survey, warily, any intruders. The view is superb – to the south-east you can see the Takar and many other glaciers.

Several hours walk will take you to the glacier in the south-west side valley but beware of the river which, due to the melting snow, may be fordable in the morning but impossible in the afternoon. The summit at the end of the valley, of which only the peak can be seen, is 7072 metres high while the mountain to the north stands at 6873 metres. There are many unnamed peaks in the area, waiting for intrepid mountaineers to be the first to climb them.

The descent from the Pensi La into the Stod Valley is steeper than the climb up from the Rangdum Gompa, but not too difficult. The road winds about with many hairpin turns, which can be cut across on

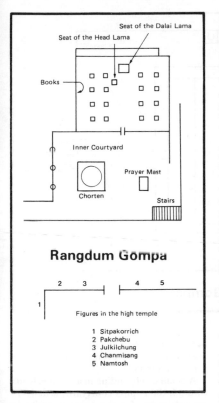

Rangdum Gompa

Figures in the high temple

1 Sitpakorrich
2 Pakchebu
3 Julkilchung
4 Chanmisang
5 Namtosh

foot, to the river below. Wild rhubarb can be seen growing on the slopes. The generally used trekking route follows the road on the left bank of the Stod (or Doda). There may now be a bridge over the river. The grass at the foot of the Pensi La furnishes a good pasturage and this is a fine camping spot, although Trakkur, shortly before the crossing of the Chinzum (Ghinzilin) is also to be recommended. Another good camping place is Chumkurmu (3920 metres).

Day 5: Pensi La-Abran

Past Chumkurmu you reach a spectacular, but short, ravine which the Chanu (Chinu) River, coming in from the left (north), has cut through a ridge. A road bridge has been built over the ravine and a temporary bridge leads down to the river and over a bridge to the other bank, up to the river terraces. The left bank route continues through Aksho (3750 metres), Chibra, crosses a tributary of the Stod and finally reaches Abran (3700 metres), the first village of the Zanskar Valley.

Day 6: Abran-Phe

From Abran to Phe, where there is a small and currently deserted gompa above the village, you pass the interesting little villages of Hamiling and Kygam, where there are only a few houses. The route is now generally heading south-east. Opposite Phe (3600 metres) the Bardur Valley opens into the broad Stod Valley. Because the Stod cannot be crossed at this point you must go further towards Padum to the Tungri Bridge, then back along the other side of the Stod, if you wish to visit the Bardur Valley with the Zongkhul Gompa or to trek over the Umasi La to Kishtwar (see Tungri-Zongkhul Gompa Roundtrip or the Padum-Kishtwar Trek).

From Phe a route goes north-east to the Rulakung La and then turns down to Hanumil on the Zanskar River on the way to Padum or past the Lingshot Gompa and on to Lamayuru (see Padum-Lamayuru Trek) on the Kargil-Leh road.

Day 7: Phe-Padum

The road to Padum leads through the very picturesque villages of Rantak Shuk, Shamuni and Tarkand to Tungri. A new road will probably be built from Tungri to the Karsha Gompa, currently a three-hour journey on foot. The footpath to Padum runs past Tungri, over the sturdy wooden bridge (stone supports) to the right-hand side of the Stod and then past Sani.

Next to Karsha the Sani (Sanee) Gompa is the most important monastery near to Padum. The gompa is unusual in that it is not built on a hill or mountain side but on flat ground and is then encircled by a stone wall in which chortens are mounted

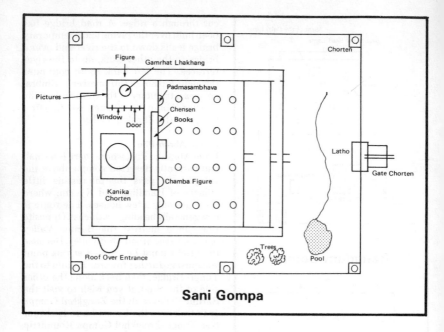

Sani Gompa

at intervals. You enter this 25-monk, red-cap monastery through a gate chorten with prayer mills. It leads to a Latho or House of God. The monastery walls have the usual symbols to ward off evil spirits and, for the same purpose, there is a goat's head filled with jewels, fortune-bringing mantras and prayer cards with 'om mani padme hum' written on them. The monastery is subject to the control of the Stagna Turku in Ladakh.

If you happen to be there at the right time, or provide a suitable donation, you may see the long ceremony in which the symbols of fortune are consecrated. The ceremony involves a goat's head being sizzled in a large pot. The value of the 'garnishings' which the monks add to the pot during the proceedings depends upon the prosperity of the person who donated the head and for whom it is supposed to bring good fortune. Look out for the goats' heads which hang outside practically

every house in Leh and other towns. In the normal course of events this symbol is renewed annually.

A small ditch, ending in a temple, leads through the gompa courtyard; it delivers enough water for the trees, a rarity in Zanskar, which grow there. The Dukhang, with its 16 columns, houses a Chamba, a Chenren and a Padmasambhava figure amongst others. The Gonkhang is a small room behind the altar, worth seeing for it contains an old figure of the Cho Rimpoche and a new bookshelf lattice work for the holy writings of Kandshur. Upstairs there are the rooms of the head lama, a storage room for tankas and, on the left side, the room of Dorje Chan.

More interesting than these first storey rooms is the old part of the gompa, which can be reached through the corridors which run right round the monastery. In this low and dark passage many small Tsatsas lie on the floor. The corridor ends in a further inner courtyard, past the large Kanika chorten where Buddhist relics are preserved. To the right of the chorten, squeezed between the main building of the gompa and the corridor, is the Gamshot Lhakhang in which Padmasambhava is supposed to have dwelt for five years. A door from the inner courtyard leads into the room. If it is locked you can still look through the window and see the Padmasambhava figure in the middle and historical scenes in half-relief on both sides.

North-west, outside the fenced-in area of the gompa, there's one of the most important cremation places in Zanskar or Ladakh – well known on account of its two-metre high dark grey boulder, on which a relief of the Maitriya has been carved. It shines from the sacrificial oil which monks and pilgrims pour over the Buddha image. Other smaller, crumbled-away stones can be seen in the semi-circle and the picture is completed by a prayer mast with fluttering prayer flags.

Ponies can be hired here from Rs 30 per day, porters cost Rs 10 to 25. In contrast to the ponies of the Kashmir Valley these are suitable for a trek through Karsha up the left side of the Zanskar, past the Lingshot Gompa to Lamayuru. An alternative stretch from Pensi La to Tungri leads up the right side of the Stod, at the foot of the Takar Glacier, south-east through Chibra, Chukarpa, Denya and Tangar, then opposite from Phe into the Bardur Valley where the route merges, at the Zongkhul Gompa, with that described under Tungri-Zongkhul Gompa Roundtrip and Padum-Kishtwar Trek. You cross the Bardur River, follow it downstream on the right bank and turn again at Ating into the Stod Valley which you then follow to Padum. This route from the Pensi La to the Tungri Bridge is shorter than that on the left bank of the Stod, but much less travelled and little known.

MANALI-PADUM

The 10 day trek from Manali to Padum can take one of two routes. One goes from Darcha over the 5100 metre Shingo La pass to Kargiakh. The alternative route continue from Darcha along the Leh road to a little beyond Sarai Kilang then turns north-west and crosses the 5345 metre Phirtse La pass, eventually meeting the first route a little north of Kargiakh. At one time it was difficult to take the first route without special permission but this no longer appears to be the case.

Manali-Darcha

There has now been a summer time bus service across the 3650 metre Rothang Pass from Manali to Keylong and on to Darcha for several years but, as on the Srinagar-Leh road, travellers often have to wait for the pass to be cleared and the road opened each summer. In Manali John Bannon organises tours and vehicles for this trip. The surfaced road ends at Darcha and the gravel road which continues north-east, all the way to Leh, is suitable for four-wheel drive only and is only open to the military. From Darcha the 5100 metre Shingo La pass leads directly into the Zanskar valley – see Alternative 2 below. To trek right through the Zanskar valley to Lamayuru or Kargil will take 16 to 20 days.

ALTERNATIVE 1

Day 1: Darcha-Mane Bar (4150 metres)

Darcha, at 3300 metres, is a control post and the police chief will want to see passes. Westwards, on the bank of the Bhaga, the good road continues to the next rest place at Sarai Valley where there is a small lake (no swimming though) to the left of the road with a good view of the ravine; a good spot for a rest.

A little beyond here the road crosses to the left bank of the river by a wooden bridge, then continues to Pataiso. The river terraces broaden out to a rolling, grassy plain while the river runs in a deep ravine. Topachani will be reached late in the afternoon, fast walkers can continue to Zingzing Bar or Mane Bar.

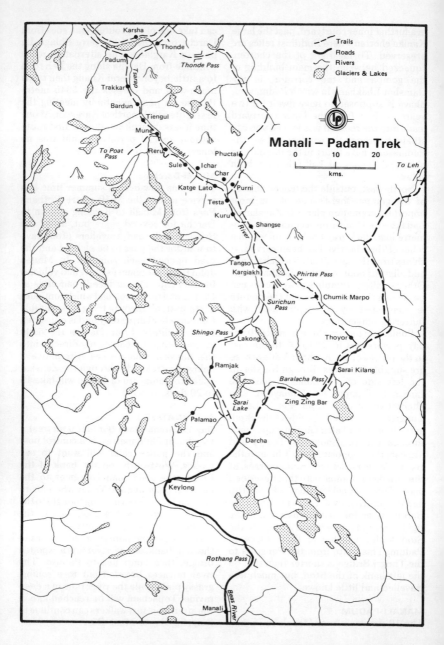

Karsha
Thonde
Padum
Thonde Pass
Trakkar
Bardun
Tiengul
Mune
(Lumaki)
To Poat
Pass
Reru
Sule
Ichar
Char
Katge Lato
Testa
Kuru
Tangso
Kargiakh
Shingo Pass
Lakong
Ramjak
Sarai
Lake
Palamao
Darcha
Keylong
Rothang Pass

Phuctal
Purni
Shangse
Phirtse Pass
Surichun
Pass
Chumik Marpo
Thoyor
Sarai Kilang
Baralacha Pass
Zing Zing Bar

To Leh

Tsarap

River

Beas River

Manali

Manali – Padam Trek

Trails
Roads
Rivers
Glaciers & Lakes

0   10   20
kms.

Day 2: Mane Bar-Sarai Kilang (4460 metres)

This day's walk crosses the Baralacha La, but although the route starts almost at the pass height the climb to the top should not be underestimated. The Baralacha La is a double pass to the east and south. Even the lower, eastward, pass is, at 4891 metres, higher than Mont Blanc, the highest mountain in Europe, and twice the height of Mt Kosciusko, the highest mountain in Australia! To the right the pass is close to the Suruf Lake and in good weather you can see snow-capped five and six thousand metre peaks. The southern pass is at 5100 metres and gives a view further southwards. The route continues to the left bank of the Yaman River, whose source is in the Suru Valley, to the Sarai Kilang camping place, a grassy oasis with a brook.

Day 3: Sarai Kilang-Debni (4360 metres)

An early start is advisable. The route, now just a track, fords the river and continues until the Keylong River, entering from the left, obstructs the route. As with all river crossings in Zanskar the earlier you cross, the lower the water level will be. Take no risks, this is a dangerous crossing. Running shoes should be worn for the crossing since they give more secure footing on the slippery rocks.

Further along the left bank of the Yaman there is a wide, grassy plain. If you take a short detour to the right to the edge of the river terraces there is a view of the deep Loess ravine of the Yaman; beware of the crumbling ravine edge. The route continues over the plain into the valley then gradually uphill towards the Phirtse La pass, the highest pass on the whole trek. First the 4280 metre Thoyer is reached, then the walk continues on the right bank of the Lingti Chu, following it upstream and across some deep side streams. After some more up and down walking Debni, the next overnight halt, is reached.

Day 4: Debni-Chumik Marpo (4600 metres)

Again it is wise to start early in order to cross the Kamirup, which enters the river from the left, at Kyonon. By mid-day the route climbs over a ridge to the right of the river; it's cut through by a cleft. Past here is the next river crossing; the Trukkar enters from the left from the Phirtse La Glacier. Trukkar is a rest stop but you should continue on to the overnight stop at the foot of the pass. From here a route branches off to the left over Kurziakpulo and the Surichun La to Kargiakh, but it doesn't gain much.

Day 5: Chumik Marpo-Shingsan (4460 metres)

Once again you should start early for this fine walk over the Phirtse La (5435 metres). On the pass crest there is a mini glacier to the left and to the right a mani stone with prayer flags. Past it there is a small, rocky peak which gives a better view than the pass itself. On clear days it extends to the Karakoram range in the north. The route now descends steeply into the valley of the Phirtse Chu to the camping place in front of a rubble slope.

Day 6: Shingsan-Kargiakh (4060 metres) or **Purni** (3750 metres)

The rubble slope has to be climbed first thing, by noon you reach a mountain from where the Zanskar valley is visible to the west and the valley of the Kargiakh Chu to the south. The latter joins here with the Phirtse Chu at Anokh, one of the three tributaries of the Zanskar. A smaller path zig-zags steeply down to the valley. The route leads to the right into the village of Shangse, with long mani walls and a small gompa on a slope up to the right. Here the route splits, you can turn south to Kargiakh (see Alternative 2) and over the Shingo La back to Darcha, or continue north to Zanskar.

A wooden bridge crosses to the left side of the river from Shangse and you continue through the villages of Kuru, Testa and Yal before a second wooden bridge, with stone supports, leads back to the right bank. Above the bridges it is possible to camp in front of Purni. A second route also leads to Purni from Shangse, keeping to the right bank all the way, but it is not so interesting because there are no villages along the way.

Day 7: Purni-Phuctal Gompa

From here the trail again follows the left bank of the Tsarap Chu, the main tributary of the Zanskar, to a swinging but stable suspension bridge – gloves are recommended when crossing. Further along the other bank a surprising view presents itself at a bend in the path – the 500 year old Phuctal Gompa. The monastery is like a honeycomb, cut into a rock under a gigantic grotto, and has 70 yellow-cap monks. The name means 'through cave'.

The library, three large and one smaller prayer rooms, the kitchens, abbot's chamber, chorten and the grave of Gangsem Sherap Sanpo, who founded Phuctal, Lekir and Rangdum, are all worth seeing. In the caves over the monastery there is a waterhole whose water level never changes; the water is said to have healing properties. There is also a stone tablet left by the Hungarian Alexander Csoma de Koros. He was one of the first explorers of Tibet and spent some time here in 1826-27.

Day 8: Phuctal Gompa-Katge Lato (3800 metres)

There is a route back along the west bank of the river to Char but it is not recommended because the Char bridge is in a dangerous condition. It is better to return along the left bank to Purni, cross the bridge and go further to the right over a ridge, past which is the Katge Lato camping place with a view over the deteriorated Char bridge, far below.

Day 9: Katge Lato-Reru (3680 metres)

There is again much variety on the day's walk. There are many picturesque villages on the bank opposite to Char – first Abnop

then Dorzong, green oases in the monotonous grey-brown, and finally the Ichar castle, reached by a hanging bridge across the valley. Certain places, with rubble hills and steep, sandy slopes, call for careful treading. Three hours further walking brings you to a camping place opposite Reru, in a side valley to the left of the main route, on green grass with a brook.

Day 10: Reru-Padum (3500 metres)

From the camping place the route goes up on the plateau and over a bridge to the town of Reru with an interesting gateway chorten. The route continues past the town on the wide river terraces towards Mune. There is a gompa on a steep hill behind the lovely little village but beware of the red-cap monks' ferocious dog! From here a route leads to the left to the 6150 metres Poat La pass, the highest and most difficult pass in Zanskar. It involves crossing a glacier.

Continuing towards Padum you cross Tema and reach the Charmoche Kore camping ground. It goes on past Tiangul to a large rock from where the Bardun Gompa is visible. This gompa was founded by Shabdru, who also founded the Hemis Gompa in Ladakh and later went to Bhutan. There are only a handful of monks working on the reconstruction of the partially ruined gompa. The climb up to the roof is worthwhile. The gompa's principal image is a Gandhara statue of the Buddha Maitriya, which is less than a metre in height and is said to have spoken.

Near the gompa there is a good camping place where a spring issues from the rocks. Two to three hours further, with the river always to the right, you will reach the wide plains of Zanskar with picturesque villages on both sides of the valley, and ahead Padum, the administrative 'capital' of Zanskar.

ALTERNATIVE 2

This description covers the route between Kargiakh and Darcha when travelling south. You can also take this route across the Shingo La heading north from Manali to Padum. It's also possible to make an eight to 10 day round trip trek from Darcha to Darcha – see Alternative 1 for details of the route from Darcha or Padum to Kargiakh. Heading south Kargiakh is the last inhabited settlement on this route until you reach Chikka (or Chica), shortly before Darcha.

From Kargiakh at 4060 metres you must head upstream as early as possible to the river crossing, above the point where a small stream joins it. You can camp by the mani walls or further uphill at Lakong (4450 metres). Here the valley branches out and a small valley to the right leads to the Shingo La at 5100 metres.

Day 2: Shingo La-Ramjak

The ascent to the top of the pass should be undertaken early in the morning. There is a superb view of the surrounding mountains from the crest of the pass, on which snow lies all year round. The highest peak, directly to the south, is 6797 metres. The descent from the pass follows the river on its right bank. The route to the next camping place, below the 'south peak' at a stone hut called Ramjak (4270 metres), is not difficult.

Day 3: Ramjak-Darcha

Set out early in the morning to the Barai Nallah which comes from the right and cross the Shingo La River at this point. If the snowfall in the last year has been heavy it is possible to cross by snow bridges as late as July but if the snow is melted you must wade across. The river is wild and rapid so this is probably the most difficult point of the whole trip.

Continue along the left side of the high valley to a good camping place where the highest trees grow at 3700 metres. A small bridge leads there over a raging mountain brook. Another brook, with a waterfall, branches off and here you can find another camping spot. Yet another one can be found past a wooden bridge over a deep

ravine. From here it is only about three hours to Darcha. Chikka, a couple of hours before Darcha, is the first habitation after Kargiakh.

PADUM-LAMAYURU
ALTERNATIVE 1 – via Zangla & Nerag

A local guide is an absolute necessity on this route.

Day 1: Padum-Thonde As the Around Padum Trek.

Day 2: Thonde-Honia

As far as Zangla the route is the same as for the Around Padum Trek. From Zangla past Honia to Nerag is difficult, especially for horses, and should be traversed in late-summer if the previous winter had heavy snow. Rain can also make this route impassable. Above the small village of Honia there is a small spring and you should overnight here whether you have come in a one-day march from Padum or have already spent a night at Thonde along the way.

Day 3: Honia-over the Shing La-Kharmapu

The steep ascent to the Shing La pass begins after Honia. The first stretch can be dangerous due to a deep cut brook which leads directly along the steep slope. In '77 I lost my pack horse with all my personal luggage here. Past the 4500 metre high Shing La you enter a valley with tufaceous limestone formations reminiscent of those in Turkey.

At Kharmapu you can camp by the river, only a few km from growing willows so that burning fuel need not be brought along. You can also camp at the foot of the double pass of Nerag La, beyond Kharmapu, but although this allows you to reach Nerag in one day the camp is at 4900 metres, just below the pass, and at this height fuel for the fire and fodder for the horses is not readily available.

Day 4: Kharmapu-foot of the Nerang La

This route is very difficult and Zanskari

guides and porters are essential. At several places you have to wade across rivers and the trail crosses steep rubble hills above wild mountain brooks. Paths must be cleared (don't forget shovels) for the horses to find their footing. At one point the route leads through a tunnel-like rock passage in the bed of a brook and subsequently under an ice cornice, even in high summer. Even past this rough stretch the actual ascent to the pass requires some skill.

Day 5: Nerag La-Nerag

The view from the Nerag La, over the village 1500 metres below and to the mountain range on the other side of the Zanskar, is superb. Shortly before Nerag you can again find burnable wood and there are some suitable camping spots above the village. Pasturage for the horses and fresh water are also on hand.

Day 6: Nerag-Yulchung-Singi La-Photosar

Two km below Nerag there is a wooden bridge across the Zanskar which is suitable for horses. Immediately on the other side of the Zanskar (3400 metres), which here flows in eastwards in a deep-cut bed towards Nimmu, the ascent towards the Singi La begins. The first saddle is at 3990 metres, the second at 3930 metres. Near Yulchung the route bends left to the Lingshot Gompa (see Padum-Lamayuru Trek, Alternative 2).

At Yulchung one can marvel at the irrigation techniques of the Zanskaris. Above the village melted ice-water from the mountain brooks is first collected in ponds and warmed through insulation, then conducted into the struggling small fields with their poor soil. There is a grand panorama to the east with waterfalls cascading down the rock walls on the other side of the Singi La or 'Lion Pass' (4850 metres). The trekking path wanders around the western valley slope through many side valleys. Mountain wanderers can take a short cut on the northern rubble slopes by cutting across the serpentine

curves on the route leading to the valley.

The valley floor is quite marshy due to the brook flowing eastwards from Photosar into the Photang River. In summer it is richly grown and provides good grazing pasturage. The route leaves the western side of the valley and crosses a small pass, then through a mountain ridge between the valley it came out of and the Photang Valley in which lies Photosar. If you arrive late do not go straight into the village but camp on the southern slope of the Photang River, opposite Photosar, where there is also pasturage for horses.

Day 7: Photosar-Shirshi La-Hanuputta

According to our Zanskari guide Photosar means 'salt-cave'. It stands at 4100 metres on a small plateau on the other side of the eastward flowing Photang River. The name touches on the fact that during the rain so much salt is washed out of the rockwall past Photosar that the fields around the village slowly become infertile due to this mineralised irrigation. Sited 50 metres above the river Photosar is an attractive place even when the peace is disturbed by loudspeakers, playing music from All India Radio. Upstream from Photosar, to the west, is the bridge over the Photang River.

The route to Lamayuru follows the Photang-Drogpo to the west, first on the southern banks then, after three km, on the northern. The route leads through terraced fields then turns north-east into a side valley of the Photang River. En route to the pass you can see marmots and rock ptarmigans. It's only a short trek to the Shirshi La (or Sirsir La) and only the last hundred metres is steep and strenuous. Above the top of the pass you find, as on every pass in Ladakh and Zanskar, a Latho ('god house') with coloured prayer flags and mani stones. The flags show the head of a horse in the middle and every Buddhist traveller will leave behind a flag with a mantra printed on it. Do not collect these as souvenirs under any circumstances! The descent from the pass into the valley of the Tang is steep but not very difficult. From here there are two routes to Lamayuru:

1. via Hanuputta and Wanla
2. through the valley of the Shillakong to Wanla

The route via Hanuputta descends from the Shirshi La through the valley of the Tang on the right river bank, high on the slope to the north-east. After some kms it crosses a bridge to the left bank where the river is wider and the path better. As in most Zanskari villages it is difficult to obtain food supplies in Hanuputta.

Day 8: Hanuputta-Wanla-Shilla-Prikiti La-Lamayuru

The route from Hanuputta to Wanla is difficult and not always passable – especially for pack animals. Past Hanuputta the route leads down to the river and forces through a narrow spot to where you can ford the river. A little later it climbs above the river to a place where it cuts deeply through the rock. At times the path ends at the water and you must continue along the bank to find a place shallow enough to cross to the other side. The path then winds steeply up the rocks where the ponies clamber like deer.

Heading north-west there are dangerous stretches where the ponies must be unloaded and led across step-by-step. The process repeats itself for a couple of hours – unload, lead the ponies across, carry the loads across, load the ponies, continue on. Finally the mountains open and the path becomes much more hospitable.

The next village offers the inviting shade of apricot trees and the route then leads along a precipice and descends to the bottom of the valley. Here one goes past field after field and large settlements until Wanla is reached. A left turn takes you into the Shillakong Valley and shortly past the village of Shilla you turn right (north). Early in the morning a part of the route in the narrow, barren valley to the 3900 metre Prikiti La ('Lizard Pass') is still in shadow – for both man and beast this is very pleasant. By noon the climb in the strong sun can become an ordeal. From the Prikiti La the route leads north-east into the Lamayuru Valley then, once cultivated fields have been reached, a short way to the west.

The Lamayuru monastery is first seen to the right on a sugarloaf mountain. The trail leads westwards from the monastery hill through the village of Lamayuru to the Fatu La-Nimmu-Leh road, on which from the Prikiti La you can already see trucks crawling. Careful – Zanskari horses are not accustomed to traffic and scare easily, the noise of movie cameras can also frighten them! You should unload them as quickly as possible on the road. From here you can take a bus or truck to Leh or to Kargil and Srinagar.

Souvenir seller at Lamayuru Gompa

Alternative Route – final day
Day 7 to 9: Photosar-Shirshi La-over the Tang River-Niuche La-into the Shillakong Valley-Shilla-Prikiti La-Lamayuru

If the Hanuputta-Wanla route is impassable then this route may be an alternative. It crosses the Tang River (4500 metres) past the Shirshi La, whereas the Hanuputta route follows this river.

Cross the river as early as possibly in the morning since the river is very rapid after mid-day. The trail then goes northwest into the side valley opposite. If you get here in the afternoon you should seek a camping spot with pasturage for the horses. The last kms to the 5050 metre Niuche La are barren and terrible for camping. On the other side of the pass, to the north-west, there is another camping possibility at 4450 metres. The route continues down into the Shillakong rivervalley which it follows to Shilla. This 20 to 25 km route is unique since the valley is so narrow that at times you have to go along the river-bed! Note the mineral layers in this ravine, indicative of the dislocation the creation of the mountain range must have caused.

Shortly before Shilla there are three unstable wooden bridges, one of which is particularly bad. The route crosses a stone bridge with a Latho to a warm spring which is said to have healing properties. From the top of the pass you can reach Shilla (3300 metres) in one day, from where the route is the same as the Hanuputta-Wanla alternative.

ALTERNATIVE 2 – via Lingshot Gompa
Day 1: Padum-Pishu

You can go via Rubruk to Yalong (Yulung) and Karsha or via Sani, the Tungri Bridge and then downstream along the Stod which is altogether a six hour trek to Karsha. From Karsha you continue on the left bank of the Zanskar to where the Stod joins with the Tsarap Lingti Chu and through Ridam to Pishu. Pishu is six hours from Karsha. There are camping spots with grass for the animals by the river.

Past Karsha the fields stop and the relatively infrequently travelled path is bordered by sandstone. The mountains creep closer to the trail; constant erosion has carved them into fantastical shapes. The geological layers are quite easy to observe. Before the village of Pishu the banks get narrower and narrower and at Pishu you can cross the river by a rope bridge, as related in the Around Padum Trek.

Day 2, 3 & 4: Pishu-Lingshot Gompa

Past Pishu the route leads at first along the bank of the Zanskar until the village of Pidmu (Pigmu or Pittu) is reached after four to five hours. Some tributaries of the Zanskar must be crossed but they should present no problem. The path then runs very close to a brook, so close that you can bargain on getting wet feet at some stage. You can stay overnight near the small village of Hanumil (Hanomul) past where the route runs through grassland. A route branches off to the left towards Rulakung and over the Rulakung La to Phe (see Kargil-Padum Trek).

The valley narrows, the path is hewn through rocks, the bank is steep and at one point, which the rocks overhang, ponies can only be led unloaded. Once past this difficult point a short climb leads over a rubble hill while to the right the Zanskar River storms past the practically vertical bank. The trail continues along the steep slopes, over which the native ponies go with great certainty.

After a few hours the path leads left to a small pass which is indicated on some maps as the Purfi La. The pass is only steep over the last hundred metres. On the north side the trail makes tight bends through grass slopes and bushes then turns right and continues over broken rocks and rubble. At a sharp bend the river and a ruined bridge can be seen far below.

With a climbing rope and poplars, which grow on the bank, you can build a makeshift bridge at a narrower point. The pack animals can, unloaded, swim the river at a wider, less rapid point. On the other side the climb begins to a small pass and at this height the trail leads along a steep canyon wall then slowly gets easier. There is grass and a good camping spot in the valley below.

Continuing upstream towards Lingshot there are snow bridges which can still be crossed in mid-summer. After a while the valley widens and the horses have no more strenuous climbing. The path then turns right and soon the pass saddle is visible with the usual mani stones and prayer flags. From the top of the Hamalun La (or Hanuma La) there is a fine view of the Lingshot Gompa on the other side of the valley. The descent, over sand hills, is steep and several hills and rises must be crossed during the descent into the valley.

After a few hours the village of Lingshot and the Lingshot Gompa are reached. Lingshot (also Lingshed) has 60 monks and is famous, in Zanskar, for its school of painting. In the gompa there are a large number of superb paintings made with bright mineral pigments.

Day 5: Lingshot-Yulchung
Past Lingshot the route leads eastwards over mountains and passes to Yulchung. Turning right here will take you back to the Zanskar Valley via Nerag.

Day 6, 7 & 8: Yulchung-Lamayuru
The last three days are as Alternative 1 for the Padum-Lamayuru Trek.

PADUM-KISHTWAR
This trek from Padum, passing over the 5234 metre high Umasi La, can only be undertaken with local porters. Since most of the porters do not understand any English it is worth discussing the route with the porters before departure, the Tourist Officer will interpret. One porter per person is recommended. Zanskari porters are faster, harder-working and generally friendlier than Kashmiri pony-

drivers so there will undoubtedly be many more trekkers using Zanskaris in the future. The price is about Rs 25 per day for a porter. They will only set out for the Umasi La in good, fog-free, weather so you should also allow Rs 10 per day for waiting time.

No great difficulties are experienced on this trek so long as you are fit, healthy and acclimatised to the altitude. The ascent to the Umasi La pass is steeper but shorter from the Padum side than the Kishtwar side. Leggings are recommended because of the snow on the Umasi La and it is also wise to have a waterproof tent. Bring food supplies from Padum although you can also get some food in Matsel and Atholi.

Day 1: Padum-Ating
Do not hire horses, which are inappropriate for this trek; see the Tourist Officer for porters. It's a pleasant march to Ating with a bridgeless glacier river to cross – the earlier in the day the better.

Day 2: Ating-shortly before Ratrat
You turn from the Stod Valley into the south-west side valley of the Bardun and arrive at the Zongkhul Gompa or ravine fortress. The foundations of this monastery is attributed to the abbot Naropa, whose ceremonial dagger in the rocks of Zongkhul attracts many pilgrims today. The monastery belongs to the red-cap sect and had 20 monks about 15 to 20 years ago; today one seldom sees more than two to three. The route from Ating leads directly to the monastery in about two or three hours along a meandering path.

The monastery is built directly on a rock wall surrounded by about 10 stone houses which, from a distance, blend in to the grey background. Like the Hemis Gompa in Ladakh, the Zongkhul Gompa has an 'eagle's nest' which can be reached in about 10 minutes from the gompa – which offers superb views from the roof terrace. It's an easy seven hour climb to the excellent Ganra rest place which also has a wonderful view.

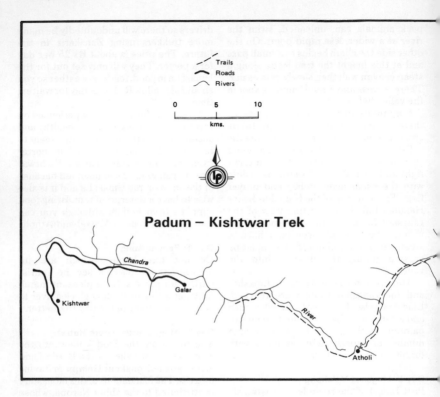

Trails
Roads
Rivers

0   5   10
kms.

Padum – Kishtwar Trek

Chandra

Galar

Kishtwar

River

Atholi

Day 3: Umasi La-shortly before Bhuswas
A 5½ hour climb takes you over a glacier
and a snowfield to the top of the pass with
its remarkable crest. On the other side of
the somewhat easier descent you go
through snowfields and then across another
glacier. The walk to the camping spot,
about an hour before Bhuswas, is about 12
hours. There is a spring, a river and grass
at the site.

Day 4: Bhuswas-Matsel
It's a pleasant eight-hour descent from
Bhuswas to a police station but nothing
will persuade Zanskari porters to go
further than here and it is difficult to hire
porters in Matsel (Machail or Machel).
For about Rs 150 you can eventually hire a

donkey to Kishtwar. Prices on this side of
the pass are significantly higher.

Day 5: Matsel-Atholi
The river valley becomes increasingly
narrow and the route more strenuous as it
leads over an unbroken sequence of
ascents and descents. Atholi is reached in
the late afternoon and the police comman-
dant is hospitable. Beware the gnats!

Day 6: Atholi-Shasho
As on the previous day the route is hard
work. It takes six to eight hours to reach
the Shasho rest place, a small, dirty,
uncared for site with three or four huts on
the mountain side. A stay in the huts is not
recommended.

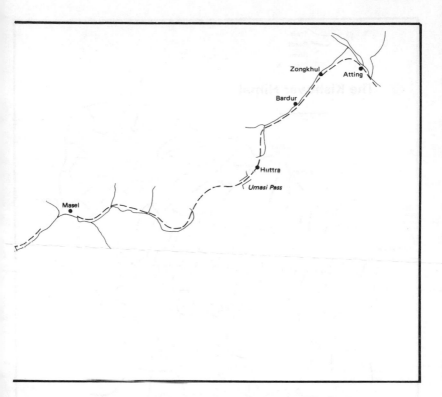

Day 7: Shasho-Galar-Kishtwar

The route continues to climb and drop and continues to be strenuous. During the monsoon it can be marshy and seem endless. Galar is reached after about seven hours and a road leads from here to Kishtwar. Work is in progress to extend this road from Galar back towards Atholi. Two or three buses go daily to Kishtwar from Galar, a distance of about 30 km. If you leave Atholi very early and travel fairly fast you can get to Galar in one day. The last bus leaves Galar about 5 pm; if you miss it you must overnight here and go to Kishtwar the next day. Long distance buses leave Kishtwar at about 6 am for Srinagar and other places.

PADUM-NIMMU

The first section of this trek as far as Hanuputta is covered in the Padum-Lamayuru Trek reports. Between Hanuputta and Wanla you turn right into a side valley, north of the Zanskar mountain chain, and continue upstream over a pass and then down a brook which is a western side arm of the Zanskar. You reach the Zanskar a few km to the north of the village of Chiling, with its chorten of Guru Padmasambhava, and follow the river's left bank to Nimmu.

A rope bridge crosses the Zanskar between Chiling and Nimmu so you can turn at Sumdo (the village where three rivers meet) into the Markha Valley. See the Markha Valley Trek in the Ladakh

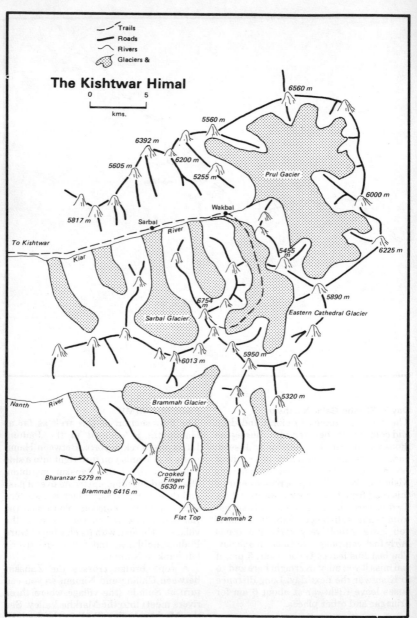

Trails
Roads
Rivers
Glaciers &

The Kishtwar Himal

0   5
kms.

6560 m

5560 m

6392 m
6200 m
5605 m
5255 m

Prul Gacier

6000 m

5817 m

Wakbal

Sarbal

River

To Kishtwar

Kiar

5455 m

6225 m

5890 m

6754 m

Sarbal Glacier

Eastern Cathedral Glacier

6013 m

5950 m

Nanth   River

Brammah Glacier

5320 m

Bharanzar 5279 m

Crooked
Finger
5630 m

Brammah 6416 m

Flat Top   Brammah 2

section and the Padum-Leh Trek. Near Nimmu, towards Leh and above the junction of the Zanskar and the Indus, there is a sturdy bridge capable of taking pack animals across the Indus. The route then goes on the right bank of the Zanskar to the Markha Valley. The direct route from Nerag through the Zanskar gorge to Nimmu is only possible in the winter on the ice of the river. The strenuous and hazardous trek lasts about five days.

PADUM-LEH – Markha Valley
This hard but very rewarding trek takes you from Padum to Zangla as on the Padum-Lamayuru Trek. At Zangla you turn right to the Charcha La pass (5200 metres) and from there to Tilta Sumdo via Tom Tokh. Here a path turns left towards Nimmu but you must turn right then in 12 to 15 km turn left towards Kurna Sumdo. To the right it goes further via Lapurbo to Kurna. From Kurna Sumdo the route continues past the Ruberung La pass (5000 metres) to the Markha Gompa in another day or two.

Here the route diverges: one route goes from the gompa to the right, past Hankar and in two days reaches Chokdo after which comes Hemis and finally along the Indus to Leh. The other route turns left from the Markha Gompa past Skiu, the Ganda La (or Kanda La) pass at 4800 metres and on to Rumbagh. From Rumbagh it crosses the 4880 metre Namlung Pass and on to Leh.

This difficult route is only recommended for the second half of August because from Zangla to Markha many crossings have to be made over large rivers. Often the water is chest high and by September it is once again too cold. See the Markha Valley trek in the Ladakh Trekking section for more details of the routes from Markha to Hemis or Spitok.

Days 1-2: Padum-Thonde-Zangla
As the roundtrip trek from Padum below.

Day 3: Zangla-Charcha Nullah
From Zangla you walk north-east, ascending the Zumling River. During the day you may have to cross the river 20 times.

Day 4: Charcha Nullah-across Charcha La
From below the pass it takes about four hours to ascend to the pass at nearly 5000 metres, marked by a chorten. Descending from the pass you follow a narrow gorge, crossing a shallow stream several times, sometimes on ice bridges and avalanche debris. At one point the gorge is less than two metres wide for about 50 metres. This could be difficult if the water level in the stream is high. You need to carry additional water for the ascent of the pass. The camp site below the pass is at Tom Tokh Sumdo.

Day 5: Tom Tokh Sumdo-near Tilta Sumdo
This hard day's walk follows a very rough, rocky and unstable trail with many river crossings – 20 to 30 in all. The walk is much more difficult if the river is high or after many recent rockfalls.

Day 6: Tilta Sumdo-below Ruberung La
Another hard day's walk with many river crossings to be made. The first 1½ hours walk to Tilta Sumdo involves a dozen crossings. Here the Khurna Cho flows in to form a major confluence and join the Zanskar River further to the north. Various nullahs join the river trail here. The turn-off for the Ruberung La is the second stream (nullah) from the left (north) after Tilta Sumdo.

Day 7: Ruberung La-Markha Valley
The ascent from here is up a narrow gorge with numerous other gorges joining it. It would be easy to take the wrong trail without a guide. The top of the pass, at 4900 metres, is reached after about three hours. From the top of the pass the path is quite clear and descends to a stream which you follow for four or five hours down to the Markha River.

Day 8-10: Markha-Chokdo-Hemis

The final three days are covered in the Markha Valley trek report in the Ladakh Trekking section.

PADUM

The locals say Padum, foreigners generally Padam. The capital of Zanskar, it stands on the southern part of a wide, fertile plain in which the Tsarap Lingti Chu (Lunak River) and the Stod (Doda) River join to form the Zanskar (Cham) River. There are only about a hundred houses in Padum, built on a barren, rock-covered hill. New houses are built in a semi-circle in the fields. The low hill, on which a fort once stood, today has only a small, insignificant gompa with its entrance facing the river. The chapel is practically empty apart from some recently painted murals.

Unlike most other Zanskaris, who are practically all Buddhists, about 300 of Padum's 700 inhabitants are not Ladakhis but Indo-Aryans like the Baltis and Lahulis and are followers of the Sunnite Muslim sect. The division into these two completely different population groups is instantly recognisable by the clothing they wear. The people are very hospitable but also shy, in the first four years after the re-opening of Zanskar to foreign visitors only a couple of hundred people passed through. Making contact with the children will result in an invitation into a house. If you wish to make a longer trek the Administration or the Tourist Bureau (yes!) will be happy to answer any questions and are very helpful with the hiring of horses (there are about 40 in Padum) or obtaining accommodation. An overnight stay in a private house in Padum will cost Rs 10 to Rs 20 per person.

There are a few shops in Padum, like Mohammed Amid's, but only the basics are available and prices are high. The government buildings outside Padum include a morse radio station which, when necessary, can call for a military helicopter from Leh, which can land near the Karsha Gompa on the other side of the Stod River. The local water is milky-white and highly mineralised and even when boiled for tea is not very palatable. In July and August stray·monsoon clouds sometimes creep into Zanskar from the plains of India and heavy showers are not uncommon in the afternoon. Therefore the excursion to Karsha should be made in the morning.

West of Padum, a good half hour's climb, is the small Tagrimo Gompa with an interesting Dukhang with a stamped clay floor. The paintings on the side walls are, unlike most gompas, not directly on the wall but on tanka cloths.

TREKS AROUND PADUM

There are a number of round trips that can be made from Padum but in any event a

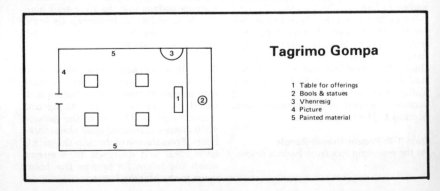

Tagrimo Gompa

1 Table for offerings
2 Bools & statues
3 Vhenresig
4 Picture
5 Painted material

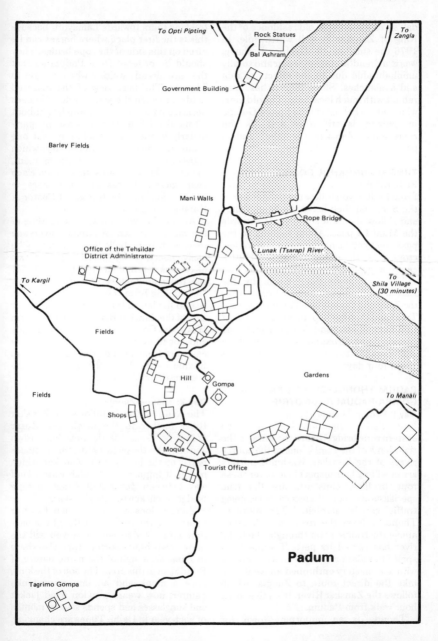

To Opti Pipting

Rock Statues

Bal Ashram

To Zangla

Government Building

Barley Fields

Mani Walls

Office of the Tehsildar
District Administrator

Lunak (Tsarap) River

Rope Bridge

To Kargil

To Shila Village
(30 minutes)

Fields

Hill

Gompa

Gardens

To Manali

Fields

Shops

Moque

Tourist Office

Padum

Tagrimo Gompa

day's excursion to the old residence of the King of Zanskar is well worthwhile. In 1976 the small castle, Gyalpoy Pothang, was in a dreadful state of repair and totally uninhabitable due to the effects of rain and avalanches. Since then it has been rebuilt with much local help. The old king, whose uncle belongs to the Spitok Gompa in Ladakh, is still alive and his son represents Zanskar in the Indian parliament.

TUNGRI-ZONGKHUL GOMPA ROUNDTRIP

From Padum you follow the Stod River to the Sani and then leave the Stod Valley and follow the Sani southwards towards the Muni La pass. About halfway to the pass crest you turn west into a side valley, cross a saddle and arrive at the Huttra camping place below the Umasi La.

The trail leads downstream by the Bardur to the Ganra camping place near the Zongkhul Gompa (see Padum-Kishtwar Trek) and then back to the Stod Valley. At Chibra Stod you head downstream to the east via Ating, Drokund, Shagur, Murkum and Turkum to Tungri. The trip takes about four days.

PADUM-THONDE-ZANGLA-KARSHA GOMPA-PADUM ROUNDTRIP
Day I: Padum-Thonde

From Padum the route leads over the eastern rope bridge, below the town on the right bank of the Lunak, one of the source rivers of the Zanskar. Kashmiri porters are unwilling to transport loads over these rope bridges. Zanskaris are the true specialists and the performance of 'oncoming traffic' can be acrobatic! The route to Thonde follows the river, at a distance above the rubble plain through which the river has carved its path. Thonde (also spelt Stongday or Stongde) is a river oasis with a monastery enthroned above it, you take the direct route to Zangla, which follows the Zanskar River. It's a five to six hour walk from Padum.

Thonde is an important town for trekking tours towards Lamayuru because this is the first place where horses can be hired on this side of the rope bridge. They should be ordered from Padum so that they are already waiting when you get to Thonde. The best view of the irrigated fields, in which the semi-circle of houses lie, is from the monastery which has about 60 monks. It's a strenuous ascent, particularly in the heat of mid-day, but one should not fail to see this monastery which shows to visitors, at least at the moment, the intact life of a monastic society. Each year sacred dances are held here in conjunction with the festival of Gostor at Karsha Gompa.

At mid-day you can see the feeding of the monastery school pupils – everyone receives tsampa balls to eat. You may be lucky enough to view the ritual purification of various ceremonial objects or you may see the manufacture of butter candles. Descending from the monastery you can see, to the left of the mountains on either side of the Zanskar River, the distant form of Karsha Gompa. A difficult, dangerous and not to be recommended route turns eastward from Thonde through the Shadi Ravine to the Phuctal Gorge – see the Padum-Phuctal report.

Day 2: Thonde-Zangla

The route to Zangla follows the Zanskar River further to the north-east. Zozar (Zazar or Tsazar) is the next large town and after this the picturesque trail continues partly on the banks of the Zanskar, which makes it impassable at high water. Half way between Zozar and Zangla a rope bridge leads across the Zanskar.

Zangla does not have much to offer apart from the rebuilt 'castle' of the one-time kings of Zanskar. Here you will see more newly built chortens than elsewhere in Zanskar, a sign of the living nature of Buddhism in this area. The son of the king, once a monk and an important tanka painter, now wears a nylon wind jacket and sunglasses and spends several months of each year in Delhi. Times are changing.

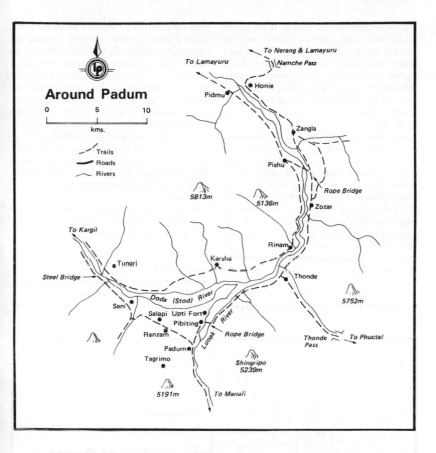

Around Padum

0   5   10
kms.

- – – Trails
—— Roads
～ Rivers

To Nerang & Lamayuru
To Lamayuru
Namche Pass
Honie
Pidmu
Zangla
Pishu
Rope Bridge
5813m
5136m
Zozar
Rinam
To Kargil
Karsha
Thonde
Tungri
5752m
Steel Bridge
Doda (Stod) River
Sani
Salapi Upti Fort
Pibiting
Lungak River
Rope Bridge
Ranzam
Thonde Pass
To Phuctal
Padum
Tagrimo
Shingripo
5239m
5191m
To Manali

If you should be invited in for a cup of butter tea (or 'sweet' tea) try to have a look at the 'palace' Dukhang. Some of the tankas in this room were painted by the king's son.

The remains of the old and decayed fortifications of the king lie on the mountains above the village. The prince of Zangla compared the site of these ruins to the head of an eagle but they did not impress us enough to want to climb the hill! We did enjoy making friends with the children during our stay with the royal family.

Day 3: Zangla-Karsha Gompa

In Zangla the Markha trek turns towards Leh (see Padum-Leh Trek) but if you wish to go to Lamayuru it is best to follow the Zanskar River further along to Honia (see the Padum-Lamayuru Trek). To return from Zangla, crossing over the river to Karsha en route to Padum, you must go some km back towards Zozar and cross the Zanskar by a scenic rope bridge. The route branches right past the rope bridge and continues past Pishu and the Lingshot Gompa towards Lamayuru (see Padum-Lamayuru) or left towards Padum.

Five to six hours ascending walk to the south-west takes you past Rinam towards Yalong and the Karsha Gompa. A direct route also leads to this gompa from Padum and over the river terrace plains to the north towards Yalong. Yalong is on the other bank of the Stod, one of the source rivers of the Zanskar, below the Karsha Gompa.

Karsha is the largest and most important monastery in Zanskar, has more than 150 yellow-cap monks and is subject to the control of the younger brother of the Dalai Lama. It is said to contain bone relics of Dorje Rinchen. The white-washed walls of the houses and chapels of the gompa, which perches like a falcon's nest on the rocks above the Stod/Zanskar Rivers, can be seen from a great distance away. A sweat-raising climb is eventually rewarded by superb panoramic views over the valley.

The chapel of the monastery, which contains a further three prayer rooms, has places for 35 lamas. Behind the seat of the Dalai Lama's brother there is a figure of Lhaso Cho Rimpoche with a golden crown inset with carnelian and turquoise gemstones. It was brought here from Lhasa in the early '60s but the three small windows let in little light to the room so it is difficult to see clearly. Karsha's most important festival is the Karsha Gostor with Cham mask dances on the 26th to 29th day of the 11th month of the Tibetan calendar – usually mid-December to early January. The library of the gompa is also worth seeing and Karsha's butter tea is widely renowned.

Near the village of Karsha there are the monasteries of Khagsar, Purang, Phagspa and a nunnery, Dorjezong, near the top of the valley.

Day 4: Karsha-Padum
You can cross the Stod by a rubber dinghy (cost is Rs 5) left behind in '76 by a German party or you can take the route

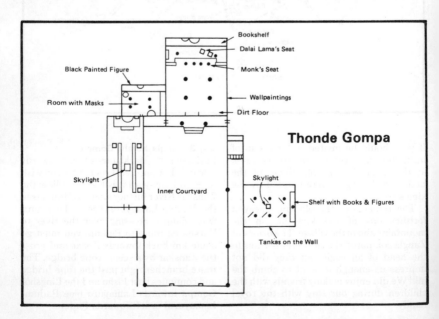

Bookshelf
Dalai Lama's Seat
Black Painted Figure
Monk's Seat
Room with Masks
Wallpaintings
Dirt Floor

Thonde Gompa

Skylight
Skylight
Inner Courtyard
Shelf with Books & Figures
Tankas on the Wall

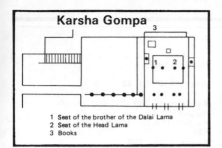

Karsha Gompa

1 Seat of the brother of the Dalai Lama
2 Seat of the Head Lama
3 Books

over Lami and Kusser towards Rankiut where you can stay overnight although Tungri is better. A sturdy wooden bridge (the Tungri Bridge) crosses the Stod and the route then follows the river westward (upstream) to Turkum (3550 metres). There is a small, but interesting, gompa with nuns above picturesque Tungri. From Tungri the route leads back past the Sani Gompa, Salapi and Ranzam to Padum.

Padmasambhava is said to have visited and blessed Sani. It has a large cemetery ground with trees and springs and in a rock face on the opposite side of the river there is a meditation cave which is said to contain a footprint. Sani Gompa also has the great stupa of Kanishka, and an image of Naropa, which can be viewed on the day

of the pilgrimage which occurs around the middle of the sixth Tibetan month. People come from all over Zanskar for this pilgrimage, wearing new clothes and their finest jewellery.

PADUM-PHUCTAL GOMPA – by the Shadi Gorge

This four or five day trek can be extremely dangerous and difficult although it might, superficially, seem like an attractive way of making a round trip Padum-Phuctal-Padum. The route from Padum runs to Thonde then eastwards (to the right) into the mountains and across the 5492 metre Thonde La. To the top of the pass the route is quite easy but from there it's hell through the gorges.

The route has not been regularly travelled for years so the path has deteriorated and much dangerous clambering plus river and mountain crossing is necessary. Horses are unusable! There is only one tiny village, Shadi, on the whole route and even that is in a side valley. Many stretches are dangerous due to the vertical rock walls and the loose rock slopes high above the turbulent rivers winding their way far below the trail. From Phuctal you soon rejoin the usual Padum-Manali route.

Index

200

Update Supplement

Some last minute additional material from Tom Harriman and Jan King (USA):

Money
There are many moneychangers in Srinagar offering a rate about the same as in Delhi. They even tour the lake on shikaras. You have to negotiate vigorously to get the best deal.

Bookshops
Good bookshops in Srinagar are the Kashmir Bookshop under the Indian Coffee House and the Hind Bookshop across the road.

Kashmiri Food
Some other vegetable standbys are *palak paneer* – spinach-like greens with fried white-cheese, *alu gobi* – potatoes and cauliflower. Aubergines may be better known to some people as eggplant, lady fingers as okra.

SRINAGAR
The museum is housed in an interesting old palace. There is beautiful papier mache work on the walls. The collection is eclectic but outstanding – early architectural relics, ancient coins and medals, weapons, costumes, fabrics, stuffed animals, you name it. Get there by shikara across the river from the bund.

Places to Stay
The *Grand Hotel*, across from Ahdoo's on Residency Rd, is conveniently situated and has doubles with fan, hot water, towels and so on for Rs 40 – if you negotiate. Rooms back from the street are quieter.

Places to Eat
The *Grand Hotel & Restaurant* has good medium-priced Kashmiri food in an old-fashioned atmosphere. It's cheaper than Ahdoo's although the variety isn't so great. For excellent ice cream, milk shakes, pizzas, mutton-burgers and many other dishes try *Caprini's* just down from the Grand. Towards the GPO on Residency Rd the *Mughal Darbar* is very good – 'better than Ahdoos and larger portions'. Just before you turn onto the Boulevard in Dal Gate the *Gateway Restaurant* has good value, inexpensive Kashmiri food.

Getting There
Bharat Transport Company in Lal Chowk has a deluxe bus direct to Delhi via Jammu-Jullander-Ludhiana and Ambala. Cost is Rs 175.

Getting Around
For Rs 10-15 an hour you can can get a shikara down the river from in front of Grindlay's Bank. Double-decker city buses to the Shalimar or Nishat gardens for 40p are good value. They're also a good way to get from Dal Gate to Lal Chowk. They run from Lal Chowk, down Maulana Azad to Dal Gate and then along the Boulevard to Shalimar and, sometimes, Harwan.

PAHALGAM
Doubles at the *Government Tourist Bungalow* are Rs 30. The *Tourist Huts*, in the pine trees around the Tourist Bungalow, are Rs 90 single bedroom or Rs 150 with two bedrooms. Just up the road from the bungalow the Yog Niketan ashram, from Rishikesh, operates in the sumer only. They offer free hatha yoga and meditation lessons and you can rent a large tent there for Rs 110 for two weeks or Rs 195 for a month. They ask for a two week minimum commitment although they're flexible. You can stay there with your own tent for just Rs 30 a month. It's restful and a good place for yoga and meditation.

The *Khalsa Janta Restaurant*, just before the Pahalgam Hotel, has excellent and reasonably priced Kashmiri and Punjabi food. The *Tabela Restaurant* across the street is good but expensive.

KARGIL
The *Naktul View*, near the Tourist Reception Centre, is cheap and quiet as it's off the main road. There are attached bathrooms and it's only Rs 10/15 for singles/doubles. The *New Light* on the main road has reasonable basic rooms from Rs 5 per person.

The *Khyber Restaurant* has reasonably priced and good Kashmiri food. The *Babu Chinese Restaurant* is popular, for some reason. Buy dried apricots from the Fruit Growers' Co-Op near the post office.

Beyond Kargil at Saspul there is now a *Tourist Bungalow* (without running water) while Pushkum (at km 218) has two seasonal tent villages in an irrigated, grassy area. At Mulbekh there are two tea shops opposite the statue. The *Nen-Dum Tea Stall & Hotel* is better than the *Nanchung Hotel & Restaurant* but they both have beds for Rs 5 and OK food. There are interesting hikes in the canyons across the river from Mulbekh.

LAMAYURU
The Tibetan *Dekung Labrong Hotel* is on the highway right above the gompa. Doubles are about Rs 20 and the cheerful restaurant is reasonably priced. The monastery has a dormitory outside the monastery proper with beds at Rs 8 and there's another non-descript hotel near the monastery.

ALCHI
One of the most interesting gompas in Ladakh. The *Zimskhang Hotel & Restaurant* is Rs 20 per person but they'll negotiate. They have electricity, good food and beer. This is a better place to stay than nearby Saspul.

LEH
The Ladakh Ecological Development Group is next door to the Hotel Tsemo-Lah and has a solar demonstration house and a fantastic library on Ladakh.

Places to Stay
The *Manzor Guest House* is a pleasant, family-run guest house with rooms from Rs 10 to 20. Nearby is the *Two Star Guest House* which is also good. They're both a hundred metres up the road from the Hotel Tsemo-Lah.

Places to Eat
More good restaurants are the *Potala Restaurant* near the mosque and the *Gangri Norbu Restaurant* a block south of the post office. Shashlik vendors set up beside the street on the corner by the mosque, below the Potala Restaurant.

HEMIS
They sell seats to watch the festival now! Rs 20 on the roof, Rs 35 for a shaded seat on a balcony. It's a good idea to arrive the day before the festival to see the gompa, buy a seat and arrange accommodation. There is no shortage of places to stay.

STOK
You can also visit the Gurphug Gompa (Rs 10 admission) which is attached to the Spitok Gompa. It's small but well maintained and worth visiting if you go to Stok.

Lonely Planet travel guides are available around the world. If you can't find them, ask your bookshop to order them from one of the distributors listed below. For countries not listed or if you would like a free copy of our latest booklist write to Lonely Planet in Australia.

Australia
Lonely Planet Publications, PO Box 88, South Yarra, Victoria 3141.
Canada
Milestone Publications, Box 2248, Sidney British Columbia, V8L 3S8.
Denmark
Scanvik Books aps, Store Kongensgade 59 A, DK-1264 Copenhagen K.
Hong Kong
The Book Society, GPO Box 7804.
India & Nepal
UBS Distributors, 5 Ansari Rd, New Delhi.
Israel
Geographical Tours Ltd, 8 Tverya St, Tel Aviv 63144.
Japan
Intercontinental Marketing Corp, IPO Box 5056, Tokyo 100-31.
Malaysia
MPH Distributors, 13 Jalan 13/6, Petaling Jaya, Selangor.
Netherlands
Nilsson & Lamm bv, Postbus 195, Pampuslaan 212, 1380 AD Weesp.
New Zealand
Roulston Greene Publishing Associates Ltd, Box 33850, Takapuna, Auckland 9.
Papua New Guinea
Gordon & Gotch (PNG), PO Box 3395, Port Moresby.
Singapore
MPH Distributors, 116-DJTC Factory Building, Lorong 3, Geylang Square, Singapore, 1438.
Sweden
Esselte Kartcentrum AB, Vasagatan 16, S-111 20 Stockholm.
Thailand
Chalermnit, 1-2 Erawan Arcade, Bangkok.
UK
Roger Lascelles, 47 York Rd, Brentford, Middlesex, TW8 0QP.
USA
Lonely Planet Publications, PO Box 2001A, Berkeley, CA 94702.
West Germany
Buchvertrieb Gerda Schettler, Postfach 64, D3415 Hattorf a H.

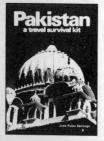